# STRENGTH
## *for Each Day*

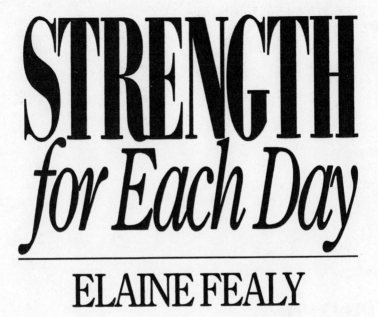

# STRENGTH
## *for Each Day*

### ELAINE FEALY

**PRINCE OF PEACE PUBLISHING**
Burnsville, Minnesota 55337

By the Same Author:

*I Will Lift Up My Eyes Unto the Hills*

# STRENGTH
## *for Each Day*

Where indicated, Scripture quotations are from the Revised Standard Version of the Bible (RSV), copyrighted 1946, 1952, © 1971, 1973 by the Division of Christian Education of the National Council of Churches of Christ in the U.S.A., and are used by permission.

## Second printing 1991

Library of Congress Cataloging-in-Publication Data
Fealy, Elaine J., 1936-
    Strength for each day.

      1. Love—Religious aspects—Christianity—
Meditations.   2. Spiritual exercises. I. Bittner,
Vernon J.  Breaking free.  II. Title.
BV4639.F39  1986     248.4     86-25187
ISBN 0-933173-08-3

*Printed in the United States of America*

This devotional is dedicated to my four children,
Julie, Cathy, Barbie and Lee,
and to my wonderful grandchildren,
Rachel Margaret Fealy-Layer, Robert Patrick Fealy-Layer
and Sonja Joy Englund.

*Twelve Steps for Christian Living One Day at a Time* was written for everyone involved in 12-Step programs and who desire a Christian approach to these steps. This book resulted from the "Twelve Steps for Christian Living," which originally appeared in the book *You Can Help With Your Healing* and a revised edition of the steps that is found in *Breaking Free*. Both of these books were written by Dr. Vernon J. Bittner.

The 12-Step programs are intended to help individuals in their *spiritual* recovery in any area of their lives that is unmanageable. To to be human is to accept our unmanageability. The Twelve Steps for Christian Living provide a framework for spiritual growth that is applicable to any area of life in which one finds oneself powerless.

Information has it that there are at least 15 to 20 12-Step programs in our society. The Twelve Steps for Christian Living is the only such program with a Christian emphasis.

This daily devotional is intended to help individuals who desire a closer walk with their Lord Jesus Christ and are willing to give reflective time to *Scripture, meditation* and *prayer*.

It is hoped that these daily reflections on God's word will help readers in their growth in a new way of living. Finding the abundant life is a lifelong process. May this help us all along the way, and may all who read this come expecting the Spirit of God to act in their lives.

# TWELVE STEPS
## for Christian Living

### Step One
We admit our need for God's gift of salvation, that we are powerless over certain areas of our lives and that our lives are at times sinful and unmanageable.

### Step Two
We come to believe through the Holy Spirit that a power who came in the person of Jesus Christ and who is greater than ourselves can transform our weaknesses into strengths.

### Step Three
We make a decision to turn our wills and our lives over to the care of Christ as we understand him—hoping to understand him more fully.

### Step Four
We make a searching and fearless moral inventory of ourselves— both our strengths and our weaknesses.

### Step Five
We admit to Christ, to ourselves and to another human being the exact nature of our sins, as well as all of who we are, including our strengths.

### Step Six
We become entirely ready to have Christ heal all of these defects of character that prevent us from having a more spiritual life style.

### Step Seven
We humbly ask Christ to transform all of our shortcomings.

### Step Eight
We make a list of all persons we have harmed and become willing to make amends to them all.

### Step Nine
We make direct amends to such persons wherever possible, except when to do so would injure them or others.

### Step Ten
We continue to take personal inventory and when we are wrong, promptly admit it, and when we are right, thank God for his guidance.

### Step Eleven
We seek through prayer and meditation to improve our conscious contact with Christ as we understand him, praying for knowledge of his will for us and the power to carry that out.

### Step Twelve
Having experienced a new sense of spirituality as a result of these steps and realizing that this is a gift of God's grace, we are willing to share the message of his love and forgiveness with others and to practice these principles for spiritual living in all our affairs.

Institute for Christian Living

# JANUARY 1

*"Those who are well have no need of a physician, but those who are sick
. . . For I came not to call the righteous but sinners."*
Matthew 9:12-13

Not only is January the beginning of a new year, but admitting our humanity and that we are in need of a savior is the beginning of spiritual and emotional growth.

Working the first step takes daring, confidence, and heart. It means that we are willing to swallow our false pride and admit that we are "sick" (powerless or sinful) in some area of our life and that we are in need of Jesus Christ who is more powerful than ourselves to heal, transform, and save us.

Accepting that we are unable to find wholeness by ourselves is the first step toward finding the abundant life. Jesus is unable to help us in the healing process unless we are willing to admit we need his healing power to transform our weaknesses into strengths.

Have we made our New Year's resolution yet? Would we consider the truth that even Jesus can't heal us unless we admit our areas of sin and unmanageability?

PRAYER:
*To begin, Lord, help us to begin . . . a new year, a new day, a new way of living. Help us, Lord, to admit that we can't do it alone. Amen.*
Step 1

# JANUARY 2

*"Great is my boldness of speech toward you, great is my glorying of you;
I am filled with comfort, I am exceeding joyful in all our tribulations."*
II Corinthians 7:4

When Paul wrote these words he must have experienced not only the need to let go, but also the joy that comes with it. Paul was an exuberant writer who wrote with great depth of feelings, both of sorrow and joy. It is important that like Paul, we not only recognize our feelings, but we find a way to express them in a constructive way with others. Unless we are willing to share our feelings and our experience of healing with others, we will cease to grow toward wholeness in body, mind and spirit.

If we express our feelings of sorrow, it is possible for him to send us comfort. If we share the feelings of guilt, he can lead us to forgiveness. If we talk about our feelings of hatred, it is possible for him to teach us to love. By expressing our feelings of loneliness and rejection, we can experience his transforming friendship and acceptance. We recognize the importance of our joys as well as our sorrows. We must seek out the good in our lives so that we can be examples of his influence in our lives.

PRAYER

*Loving Friend and Counselor, help us to be willing to share our feelings with you and others. Let us not be ashamed or afraid of whatever we feel. Remind us of your life and the many feelings of others. Help us to listen with our ears, our eyes, our minds and our hearts. Amen.*

Suggested for Step 3

# JANUARY 3

*"Love never faileth."*
I Corinthians 13:8

Sometimes when we hurt one another or when we have been deeply hurt by someone we loved and trusted, this verse may be difficult for us. Broken relationships often cause us to wonder if there really was any love at all, or if loving truly accomplishes what we thought it would. We need to remember that love is a bond that cannot be broken. Even when we love someone who is for some reason incapable of accepting our love, "Love never faileth." The impact of true love (Christlike love, not romantic love) leaves an imprint on everyone it touches.

Some people may not respond to our love and may even scoff at us, but if we continue to love unconditionally, it will have a lasting effect on them. Certainly it will touch them in a more positive way than if we were hateful or angry. It is important that we remember, even in the midst of the most painful relationships, that love does work. It can change them. In fact, it is the only thing that can change them.

It is also important to remember that during the time we are waiting or hoping for this relationship to be renewed, we are never alone. The love of God is ever with us to sustain us and comfort us. Even when things do not work out the way we wanted them, God can give us peace and help us to continue to be loving. He will help us to practice tough love when that is what is best.

PRAYER:

*God of love, we ask that the strength and goodness of your love be very real to each one of us. Help us to show that love, not only to those who are precious to us, but to strangers and enemies as well. Whatever may occur in our lives, teach us to remember that love never fails. We thank you for your supreme example of love for us through your death on the cross. May we love one another as you have loved us. Amen.*

Suggested for Step 8

# JANUARY 4

*"He who finds me finds life."*
Proverbs 8:35

There is a healing power in confession. When we seek out our Lord and pour out our pain and confusion, he fills us with his Spirit. His presence is like a life stream flowing through us that heals and renews us. When we are open to this life-giving presence, we are in the process of being made whole. We must be willing to seek him with a penitent heart and be open to his healing. He promises that once we find him, we will also find life in him.

As we accept and acknowledge this healing potential, our bodies, minds and spirits respond to this positive affirmation. We begin to get better and feel the changes taking place in our lives. Disease can be improved or even cured when we allow him to go to work in us.

Confession helps us with the housecleaning process that is so necessary in order to change our destructive life styles. We must be willing participants. Can you believe that he is able to heal? Are you willing to put your life in God's hands and be healed in whatever areas he sees that need healing? Will you believe it when he heals you?

PRAYER:

*Gracious Father, your strength never fails us. You provide resources for us that are adequate for each day's need. We thank you for that. We remember others this day who are in need of healing. Touch them and heal them with your love. If we can help, use us, and if we cannot help or they will not let us, we need to know that, too. Amen.*

Suggested for Step 5

---

# JANUARY 5

*"Better is the end of a thing than its beginning;
and the patient in spirit is better than the proud in spirit."*
Ecclesiastes 7:8

There are many things that keep us from having a more spiritual life style. One of those things is a lack of patience. We lack patience with our Lord, with others and especially with ourselves. We want what we want *now!* Once we reach the point where we recognize that some changes need to be made in our lives, we want it all to change suddenly. We become very irritated with ourselves and others when things do not go as we planned. Once we have made an honest commitment to let Christ heal our defects of character, we can easily lose patience with the process of change.

We need to remember that it took us a long time to become the way we are today. It will likewise take a while for us to change those areas of our lives that we do not like. Quite often we have a different timetable than our Lord has, and we need to be patient with the process.

In some cases we need to learn new ways and attitudes about life. In some cases we need to "unlearn" old, destructive ways that keep us from being more whole. Some of us will need to learn an almost totally new life style if the background we came out of was dysfunctional. Our Lord is patient as we work to change for the better, and we need to be gentle with ourselves.

P R A Y E R:

*Lord, great Counselor and Teacher, we thank you that we can change our lives and become better people. We thank you for your guidance and encouragement during this process of change. Help us to be patient with ourselves and others during the process of change and renewal. Remind us, when we need it, that "all things work together for good." We are part of a divine plan and we need to trust in you as the Master Architect. Thank you for the possibilities for change. Amen.*

Suggested for Step 6

---

# JANUARY 6

*"If God is on our side,
who can be against us?"*
Romans 8:31, *The Living Bible*

We do a lot of needless worrying because we do not take this verse seriously. God is with us wherever we go. He is within us, and he is all around us. Although we may have real reasons to be afraid at times, he is always with us. With every step we take, he walks with us. He urges us to make good judgments as we handle difficult situations in our lives.

We live in a violent world—a world where sick, immature people hurt us without provocation. After a mugging several years ago, I spent a year in the hospital and subsequently had many unsuccessful surgeries. I was left with an ugly disease and permanent disability that profoundly affected my life. At the time I was being assaulted, and for some time after, I wondered where God was when I needed him.

Over the years that I have had the disease, I have discovered the importance of this verse. God was always with me, even when I was unaware of his presence. I was seriously ill, enough to become dangerously underweight, and nearly died on two occasions. I am very much aware that God not only helped me to survive all those surgeries, but he healed me spiritually and emotionally. That made physical healing sufficiently possible so that it is no longer necessary to spend my life in the hospital. I continue to have the disease, but it is no longer a burden to me like it was before. All that has happened has been a genuine blessing.

P R A Y E R :

*We thank you, Protector, for being greater than any evil force that we may come up against. We thank you for your presence, protection and love. We appreciate that you are always with us and because of that, nothing that comes against us can defeat us. We can win if we are just willing to turn to you for our strength. Amen.*

Suggested for Steps 1 and 2

---

# JANUARY 7

*"If you abide in me, and my words abide in you, you shall ask what you will and it will be done unto you."*
John 15:7

What do these words mean for us today? What is Christ asking of us? First of all, we are reminded that Christ and the Father are one. He urges us to dwell in him. We are assured that if we have faith and practice our beliefs, he will dwell in us. We are told many places in the Bible that if he abides in us, that will make all the difference in our lives. Knowing his presence in everything we do will enable us to love because we are being loved.

How do we abide in Christ? Certainly we need to follow the word of God as found in the Bible. We need to spend time in prayer and meditate on the meaning of God's word for our lives. We can experience his abiding presence through fellowship with other Christian people, such as in our 12 step groups. Abiding in Christ means that we are willing to love all others regardless of whether they are friends or enemies.

We need to practice the presence of Christ daily. When we practice unselfishness, we discover Christ. When we share our lives with others, he dwells in us and we in him. When we practice love and forgiveness, he abides in us. When we turn our will and our lives over to his care, he dwells in us. Whenever we practice Christlike loving and living, his presence is with us, and that makes all the difference in the world.

P R A Y E R

*Precious Lord, help us to practice your presence every single day. Abide with us so that we will live our lives according to your will. Help us to discipline ourselves so that we stay in touch with you at all times, and give us the good sense to turn to you for guidance. Thank you for your presence and the continued comfort you give. Amen.*

Suggested for Step 10

# JANUARY 8

*"But I have prayed for you that your faith may not fail;
and when you have turned again, strengthen your brother."*
Luke 22:32

We live at a time in history when too many people ignore this verse. Stories are reported in the news in which people stood by while another person was being beaten or murdered. We are reluctant to get involved because we are afraid of what might happen to us. We even worry that if we get involved, we may be called into court to testify and that would cost us time and money. That person being attacked may die, and yet we hesitate to get involved.

Christ did not show us that kind of example when he was on this earth. He became involved in situations that caused him much public criticism. It cost him his life because he was committed to ministering to people at their point of need. His own safety was not as important to him as showing others how much he loved and forgave them.

We can strengthen others in many ways by our own example. Surely you have wept because of sorrow in your life. You can share that with another sorrowing soul. Have you ever failed at something that was really important to you? Share that, so others may gain from your experience. Sharing our weaknesses as well as our strengths is the most powerful witness we have of our Savior's love.

PRAYER:

*Loving Savior, help us to take the risk of sharing with those around us. Let us be willing to strengthen them by being willing to share who we are, even at our most vulnerable times. Give us the courage to share your love through the witness of our own experience. Amen.*

Suggested for Step 12

---

# JANUARY 9

*"By little and little I will drive them out from before thee,
until you will be increased and inherit the land."*
Exodus 23:30

In this story from Scripture, we are reminded that the people of Israel did not gain possession of Canaan in one great, quick victory. It took many years of fighting. We need to remember this as we work on making changes in our lives. When we become aware that we need to change some area in our lives, we quite often become impatient. Once we are aware of the need for change, we do not understand why it will not happen immediately.

Unfortunately, will power alone does not change our destructive life styles. "Old habits are like living organisms, and they die hard." As Christians, we are growing and changing with the help of God, but we are not perfect. We will never achieve perfection on this earth, and we need to be patient with ourselves and others.

With the help of Christ, we can change those areas of our lives that need changing. However, some of our bad habits have had many years to get a foothold in our lives. We need to realize that some of our negative thoughts and attitudes were taught to us as children. It will take time and patience to learn a better way to do things.

PRAYER:

*Lord, we thank you for the ability to change and become better persons. Help us to remember that change takes time, but that "little by little" we will accomplish our goal. Make our hearts strong and help us to take one day at a time with your help. Let us be patient with others that we think need changing. We put them in your hands and let go of our judgments of them. Amen.*

Suggested for Step 7

---

# JANUARY 10

*"Be at peace among yourselves."*
I Thessalonians 5:13

These are wise words and certainly ones that we should practice, but it is not as easy as it might seem. We come from different backgrounds. We all have different personalities, and we all react differently to various situations. Even when we are aware that we are not acting in Christian love, we cannot always change our behavior. We get so personally involved in differences of opinion that we get into a battle to see who can win.

We need to stop and look at our own behavior and see what it is we are doing. We can control our feelings, and we can give Christ first place in our hearts and lives. We can let go of the pettiness in our lives and replace it with an attitude of love. We can come out victoriously no matter how immature the other people are that we are dealing with.

Even if we are already embroiled in the midst of a conflict, we need to pull ourselves out of the heat of that situation and see what we are doing. We need to turn to our Lord for guidance and be honest with ourselves as we assess our own involvement. Some disagreements are not worth the energy we waste trying to prove our point. We need to resolve the conflict in Christian love as soon as possible. If we cannot agree on a resolution, we need to be honest about that and then let go of the angry feelings.

PRAYER:

*Loving God, help us to practice peace with one another. When we get involved in personality conflicts, help us to be willing to work at resolving them quickly. Help us to resolve them with love and caring so that we reflect your love in us. Help us to love others unconditionally, as you love us. Amen.*

Suggested for Steps 8 and 9

# JANUARY 11

*"He who trusts in the Lord is safe."*
Proverbs 29:25

This verse used to make me very angry. I felt that I trusted very seriously in the Lord, and yet bad things continued to happen to me and my loved ones. Then I would start to doubt the love of God, or else I would believe that my faith was inadequate and I was being punished. I realize now that God hadn't forsaken me and I hadn't failed him. I also learned that even when terrible things happened in my life, God was there with me.

I had to stop blaming God for all the bad things that happened to me. I realize that there is evil and disease and hurtful people in this world, and my life is affected by those events and people over which I have no control. I needed to accept my powerlessness and turn to God for strength to deal with the trials, not avoid them.

This verse does not mean that our life will be trouble-free. It does not mean that if we trust in the Lord, we will always be safe and no harm or hurt will ever come to us. As long as we live, we will be exposed to hurtful, sometimes frightening events in our lives. For me, this verse promises that no matter what might happen to me, or how terrible it is, I can find safety, peace and healing in the presence of God. That is a powerful promise for me!

PRAYER:

*God of love, we thank you that wherever we go, you go with us. We thank you that we can feel safe and secure in your care regardless of the circumstances of our lives. Help us to look beyond our pain and see in it an opportunity to grow in your love. Help us to share the promise of this verse with others. Amen.*

Suggested for Step 2

# JANUARY 12

*"Casting all your cares upon him; for he cares for you."*
I Peter 5:7

This is a favorite verse for many people because it offers so much hope and comfort. When our lives seem unmanageable, we know that we can count on our Lord for management. When our lives are struck by pain, we know that we need not carry this burden alone. He *cares* for us! That is a promise for the present moment. We need someone to help carry the load.

We may not be entirely relieved of our cares, but we have a partner in our sorrow, and just knowing we are not alone is comforting. Perhaps this is to be a time of growth that will only come about through experiencing these difficult times. We need to be willing to do our share in dealing with our burdens. Our Lord does not always "zap" us with instant healing.

As we look back on difficult times in the past, we should be able to find something good in all of the experiences we have had. Our burdens can either be a stumbling block or a stepping stone. Our attitude and our faith will determine which it is. God uses the tragedies of our lives as opportunities to grow in his love. We need to work toward having complete trust in his will for our lives.

PRAYER:

*Eternal Father, your goodness and mercy never change. You are the same yesterday, today and forever. We thank you for that. You give us confidence and strength for whatever challenge we face. You quiet the storms in our souls and help us to meet life's demands with untroubled hearts. You give us our portion of peace that is more than sufficient. Thank you for your love. Amen.*

Suggested for Steps 8 and 9

# JANUARY 13

*"And all things, whatsoever you shall ask
in prayer, believing, you shall receive."*
Matthew 21:22

We misuse this verse because we want to believe that we will receive whatever we ask for if we have faith. But "having faith" also means that we must accept that what we have asked for may not be the same as God's plan for us. This is especially true when we are asking for a much-desired healing.

Certainly Christ wants health and wholeness for us, but we must remember that other factors affect our health or illness. The world has many adverse effects on our bodies and minds. Evil has much to do with whether we are sick or well and whether or not we are healed. Besides, every one of us is going to get sick and die of something someday.

There are even some people who do not believe they deserve healing, and so they block their own ability to be healed. They are living a self-fulfilling prophecy. They believe they deserve the worst in life, and so they help that to come true. This may be an unconscious thought, but it is a powerful force in our lives.

PRAYER:

*Great Physician and Healer of all hurts, we ask that you will help us to believe that we deserve to be whole. Help us be willing to participate fully in the healing process. We need to let go of destructive thinking and trust in you completely. We need to believe that you created us for health and wholeness. Amen.*

Suggested for Step 11

---

# JANUARY 14

*"For a great door and effectual is opened unto me and there are many adversaries."*

I Corinthians 16:9

Doors are very important in our lives although we don't always believe that. Sometimes doors close on a part of our life that we are not yet ready to let go of. It may be a career change, the end of a marriage, children leaving home or the loss of a significant person in our life. We may have been so satisfied with the way life was that we do not want life to change.

Whenever doors are closed to us, new doors usually open for us. This is a gift from God. We do not always consider these new doors in a positive light. We fear the unknown, and we are afraid to take the necessary risks to go through those doors. We need to trust that if God opens a new door for us, he will also help us in that new experience.

We should not fear the new doors that open up for us in life. They offer us new opportunities and fresh, new experiences. They challenge us to stretch and grow beyond our present limitations. We may be challenged to develop new relationships. We may be asked to serve God and others in a new way. We may be expected to develop and share new gifts. What doors have closed in your life? What doors have opened in your life? Let's journal about this area of our lives as we work on the fourth step.

PRAYER:

*Loving Father, we thank you for doors, those that close and those that open. Give us the courage to risk going through open doors and the serenity to close those doors that must be closed. Help us to share our doors with others so we can encourage them to take risks with your help. Amen.*

Suggested for Step 4

# JANUARY 15

*"It is good that a man should both hope
and quietly wait for the salvation of the Lord."*
Lamentations 3:26

It is not easy to both hope and quietly wait for the salvation of the Lord. The word salvation is also interpreted as "healing." I think we need to have hope before we can even begin to quietly wait. In the midst of our pain, it is not always easy to find hope. Sometimes our circumstances are so complicated and so filled with despair that we cannot see any hope on the horizon.

In order to have hope, we first have to have faith. We have to believe that no matter what happens in our lives, Christ has the power to lift us out of the darkest circumstances to a better place with him. We need to believe that Christ can bring us beauty out of the ashes of our despair.

In order to quietly wait for the healing of the Lord, we need to pursue with our hearts and minds those things that bring us closer to him. Sometimes the way we experience him the best is in the fellowship of Christian friends. We can also seek guidance during this time through prayer and meditation. He will quiet the tremblings of our spirit in those quiet moments with him. To give up worrying does not mean that we don't care; it just means that we trust him to care for us.

P R A Y E R:

*Lord of healing, we thank you for helping us to have the faith that teaches us to hope even in the most difficult times. Be with us as we quietly wait before you. It is not easy because we want action now! We want our miracle today! Help us to appreciate the miracle of your love without demanding more. Help us to love you and love ourselves. Amen.*

Suggested for Step 3

# JANUARY 16

*"He was wounded for our transgressions,
he was bruised for our iniquities,
the chastisement of our peace was upon him,
and with his stripes we are healed."*
Isaiah 53:5

It is important for us as Christians to take time out periodically to image in our minds a journey to the foot of the cross. This will remind us of how much Christ loves us and how much suffering he endured for our sakes. We are able to see him looking down from the cross. We can see a gentle, loving face filled with warmth and love.

Our minds shift, and we are reminded of the time he spent praying in the garden of Gethsemane before he was taken away. This points out the importance of time alone with God, especially when we are in a crisis. Christ must have felt very alone and fearful that night, for he knew what was to come. We are reminded that even from the most painful of circumstances—the cross—there is a gain—the resurrection. For without the crucifixion there would have been no resurrection.

Remembering the cross calls to mind that before Christ could truly live and be helpful to others, he had to die. We must also recognize that there is a part of us that must die before we can truly live for Christ and serve others. Think about your own life for a moment. What area of your life needs to die? Is it greed, anger, self-pity, envy, guilt or fear? Or is it some other area of your life that needs to die before you can help yourself and others?

PRAYER:

*We thank you, Lamb of God, for your death and resurrection. Help us to be willing to receive all that you have done for us. Help us to share with others all that you have done for us. May we share with others your infinite love and concern. Help us, Lord, to be open to the crosses in our lives so that they can become stepping stones rather than stumbling blocks. Amen.*

Suggested for Steps 11 and 12

# JANUARY 17

*"He who thus serves Christ is acceptable to God and approved by men."*
Romans 14:18

It is important to every person to feel accepted. We all want approval. We want to be accepted as individuals, and we want *what* we do and *who* we are to be accepted by others. It is very important to our self-worth to believe that others approve and accept us and what we do. Sometimes we try too hard for acceptance and give our power away to other people to decide whether or not we are worthwhile. Then we get angry because we feel abused or unappreciated.

It is even more important that we are able to accept ourselves and approve of ourselves. If we do not accept ourselves, we often make it easy for others to reject us. We need to learn to accept ourselves if for no other reason than the fact that we are children of God and he accepts us as we are.

Some people fear rejection because of their past. They fear if people knew the history of their lives, they would reject them. They refuse to share the pain of the past because of the fear they won't be accepted. Quite often they were victims in the past who took the responsibility for the pain that others caused them. We will never achieve wholeness unless we are willing to share with others our journey of pain. Then healing can begin.

PRAYER:

*Merciful God, thank you for your acceptance of us just as we are. Help us to accept ourselves with the love you have for us. Help us to refrain from worrying about what others think about us and just do the best that we can with your help. Amen.*

Suggested for Steps 8 and 9

# JANUARY 18

*"See, I have set before you this day life and good."*
Deuteronomy 30:15

What a beautiful thought this is with which to start the new day for each one of us. It offers a day of good, regardless of whatever the circumstances of our lives might be. There is a promise of life and good and hope because our Lord will be with us each step of the way. It need not be a day of suffering from anxiety and needless worry. The Great Comforter gives us his assurance that he "will never leave us or forsake us." He invites us to give him our burdens.

This day that he sets before us full of life and good is a gift to us. We did not earn it. We do not deserve it. He gives it freely because he loves us and wants us to be happy. He desires what is best for us. It is our responsibility to make the most of each day he gives us. We should accept with gratitude this day of love.

PRAYER:

*Great Creator, we thank you for the gift of this day. Help us to use it to the fullest and to give you the glory and praise for what we make of it. Help others whose days seem painful and limited. We pray that they will turn to you for guidance and strength. If we can be helpful to them, let us serve in any way we can. Help us to remember, "This is the day which the Lord has made; let us rejoice and be glad in it." Amen.*

Suggested for Step 6

# JANUARY 19

*"God is our refuge and strength, a very present help in trouble.*
*Therefore we will not fear, though the earth be removed,*
*and though the mountains be carried into the midst of the sea."*
Psalm 46:1-2

The Federal Bureau of Investigation (FBI) frequently lists the ten most wanted men or women at large in the United States. There is always one person who is listed as "Public Enemy Number One." He or she receives a great deal of our time and attention. The person's photo hangs in all the post offices, and many law enforcement officers are after him. He keeps that position until he is either captured or killed. Once he is locked away, someone else becomes Public Enemy Number One and we no longer fear him.

As Christians, we also have a Public Enemy Number One. That enemy is fear. It takes up a great deal of our time and energy and keeps us from being more whole. Fear can overshadow our faith. Fear can paralyze us so that we are unable to keep our balance. Fear can keep us from taking risks that are a normal part of our everyday life.

In times of uncertainty, when all of us are affected by fear, we need to have a belief that offers not only abiding certainties for today, but also a sustaining faith for tomorrow. By faith we can overcome fear. That faith can motivate us to turn to our Lord sooner, before our fear overwhelms us. Faith assures us that God is our refuge and strength and that indeed we need not fear anything, even death!

PRAYER:

*Eternal God, our Father, you are our refuge, and we put our trust in you. Come close to each one of us and strengthen us. Be our helper. Comfort us in times of trouble. Give us wisdom in place of doubt and courage instead of fear. Help us to be worthy of your love. Help us to see you as the answer for our times of trouble. Grant that we may help others who are afflicted by fear that they, too, might see you as having the answer. Amen.*

Suggested for Step 1

# JANUARY 20

*"Blessed are those whose iniquities are forgiven, and whose sins are covered."*
Romans 4:7

Have you ever carried the secret of something you did that was wrong for a long time? You wanted and needed to tell someone, but you were too ashamed or too scared of the consequences. The longer you carried your secret, the guiltier you felt. Before long, you could hardly think of anything else. It disrupted your sleep and kept you from feeling at peace.

Perhaps it was a lie you told one of your best friends. Maybe you were unfaithful to your spouse and you feel terrible about it. Perhaps you had promised to stop drinking and have been sneaking your drinks.

Or, maybe you took something that didn't belong to you. Whatever it is that you did wrong, you are having a difficult time living with it.

The only way we can find peace is by admitting what we have done wrong and making amends to those we have hurt. We must be willing to confess our wrongs not only to God, but also to another human being. By doing that we will be able to break with the sins of the past and experience forgiveness from God and others.

PRAYER:

*Loving God, we thank you that we can confess our sins and experience forgiveness. Help us to be willing to admit our wrongs sooner so that we can experience serenity and the peace that only you can give. Thank you for your unconditional forgiveness. Amen.*

Suggested for Step 5

---

# JANUARY 21

*"Ask, and it shall be given you;
seek, and you shall find;
knock, and it shall be opened to you."*
Matthew 7:7

Ask. Did you realize that the first letter of each word, *ask, seek* and *knock,* combines to spell the word *ask?* At least that is the case in English. Perhaps it is a special way our Lord reminds us not only that we can ask, but that we must ask if we expect to receive. He encourages active communication. He constantly reminds us that he loves us. He constantly leaves the way open for us to approach him. He reminds us that we can only reach God through him. He is our Middleman. He is the bridge between heaven and earth.

If parents truly care for their children, they permit and encourage open communication. They provide an environment that is conducive to two-way communication. They do not communicate only as authority figures to a young child. They communicate in such a way that they encourage their children to risk being open and honest. In doing so, they provide an opportunity for growth.

Our Lord, too, is a parent and a teacher. He loves us in a way that no earthly parent ever could. He wants us to feel free to ask, seek, knock, so that we might more fully understand his will for our lives. Even though he knows our needs before we ask, he wants us to know that he cares enough to give us an audience. He listens and cares!

PRAYER:

*Thank you, Lord, for your special gift to us of listening when we pray, asking in your name. Amen.*

Suggested for Step 11

# JANUARY 22

*"I am the way, the truth, and the life."*
John 14:6

This is such a plain and simple truth that I wonder why we struggle so much to find peace when we are promised all we need. Often our lives are too complicated and too busy to see this simple truth of love. At times our appetites cry out for more fun, more excitement, more success, more possessions. Some of us buy things to feel better, or we stay busy to feel fulfilled. Many of us live a hectic, scurried life because we believe that is the way to happiness. Worry walks with some of us most of each day. Fear haunts our hearts and robs us of creative energy. For many, burdens seem to multiply faster than we can deal with them. We feel bruised and wounded and sometimes without hope.

We need to spend quiet time each day away from our hectic world and hear the voice of our Master say, "I am the way, the truth, and the life." We need to listen to that voice and the promise that comes with it. Our Lord lived a simple life without a lot of gadgets. He was often surrounded by stress and hurt caused by those he loved. Yet, he found peace and was able to say to us, "I have overcome the world." He always took time with his Father in prayer and meditation. He took time to love and serve others. His mind was not on his own pain, but on his final goal.

PRAYER:

*Lord, we make our lives so complex that we spend all of our time in emotional responses to it. Help us to live simply and find in you and your life the key to a nobler life. We ask for your blessing and your help. Be with us, Lord, and fill our hearts with your peace. Amen.*

Suggested for Step 2

# JANUARY 23

*"O my soul, do not be discouraged.*
*Do not be upset. Expect God to act."*
Psalm 42:11

Do we expect God to act on our behalf? Do we have expectations of good, or are we in the habit of expecting only negative things to happen? How we think, what we expect in life, what our attitudes are, can make a difference in what we *receive* and how we *perceive* things. Do we expect healing when we ask for it? Do we expect God to act and heal that special need in our lives? Do we expect God to fill us through and through, bringing healing to every part of us physically, emotionally and spiritually?

If we expect great things in our relationships with others, we may be willing to put more into those relationships. We can help bring our expectations to a successful conclusion.

Today we will expect great things in our lives, and by expecting them in a positive way, we will help them to happen. We will expect to be happy today and work toward that goal. We will expect to love others and to be loved in return and act accordingly. We will expect better communication and practice what we seek. When we do these things with commitment, we can also expect God's approval.

PRAYER:
*Thank you, Lord, for expectations and for those expectations that you fulfill for us. Keep us mindful that you have promised that you will always be with us and love us. That is a blessed expectation! Amen.*

Suggested for Step 6

# JANUARY 24

*"My presence shall go with thee*
*and I will give thee rest."*
Exodus 33:14

Just as yesterday's verse, this verse gives us much comfort and assurance. It reminds us of the omnipresence of God. Wherever we go, he goes with us. We live in his protective presence. We can feel secure with this awareness, that wherever we go, he will go with us and will give us rest. We rest in the assurance of his presence.

Even on those days when our lives seem harried and filled with fear and anxiety, we can claim his promise and tap into the strength that he offers. We do need to be open to his will for our lives. We do need to acknowledge our faith in his faithfulness through our prayers of petition as well as thanksgiving. We need to believe and then act on our belief.

There is no problem too great or too small for our Lord to care about. He cares about everything that affects us. He promises daily, "My presence will go with you, and I will give you rest."

PRAYER:

*Thank you, Great Comforter, for your presence in our lives. Thank you for the rest you give us when we are weary. Thank you for your willingness to guide us even when we resist your help. Help us to be more aware of your presence and willing to turn to you sooner. Help others to know your presence and acknowledge you as their Lord. Amen.*

Suggested for Step 3

---

# JANUARY 25

*"Arise, shine; for your light has come,*
*and the glory of the Lord has risen upon you."*
Isaiah 60:1

If we are going to share the message of God's love and forgiveness with others, we must be willing to become his light in a dark world. Just as the sun lightens and brightens all that it touches, we must be willing to be used by God. Whatever the sun touches it warms and gives beauty and growth.

We can become light to enable other people to grow. If we are committed to Christ, his love shines in us and through us and can be seen by others. We must also remember that if the sun becomes too intense, it can damage all that it touches. So too, we must be careful that the light, the love we project, is a healthy, nurturing kind of love. We can become too intense and turn people off. Then we become another person's darkness instead of light. Perhaps the best witness we can be is that expressed in the song some of us sang as little children, "I'll be a sunbeam for Jesus, to shine for him each day. I'll be a sunbeam for Jesus at home, at work, at play."

Let us take time today to think about our witness. Is it a testimony of light or of darkness? Is there anyone for whom we have refused to light the darkness because of anger, unforgiveness or pettiness? Are we willing to change that which is blinding us from becoming true children of light?

PRAYER:

*Lord, too often we stand in the path of our own light, wondering why it is so dark. Help us to turn to you for light as a revealing and healing source of* power. Help us to be light that does not just call attention to itself, but rather illumines everyone upon whom it falls. Let us seriously practice your challenge to us: "Let your light so shine before men that they will glorify your Father in heaven." Thank you for lighting the dark areas of our lives so that they may be healed. Amen.*

Suggested for Step 12

# JANUARY 26

*"Surely goodness and mercy shall follow me all the days of my life, and I will dwell in the house of the Lord forever."*
Psalm 23:6

Do we believe that goodness and mercy can be part of our everyday lives for the rest of our lives? For those with tragic childhoods, that can be a very difficult challenge. In a way, many people become addicted to tragedy, rejection and the wrong kind of excitement. They only know how to act when things are really unmanageable. They can survive under very difficult circumstances but do not know what to do when things go well. They are programmed to believe that all will go wrong eventually, *again.*

For those of us who have been programmed this way, let us begin to restructure our lives. We need to change this destructive character trait. We need to start believing in goodness and mercy. We need to believe that with the help of our Lord, our lives can be more positive. We need not spend the rest of our lives in despair, expecting and feeling rejection and chaos. Although we may never *forget* the past, we can *forgive* the past. Once we have dealt with the hurt, anger and guilt and have forgiven those who hurt us in the past, we can concentrate on our new life. We can plan and live a life of hope and serenity with the help of our Lord.

P R A Y E R:

*Divine Redeemer, help us to believe in goodness and mercy. Give us the courage to change the things we need to change. Help us to live a life of hope, not despair. Help us to practice a positive attitude so that others can see in us the hope available in change. Be with us, Lord! Amen.*

Suggested for Step 7

# JANUARY 27

*"Now may the Lord of peace himself give you peace at all times in all ways. The Lord be with you all."*
II Thessalonians 3:16

If we just take the time to think about our lives, we will realize how wonderful the promise in this verse is. We are given the blessing of peace in many ways, and we do not always recognize or acknowledge the source. Peace is a gift to us from God. He stills the storms in our lives and gives us a peaceful place in which to rest.

We can choose to live in peace, or we can choose to live in chaos. God is willing to give us peace, but we need to let go of the chaos and trust him. We need to let go of the turmoil of the past and the anxiety for the future and rest in the peace he offers. But this peace has a price! We must put complete trust in him and turn over our will and our life to his care. We need to have faith that he will do what is best for us.

The more we practice letting go and turning everything over to God, the easier it will become each time we reach that point. We will gain more confidence each time we trust him to take over our lives and handle them according to his will for us. We need to journal about the things we need to let go of.

P R A Y E R:

*Help us, Giver of peace, to let go of the hurts of the past and the anxieties of the future and to accept the peace you offer. We accept the healing you offer and the peace it brings. We are at peace, for we know we are always in your presence. We thank you for your gift of peace. Help us to share it with others.*

Suggested for Step 3

---

# JANUARY 28

*"Do you know that your body is a temple of the Holy Spirit within you, which you have from God, and you are not your own?"*
I Corinthians 6:19

How seriously do we take this verse? If our bodies are temples of God, surely many of us have to admit that we do not take very good care of them. In fact, we are very abusive toward them. We eat more than we need and become seriously overweight. Or we eat inadequate or improper food, and our bodies and minds suffer as a result. Many of us drink or smoke even though we know it is bad for our health. Some give or sell their bodies for sexual pleasures. Very few of us fully appreciate the gift that God has given us.

Our bodies are wondrous, intricate mechanisms with many working parts that we take for granted unless one part breaks down. Then we may panic and realize too late how important taking good care of our temples really is.

P R A Y E R:

*Loving Master, we thank you for a body and for all its magnificent working parts. We thank you for a strong heart and strong lungs. We thank you for our senses of hearing, smell, taste, touch and sight. We thank you for our limbs. Help us to be committed to taking better care of our bodies, your temples. We pray for others who are struggling with poor health. Touch them with healing and comfort. Amen.*

Suggested for Step 10

# JANUARY 29

*"Therefore turn thou to thy God:*
*keep mercy and judgment,*
*and wait on thy God continually."*
Hosea 12:6

For those of us who believe we can solve our own problems better than anyone, including God, this verse has an important command. None of us has walked in his own strength for very long before his strength has given out. Our circumstances are often too much for us to handle, but we may be too stubborn to admit we need help.

We are perplexed by problems, torn by dissensions, wearied by our burdens and sorely tried by life's temptations. We forever seem to be in a struggle between our ideals and our actual circumstances. We exhaust ourselves in body, mind and spirit by trying to find our own solutions. Sometimes we have little success, and often times we experience great failures.

We simply are not equal to the task. To whom can we turn? We can turn to friends, and certainly if they have understanding, love and forgiveness, they might help. But if they are too overwhelmed with their own problems, they may not be in the best place to help us.

We need to turn to God *continually*. He knows us better than anyone else could ever know us. We need to be willing to trust in him so that we can "let go and let God." We need to turn to him in obedience and listen for his will for our lives. Then we will experience the joy that comes with the feeling that our lives are once again manageable.

P R A Y E R:
*Dear Lord and Father of us, thank you for your guidance. Teach us to have discerning minds. Recover us when we wander away. Assure us of your nearness so that we will let go of our fears. Amen.*
Suggested for Steps 2 and 3

# JANUARY 30

*"Take my yoke upon you and learn of me;*
*for I am meek and lowly in heart*
*and you shall find rest unto your souls."*
Matthew 11:29

This is a good verse to keep in front of ourselves as we take an inventory of our lives to see what needs to be changed. Our Lord is the finest example of a loving person that we will ever find. When we feel impatient or quarrelsome, we need to remember Christ's example when he walked this earth. He had many reasons to be impatient with people. Yet for the most part, he showed love and acceptance of others. Even when he drove the money changers out of the temple, he was teaching them the truth in love.

When we have been deeply hurt by someone we loved and trusted, we need to remember how our Lord handled situations of that kind. He did not turn against them, disown them or look for ways to get even with them. He did not isolate himself to prevent further hurt, as many of us do when we have been hurt. He did not gossip or complain to others about how terrible they were or how abused he was. He forgave them. He loved them. He continued to risk being vulnerable even though he had been hurt.

PRAYER:

*Lord, you whisper to us, "Learn from me; for I am meek and lowly in heart." We thank you for all that you taught us when you walked this earth. We ask you to continue to teach us love, acceptance and forgiveness. We want to share our lives as you shared yours with so many others. We want to be examples of your love living in us and shining through us to others. Help those who feel unloved, and let them be open to your love for them. Let them take the risk of being vulnerable enough to receive your love so that they might be healed. Amen.*

Suggested for Steps 4, 8 and 9

# JANUARY 31

*"Bring the full tithes into the storehouse,
that there may be food in my house;
and thereby put me to the test, says the Lord of hosts,
if I will not open the windows of heaven for you
and pour down for you an overflowing blessing."*

Malachi 3:10

Christ has proven his love to us over and over again. When we find doors and windows closed to us, he opens another one, most often one that is better. He has always poured out an overflow of blessings even though we haven't always acknowledged or appreciated them. Let us take time now to say, "Thank you, Lord!"

He provides us with an abundance of faith when we put our lives into his hands. Our faith comes from his divine love and from the power of the Holy Spirit within us. It is always available to us, but we must put it to use in order for it to work. We must have confidence and faith in our God-given courage, abilities and talents. Because of our faith and God's precious love for us, our lives will be filled with goodness and joy.

We need not fear the unknown. He has our lives in his hands and wants the best for us. Our days are filled with love as long as we allow his Spirit to dwell within us. Difficulties don't confound us, for solutions come more easily as we trust him.

PRAYER:

*Help us, Lord, to put our faith in the goodness inherent in you and in others. Help us not only to look for the faults in people. Help us to respond in a loving manner and by our own attitude, to invite others to respond in a loving way toward us. Bless us through our faith in you to be a blessing in your name. Amen.*

Suggested for Step 2

# FEBRUARY 1

*"All things are possible to him who believes."*

Mark 9:23

This verse speaks of the power of Christ to "transform our weaknesses into strengths." This is the emphasis of the Second Step.

Sometimes February seems to be such an ominous month. In Minnesota where I live, it seems so cold, snowy and long. Minnesotans often say that when February is over, the worst of the winter is gone.

There are times when February seems endless. Similarly, there appears to be no end to the recurrence of our weaknesses. They seem, at times, to be continuous. But we are told that all things are possible. Can we accept this? Can we move in faith and anticipate the transformation of our weaknesses into strengths?

We need to believe that Christ is with us and if we labor together, we will not fail. To doubt that the *Spirit* who came to us in the person of Christ has the power to change us is to ignore God's presence. If we neglect to accept this promise, we set ourselves up to fail because we do not create an atmosphere for the omnipotent power of Christ to act on our behalf. We forget His love and concern for us. We forget that in the severest month of the year, we also celebrate Valentine's Day, a day that reminds us of love. God loved us first! This gives us the power to love others.

We need to trust God's love to transform, to warm our hearts, even in the middle of winter.

PRAYER:

*Lord, help us to turn to You. May we experience confidence that assures us that You can transform us. Let us be open to allow the freedom and the time to work in us . . . so that we experience Your gift of faith and rejoice in it. Amen.*

Suggested for Step 2                                    Vernon J. Bittner

# FEBRUARY 2

*"I consider that the sufferings of this present time
are not worth comparing with the glory
that is to be revealed in us."*

Romans 8:18

When we are willing to be open to the lessons that suffering teaches, we can gain much. That is difficult to do while we are in the midst of suffering, however. Our pain or loss so totally envelopes us sometimes that we cannot see the light shining from our Lord. We do not hear his assurances, "Cast your cares upon him," "Lo, I am with you always; I will never leave or forsake you," and so many more. We need to relax our pounding hearts and quiet our racing minds. We need to trust him for strength.

Perhaps you have visited with someone who has found blessings in suffering. Conversely, there are those who only become more bitter, cynical and depressed in their suffering. They turn away from our Lord instead of toward him and so compound their problem.

If we look at the suffering of Christ, we have a magnificent role model. As he prayed in the garden of Gethsemane, he knew what his fate was to be. He knew the suffering he would have to endure. He prayed, "Let this cup pass from me." On the cross he cried out, "My God, my God, why hast thou forsaken me?" Yet he endured his suffering for the greater glory, the redemption of our sins. In triumph he turned to his Father for strength and placed himself totally in the hands of God.

P R A Y E R:

*Lamb of God, your suffering was greater than we will ever have to endure. Thank you for showing us how to endure suffering by your own example. Grant that we may turn to you so that we too may claim the victory of this verse. Teach us to help others when they are suffering. Bless us to be a blessing as wounded healers. Amen.*

Suggested for Step 1

---

# FEBRUARY 3

*"The Lord is my shepherd, I shall not want;
he makes me lie down in green pastures.
He leads me beside still waters;
he restores my soul."*

Psalm 23:1-3

As we read the 23rd Psalm we know his peace is blessing us right now. We feel him restoring us in body, mind and spirit. We relax and feel the blessings of his peace. We willingly let go of our hurtful, troubled thinking and of our anxious, fearful feelings. We seek understanding and fulfillment and know that it can come only from him.

We need to learn to trust our Lord, but it is hard if we have been hurt by the important people in our lives. When this happens, we often hesitate to trust. We need to risk turning to him with a trusting heart and allow him to direct us. Then with joy, we release ourselves into the healing stream of life. We accept with gratitude the healing he offers. We feel the assurance that he is sustaining us in all that we do. We feel that all is well. In the words of the hymn, "it is well with my soul."

We need to spend more time in the entire 23rd Psalm. It has many wonderful promises that can calm our troubled spirits. We should also share this gift with other people who may need the strength of these promises. Let's take time to meditate on the 23rd Psalm and then do some journaling on what it means in our own personal life.

PRAYER:

*Thank you, loving Shepherd, for leading us out of the troubled waters and beside the still waters. Thank you for restoring our souls. Thank you for your constant awareness of our needs even as they constantly change.*

*We pray that others will experience the peace of still waters. We pray that they will be open to you for restoring their souls. Help them to see the gentleness that you offer as their loving Shepherd. Amen.*

Suggested for Step 2

---

# FEBRUARY 4

*"By this all men will know that you are my disciples,
if you have love for one another."*
John 13:35

When we think about this verse, we realize our need to show love for one another if we are to represent our Father. We need to take the time to alert ourselves about the lives of others around us. We need to offer our help and our love wherever it may be needed. Let us offer without waiting to be asked, because some people are too timid to ask for help.

Jesus taught us by his own example how we should treat other people. He taught us how to love the unlovable. He taught us how to forgive those who are difficult to forgive. He has told us in the Bible how we can live lives of love and concern for all types of people. He has promised that he is with us no matter what we might be struggling with in life. We need never feel alone. He is as close as a prayer.

There are so many needy people and many causes that could benefit from volunteers. We can share our lives in so many important ways if we will just be willing. Hospitals, nursing homes, prisons, churches and so many other helping organizations need volunteers to help all the people they serve. We can share our time and our lives with others and show the love of God by our willingness to get involved as volunteers. Let us think seriously this day about ways in which we can help others and thereby show the love of Christ.

P R A Y E R:

*Lord, forgive us if we have been too busy to help friends or strangers or too busy to listen to them. Forgive us for not treating others with love as you would have us do. Help us be willing to lend a helping hand to someone in need. Let us not waste hours or days in things that are not worth the waste. Help us to make our time count in dealing with others so that they can see a reflection of your love mirrored in us. Bless us to be a blessing. Amen.*

Suggested for Steps 4 and 12

# FEBRUARY 5

*"Wait on the Lord; be of good cheer,*
*and he shall strengthen your heart;*
*wait, I say, on the Lord."*
Psalm 27:14

It is not always easy to wait on the Lord and be of good cheer. When we struggle through life's difficulties, we often get buried in self-pity and feel we must find our own way out. We soon discover that we are unable to solve our problems on our own and eventually turn to our Lord for help and consolation. How much better it would be if we could just remember the words of this verse and turn to our Lord sooner!

We need to discipline ourselves to spend a part of each day in prayer and meditation, seeking our Lord's will for our lives. We need to remember the words, "He will strengthen your heart," and take confidence in that promise.

During trying times especially, we need to seek out our Lord's guidance and comfort. He can quiet a fearful, anxious heart sooner than any other means we may try. He is the Great Physician! Drugs will give us temporary relief, but they will not ultimately tranquilize our troubled spirits. He will give us peace and assurance without a hangover. Will we trust him that completely? "Wait upon the Lord!"

PRAYER:

*Almighty God, grant unto us today the gift of your Spirit so that our minds may be enlightened by your truth and our hearts made pure by your presence. Help us to be of good cheer and patient as we wait upon you. Grant that we may grow daily in the grace and knowledge of your love for us. Amen.*

Suggested for Step 11

# FEBRUARY 6

*"O that thou hadst hearkened to my commandments!*
*then had thy peace been as a river,*
*and thy righteousness as the waves of the sea."*

Isaiah 48:18

One of my hobbies has been to research the story behind some of our famous hymns and their writers. This verse reminds me of one of those hymns, "It Is Well with My Soul." The writer, Horatio Spafford, was a lawyer in Chicago in 1871 when the great fire swept through, and he lost all of his material possessions. Two years later, he sent his wife and four children on a trip to Europe while he rebuilt the business. Their ship collided with another in mid-ocean, and the four children drowned. His wife cabled home to tell him that she alone had been saved. His reply to this tragic news was "It is well. The will of the Lord be done!"

It was at this time that he wrote the hymn. I would like to share some of the words with you.

*"When peace like a river attendeth my way*
*And sorrows like sea billows roll:*
*Whatever my lot, thou hast taught me to say*
*It is well, it is well with my soul.*

*"My sin — O the joy of this glorious thought —*
*My sin, not in part, but the whole,*
*Is nailed to the cross, and I bear it no more;*
*Praise the Lord, praise the Lord, O my soul!"*

We can have the kind of faith that praises God even in the midst of difficult circumstances. But we must have a faith that is deeply rooted and well-nourished. Otherwise it will not be strong enough to survive when the first storm comes along.

PRAYER:

*Thank you, Lord, for those who inspire us by their example. Help us to take courage in this man's experience so that we too can say, "It is well with*

*my soul!" Grant that we may share our sorrow with others as this man did so that we use our brokenness to minister to others who are broken. Amen.*
Suggested for Steps 1, 2 and 6

---

# FEBRUARY 7

*"He knows what is in the darkness."*
Daniel 2:22

There is darkness in each of our lives at one time or another. Sometimes it is the darkness of illness, or the darkness of grief from an overwhelming loss. Sometimes it is darkness from guilt that we carry over something that we have done that was wrong, or something that was done to us that causes us shame.

For many, there is much darkness associated with the past. It may be our recent past or all the way back to our childhood. For some, there is much shame from experiences of incest or other abuses. When we struggle to keep painful pasts buried, we only make the problem more severe. Healing cannot happen unless we are willing to bring the darkness into the light. We need to clean out the dark corners of our lives.

Christ knows what is in our darkness. He knows the feelings of guilt, grief, shame or fear that we live with as we continue to live our lives with our pasts hidden. We need to confess our fears and feelings of inadequacies to our Lord and to another trusted person, perhaps a professional counselor, in order to humanly experience acceptance and forgiveness.

PRAYER:

*Lord, we are thankful that you know what is in the darkness. It is comforting to know that nothing is hidden from you. You accept us, no matter what is in our darkness. Give us the courage to deal with those areas of darkness, and let your light shine in for healing. We confess our need and acknowledge our gratitude. Amen.*
Suggested for Step 5

---

# FEBRUARY 8

*"If you abide in me, and my words abide in you, you shall ask what you will, and it will be done unto you."*
John 15:7

Certainly these words are not only a comfort to us, but they are an assurance that regardless of the circumstances of our lives, we may have serenity. We are promised a more abundant life and given the secret to a steadfast life. We have poise, calmness and assurance as we practice the presence of Christ. If he truly abides in us, we will have the fruits of the Spirit: love, joy, peace, strength and power.

How do we abide in Christ? First, we follow the word of God as set forth in the Bible. We practice his presence when we spend time in prayer and supplication. We abide in him when we fellowship with other Christians. We discover Christ when we practice unselfishness, love and forgiveness. We need to keep our minds fixed on God and allow the Holy Spirit to fill us and guide us.

Once we allow ourselves to "feel" the experience of abiding in him, it will be so rewarding that we will want to experience that same feeling time and time again. It is also important that we share this feeling, this peace, with others so that they too might desire the same experience.

P R A Y E R:

*Dear Lord, we thank you for your presence in our lives and for the peace that it brings. Help us to stay ever close to you and to realize the importance of your abiding in us. Forgive us for getting so distracted with our own lives and the world around us that we lose the priority of letting you abide in us. We want you to be our priority. Grant us the patience and commitment to make that possible. Grant that others may see beauty in us because of your abiding presence so that they too may seek this life. Amen.*

Suggested for Steps 2 and 12

---

# FEBRUARY 9

*"For I the Lord do not change."*
Malachi 3:6

It is good to know that our Lord does not change. He is ever constant. He is reliable. We need that assurance as we struggle with those areas of our lives that are destructive. As we work on our shortcomings, we are comforted by his constancy. Change need not be fearful or harsh if we trust in our Lord. We are aware that because we have the Spirit of God within us, we have the courage to change. We need to internalize his presence and his power.

As we discipline ourselves to trust in the Spirit of God, we realize that we can grow through any change with grace and serenity. We need not be rigid in our thinking. We need not be judgmental of our own lives or of others', for the Lord helps us to be flexible. We can adapt to any circumstances in our lives if we are willing to allow him to teach us acceptance. Our lives can have harmony even in the midst of change.

We have a responsibility, first, to be willing to change, and second, to be committed to trust him to help us through that change process. We need to begin to listen to the voice of the Holy Spirit as it guides us.

PRAYER:

*Constant and loving Companion, we are thankful for the promise that you never change. We thank you that during our own difficult times of change, we have your promise as Lord and Friend that you are ever-present. Grant us the courage to look at our lives with a microscopic lens and the determination to change what needs to be changed. Help us to be available to others who struggle to change those dark areas of their lives. Amen.*

Suggested for Steps 7 and 10

# FEBRUARY 10

*"Teach me to do thy will;*
*for thou art my God: thy spirit is good;*
*lead me into the land of uprightness."*
Psalm 143:10

In praying this prayer, we must recognize that we already know a great deal about God's will for our lives. We are not asking him to teach us his will, but to teach us *to do* his will. The Bible is full of instructions that we might know his will for our lives. The Ten Commandments, the Beatitudes, the Lord's Prayer, the 23rd Psalm and many more teach us about his will for our lives.

So with this verse as a reference, we start at a point of humility, admitting that we are not always wise, strong or obedient. We know that we will probably make mistakes, but that does not stop us from working on changing our destructive life styles. We know that the only way we can achieve serenity is to do the will of God. That not only requires humility, but it requires that we surrender ourselves completely to God. It requires that we set aside our own wills for our lives and commit ourselves to "let go and let God." That is not easy, but if we are sincere, God will help us make it possible.

PRAYER:

*Lord, we surrender this day completely into your hands. That is not easy, for we are accustomed to doing things our own way. Teach us to do your will and help us to keep open hearts and minds so that we are willing to listen to what you say to us. Bless others who struggle and help them to surrender their lives into your care. Amen.*

Suggested for Step 3

# FEBRUARY 11

*"Whosoever hearkeneth unto me shall dwell safely
and shall be quiet from fear of evil."*
Proverbs 1:33

We fear many things in a lifetime. Some people live so continuously with fear that they do not know what life is like without it. They fear getting cancer. They fear losing their spouse or child. They fear they are inadequate. They fear financial insecurity. They fear success, and they fear failure. They even fear *fear*. They are so preoccupied with the feeling of fear that they do not turn to the source of their security, our Lord.

Fear can only be overcome by facing it. We must be willing to risk trusting our Lord to see us through any circumstances. That involves our willingness to be vulnerable. That means we need to try to do just exactly what we are afraid to do. Understanding the source of our fear is an important part of overcoming it. If we can understand its origin, we will be able to face it with the help of Christ and overcome it.

We are promised that we can dwell safely in his love. We are assured that we can experience quiet from fear of evil. In order to claim those promises we need to turn our wills and our lives over to the care of Christ and trust that he will care for us. We need to realistically look at our fears and decide which are real and which are irrational. Some fear is good because it protects us at times when we might become careless. Other fears are real, and we need Christ's strength to face them.

PRAYER:
*Gentle Savior, thank you for your promise of safety and quiet from fear. Help us to turn to you whenever we are afraid. You are our Light. You are our Protector. You are our Shield and Sword. We thank you for being so many things for us in our time of need. Amen.*
Suggested for Steps 1 and 3

# FEBRUARY 12

*"Their sins and iniquities will I remember no more."*
Hebrews 10:17

Our sins are not only forgiven, but this verse promises us that our Lord remembers them no more. Unlike many of us, when our Lord forgives us, he does not keep throwing the wrongful acts back in our faces to punish or humiliate us. We are forgiven, and that is the end of that! Our Lord is willing to forgive and let go of the evil once and for all. Why are we so unwilling to treat ourselves or others with this same kind of love? We often go on feeling guilty for something we did years ago. Christ has already forgiven that deed (regardless of how terrible it was), so why do we refuse to forgive ourselves? Why must we go on punishing ourselves?

Or, many times when someone has hurt us, we just go right on carrying a grudge. We say we are willing to bury the hatchet, but then we leave the handle sticking out for easy access. That way we can clobber them again for hurting us. If Christ has forgiven them, why don't we? We need to explore these areas of our lives. Let's take some time out for journaling and forgiveness. We need to be honest about why we don't forgive ourselves or others if we are ever going to work through the process of forgiveness.

PRAYER:

*Lamb of God, you died for the sins of all. Help us to accept that forgiveness in all areas of our lives. Help us to forgive ourselves and help us to forgive others when they hurt us. Help us to be honest in our journaling so that we can learn what gets in our way of complete forgiveness. Remind us that we are forgiven only if we forgive! Amen.*

Suggested for Steps 8 and 9

---

# FEBRUARY 13

*"May you be strengthened with all power,*
*according to his glorious might,*
*for all endurance and patience with joy."*
Colossians 1:11

We have meditated in this book on renewal and the healing it can bring. This verse once again promises us that we will be strengthened with God's power. We can feel assured that the strength of the Lord is with us, around us and within us. We need only to accept this power he gives so freely and put it to use in our lives. Once we believe, we will feel this power surging through us.

Prayer and meditation are the ways in which we gain this greater strength. We need to take ourselves aside, out of the everyday stress, and spend a quiet, reflective time with our Lord. If we do this with a committed attitude, we will be filled with his serenity and feel an assurance that we can, indeed, "do all things through Christ who strengthens [us]" (Philippians 4:13).

Prayer and meditation require a discipline that we do not always have. We have to want an intimate relationship with our Lord more than we want anything else in life. We have to practice the precious presence of our Lord and empty our hearts and minds of all other concerns.

PRAYER:

*Lord, we thank you for the strength you give us each day. We are grateful that you fill us with the power of your love. Help us to appreciate this love which is so great and share it with others. Amen.*

Suggested for Step 11

# FEBRUARY 14

*"He that loveth not knoweth not God;*
*for God is love."*
I John 4:8

Today is Valentine's day! Traditionally it is a day of hearts, flowers, candy and pretty words. It is nice to have a day set aside to show our love, but somehow we need to show our love every single day. Today we will make a commitment to love one another. Today we will take the time to say, "I love you." We will appreciate one another on a daily basis. We will reach out and touch—reach out and hug and be available to one another.

We will practice unconditional love, a love that says, "I love you no matter what you do. I may not like what you do, but I love you and accept you and want to be available to you whenever you need me." We will let go of the hurt feelings we have been holding on to for so long and forgive others for whatever they have done to us.

We will remember that unconditional love means not only loving, but forgiving unconditionally. It means not judging others, but leaving judgment up to our Lord. Love means patience, tolerance, acceptance and reconciliation. It means remembering to take our friends before our Lord in prayer and ask for their healing. It means that we do whatever we can do to help and then put them in God's hands. We do not desert them, and we do not criticize them just because they refuse to change in the way that we want them to.

PRAYER:

*Teach us to love, O Lord, as you have loved us. We can only love ourselves and others if we truly love and obey you. Help us to be open to your will for our lives. Help us to be open to loving others and being loved in return.*

*Thank you for love! It is the stuff real life is made of. Amen.*

Suggested for Step 12

# FEBRUARY 15

*"Blessed are they that keep his commandments,*
*and seek him with their whole heart."*
Psalm 119:2

This verse says we will be blessed if we keep his commandments and seek him with a whole heart. That is a pretty big challenge. We struggle to keep his commandments and fall short of one or more of them at any given time. We make a lot of promises to our Lord that we do not always keep.

The last part of the verse is even more challenging if we are willing to be honest with ourselves. Do we ever truly seek him with a whole heart, or do we hold back parts of ourselves that we prefer to keep under our own control?

Do we seek him only when we are in trouble, or do we seek him often in a spirit of gratitude? Is our God a God of all times or merely an emergency God? We can claim his love and his promises for our lives if we are willing to seek him with a whole heart. But we must seek believing, seek trusting, seek with faith, seek expecting that he will hear and answer.

P R A Y E R:

*Help us, gracious Lord, to seek with a whole heart and to strive to keep your commandments. Help us to be available to others who seek you. We want to live lives that are pleasing to you, but we need your help. Grant that we may turn to you for guidance every day. Amen.*

Suggested for Step 7

# FEBRUARY 16

*"Yea, the Lord will give what is good."*
Psalm 85:12

If we are willing to take this verse seriously, not only to believe it, but to practice it, we will probably experience more abundance in life. We will also be more receptive to seeing some good in every situation, regardless of how difficult that may be. But that takes a lot of faith! First of all, we will have to change our attitude because the way in which we approach life can have a profound effect on the way we feel. It can also determine how successful our efforts will be.

"Believe and you shall receive" is a promise our Lord gives us every day. He wants us to live life more abundantly! Perhaps we would if we made a fresh commitment every morning to say, "I believe in good because my Lord has promised it" and keep that thought throughout the day. An attitude like that could change us so we would have a more positive view of life.

Whenever we face a difficult situation, we need to see it as an opportunity to change our negative feelings into positive feelings. We need to believe in the good that our Lord offers. Tragedy and sorrow can help us to experience God's goodness and much joy.

PRAYER:

*Precious Lord, we want to see the potential for good in all situations and in all persons. Help us to learn to trust in you so completely that we will not get buried in negative thinking. Help us to expect good and to recognize good when we see it in ourselves or in others. Thank you that even in the most difficult circumstances we can see and experience good. Thank you for your love, which makes that possible. Amen.*

Suggested for Steps 1 and 7

# FEBRUARY 17

*"Let the righteous rejoice in the Lord,*
*and take refuge in him!*
*Let all the upright in heart glory!"*
Psalm 64:10

This verse encourages us to trust and praise him. If we really trust him, we will trust him enough to "let go and let God." To let go does not mean that we abandon our responsibility, but rather that we do all that we can in any situation and leave the rest in his hands. It is important that we understand that letting go does not mean giving up. It means that we help our Lord to help us.

We can practice this letting go in complete trust by starting each morning with a fresh, new commitment. We need to state boldly, "I let go and let God, and I am free from anxiety, stress and strain." We need to quiet our minds and relax our bodies and reaffirm this commitment whenever tension starts to build up. We need to remember that God is always with us. He is in charge. We can trust his power to work in us. We need to believe and accept that God created us to live our lives abundantly, not filled with stress.

PRAYER:

*Precious Lord, we thank you for your comfort and guidance. Help us to be committed to letting go. We thank you for the peace and wholeness we experience as we feel the sense of strain being released from our bodies and minds. We thank you for healing. We pray for all who struggle to let go of the control of their lives. Help us to learn to trust in you more completely so that we might be good examples of your love. Amen.*

Suggested for Step 3

# FEBRUARY 18

*"Repent therefore, and turn again, that your sins may be blotted out, that times of refreshing shall come from the presence of the Lord."*
Acts 3:19

There is a saying that goes "Confession is good for the soul." If you have carried a burden of guilt for some time, you know the truth of those words. Once we confess, we experience the "times of refreshing" that come from the presence of the Lord. Unfortunately, many people feel their sin is too great to be forgiven and continue to carry the burden throughout their lives.

There are many examples in the Bible of those who felt they had committed the unpardonable sin. Peter denied Christ three times and felt so terrible that he went out and wept. The woman found in adultery was about to be stoned to death. Christ said after she confessed, "Your sins are remembered no more." One of the men hanging on the cross confessed his sins just before he died. Because of Christ's death on the cross, their sins and ours are forgiven, forgotten and buried.

Once we have confessed our wrongdoing to Christ or to someone we have hurt, we experience a feeling of refreshment. We are given a new chance, a new beginning. Why are we so reluctant to admit to Christ, to ourselves or to others our wrongdoings when the result would be forgiveness and new life? It may be false pride, shame, perfectionism or fear that stops us. Only you can answer for yourself! We need to journal about this area of our lives.

PRAYER:

*Great Redeemer, we thank you for your mercy this day. Help us to be more willing to admit our wrongs, experience forgiveness, commit ourselves to a more spiritual life style and share the joy of forgiveness with others. Amen.*

Suggested for Step 5

---

# FEBRUARY 19

*"My righteous one shall live by faith, and if he shrinks back, my soul has no pleasure in him."*
Hebrews 10:38

First of all, let us say boldly that we *do* believe, we *do* love him. He is important in our lives. Faith is not always easy for us. Intellectually we know that the only time we have peace in our lives is when our faith is active and we accept without a doubt that he is there with us. When our faith is faltering, we have only fear and doubt remaining. That is not enough to carry us through.

Think about these words: "Faith still believes when reason and common sense say that it shouldn't, and then *hope thrives* because faith believes!" We need that hope, and in order to have hope, we need an active, participating faith. In order to have an active, participating faith, we need to stay close to our Lord. We need to trust him with our lives.

There are many days when faith comes so easily and is such a wonderful gift, but some times there seem to be far too many days when our faith is a constant struggle. We want to learn to have faith even when common sense and reason say that we should not.

P R A Y E R:

*Dear Lord, this is our prayer for this day, for ourselves and for others. Help us to believe with simple, childlike faith because you have shown us that it really works. Bless others who struggle as we do and touch them with the healing balm of faith. Amen.*

Suggested for Step 2

# FEBRUARY 20

*"Not that I have already obtained this or am already perfect; but I press on to make it my own, because Christ Jesus has made me his own."*

Philippians 3:12

We need to recognize that we will never reach perfection while we are on this earth. We often frustrate our own and our Lord's efforts to change us when we believe we must be perfect. We need to strive to do our best, but we also need to accept the times when we will not succeed. It may not be that we failed at our goal, but simply that our aim was too low or too high. We need to set new goals with our Lord involved in the goal-setting process. He knows what is best for us, and he knows our needs and our abilities better than anyone.

Change takes time, but we do not allow ourselves an adequate amount of time to change. It took us a long while to get to the place where we are in life. A lot of other people contributed to who and what we are today. Some people contributed good, while others exerted bad influences and left ugly scars embedded deeply in our hearts and souls. We need to allow ourselves time to change, time to "unlearn" some things and learn new things. We need courage to try our new behaviors. We need positive people to give us their honest evaluation. We need constructive feedback, not just put-downs. Our Lord is ready and willing to help us change our lives so that we are more pleasing to him. When this occurs, we are able to love ourselves as we ought.

PRAYER:

*Loving Savior, we thank you that we need not be perfect. You accept us just as we are and love us as your children. Help us to be patient with change, not only with ourselves, but with others as well. Amen.*

Suggested for Step 6

# FEBRUARY 21

*"Love is patient and kind;*
*love is not jealous or boastful."*
I Corinthians 13:4

This verse can be very confusing. If love is patient and kind and we do not feel patient and kind when someone has hurt us, does that mean that we are not loving? We may still feel love toward that person if we do not hate him or wish him ill. Yet, we lose patience and then we may avoid him and isolate ourselves. Does our hurt block that love, or is it possible that we can still love him even in our hurt?

We need to ask our Lord to help us to see how he would have us live. Most of the time, the hurt or rejection blocks our patience and dims our expression of love. We know that love can unlock the door to patience, so we need to choose to love him. Can we be kind even in difficult circumstances? With God's help, we can be if we don't take it personally or allow the feelings of others to determine our value as persons.

We know we need to be open to change some of our stubborn character defects and be open to people's caring. That is not easy because it is not easy for us to trust. We may have been hurt many times by people who seemed to invite and promise love but instead hurt us. Who can we trust besides God? What must we do to find a lasting, caring love? We do not ask for romantic love, just some truly caring human love. We need to risk. The only way to learn trust is to risk trusting.

PRAYER:

*Help us, caring Friend, to let go of our expectations of people that are not reasonable. Grant us healing from the hurt that others have caused because they were insensitive. We know they must be hurting too, or they would not hurt us. Help us to take an honest look at ourselves and accept our own shortcomings. Then, help us to trust even when it demands taking a risk. Amen.*

Suggested for Steps 8 and 9

# FEBRUARY 22

*"Peace be within your walls,*
*and security within your towers."*
Psalm 122:7

This verse reminds us of what we all want in our lives. But the truth is that in many homes, there is no peace or security. Some people live in constant fear of physical danger from those who are supposed to love them. Child abuse and abduction have reached alarming proportions in our country. Children are taught to live with fear and mistrust of many people. Family violence affects more and more families. We seem to live in brutal, frightening times.

We wonder why this is happening in such alarming proportions. We wonder if there is any solution to this problem that damages so many lives.

But our Lord said, "I have come that you might have life and have it more abundantly." He wants us to have peace and security within our walls. That is only possible when we possess his love within to guide us.

P R A Y E R:

*Lord and Protector, we thank you for the peace that is possible when we truly love you. We thank you for the security that you promise us. Help us to love one another and not to abuse one another. If we need healing in that area, let us have the courage we need to get professional help to make those changes happen. Amen.*

Suggested for Step 1

# FEBRUARY 23

*"Be glad and rejoice forever in what I create."*
Isaiah 65:18

When we take time out for prayer and meditation, we need to take the time to thank God for all that he has created for us. There is so much splendor all around us, and most of these beauties of nature are free to enjoy. We can see God's hand in everything around us. Even something as small as an ant can be a wondrous sight to behold as we see how diligently it works. The sky, the ocean, flowers and all other gifts from God add to the beauty of our lives.

We need to be glad and rejoice in these gifts. We need to develop a new awareness and new sensitivity so that we do not waste these wondrous blessings from God.

He has given us many good and wonderful gifts. Too often we ignore them and struggle to accumulate more material possessions than we could ever use. From time to time, we need to slow down and appreciate the grandeur with which God has surrounded us.

PRAYER:

*Loving Creator, this day is a special day because of your love. The beauty all around is a gift from your hands. You created it for us to enjoy. We have not earned all that you have given us. Help us to be ever mindful of your blessings to us and to share them with others. Help us to preserve our resources and not waste them. Amen.*

Suggested for Steps 4 and 11

# FEBRUARY 24

*"Instantly Jesus reached out his hand and rescued him. 'O man of little faith,' Jesus said. 'Why did you doubt me?'"*
Matthew 14:31

This familiar passage is from the story of Peter when he was out on the Sea of Galilee. As long as his gaze was fixed on Jesus, he was able to get out of the boat and walk on water. Once he started to think about how inadequate he was and how impossible the situation was, he immediately began to sink. Christ gave him the confidence he needed to do something difficult. There is a lesson in this for all of us.

As long as we look to the Master for guidance, we are given the confidence to do what we must do. When we let go of his hand and start to walk on our own way, we often get lost and our thinking becomes muddled. If we are to do his will, we must keep our minds on him. Otherwise, like Peter, we lose sight of him and sink.

This is especially true during the process of change. At first we decide to change because there is pain in our lives that makes us uncomfortable. Then as we start to change, we think we have to do it all by ourselves and find that we are not able. False pride can get in our way and cloud our view of the Master. We may lose sight of our goal until we realize once again that it is Christ who transforms us.

PRAYER:

*Lord, we thank you for standing by us just as you stood by Peter. We are grateful for your presence and the confidence you instill in us. Help us to keep our eyes fixed on you so that we will not lose sight of our goal, our transformation. Amen.*

Suggested for Step 7

# FEBRUARY 25

*"In the beginning*
*God created the heaven and the earth."*
Genesis 1:1

Think about this verse. If only we could remember that God *was* from the very beginning! Instead of stumbling along in our own isolation, we need to remember that our Lord has been there from the beginning and we need to seek his help in all that we do. Before we get so buried in separation and the belief that we can do it alone, we need to remember to turn to our Lord for help. Instead of looking only at our faults and feeling unworthy, we need to turn to our Lord and accept the good that has been in us since our creation. We need to trust that we can begin fresh each day. We can begin anew in God because he has made it possible.

We can begin again with God at the beginning of all that we do. We can leave the past mistakes in the past because he encourages us to go on. We can forgive the hurts of the past because we have seen the greatest example of forgiveness: the death and resurrection of Christ. We can let go of the past and let God take charge today! This is the day to begin, and we are ready to see new visions, to feel new hope and to dream new dreams.

P R A Y E R:

*Loving God and kindly Shepherd, help us to let go of the past and give you our wills and our lives today, for you know what is best for us. Help us to put you at the beginning of everything that we do. Help us to forgive past mistakes, our own and others', so that we can truly believe with new vitality. Let us be available to others who struggle to begin anew. Amen.*

Suggested for Step 3

---

# FEBRUARY 26

*"Bless the Lord, O my soul,*
*and forget not all his benefits."*
Psalm 103:2

It is easy to forget all of God's benefits to us, especially when things are going well and we feel good about life. We may enjoy perfect health and never appreciate what a blessing it is until one day a serious illness afflicts us. Many of us discover too late how wonderful good health is and also learn that once it is severely affected, nothing can restore it short of a miracle from God.

We may take our loving friends' relationships for granted without taking the time we should to say, "Thank you" or, "I love you." Then without warning, death takes a friend or a loved one and the void is so vast that we do not know how to fill it. Or, perhaps a foolish quarrel may sever our bond and both parties are too full of pride to say, "Please forgive me. I really care about you." Then we feel the loss, when often we have failed to appreciate them in the first place.

Let us commit this day to our Lord in gratitude for all his benefits. Let us appreciate our health, our friends, our family, our employer, our government. Most especially, let us truly appreciate the love of God through Jesus Christ, his Son. Let us take time to count our blessings.

> *"Count your many blessings,*
> *Name them one by one;*
> *And it will surprise you*
> *What the Lord has done."*

PRAYER:

*Lord, we confess that we do not always take the time to talk to you and to thank you for all that you give us. We ask for your forgiveness for our lack of appreciation for the things that we take for granted every day. Help us to appreciate them more fully and give you thanks. Teach us to be aware of our blessings without being reminded. Amen.*

Suggested for Step 5

---

# FEBRUARY 27

*"Let your conversation be without covetousness;*
*and be content with such things as you have;*
*for he has said, I will never leave you, nor forsake you."*
Hebrews 13:5

There is probably no human condition as devastating as loneliness. People of all ages feel lonely for one reason or another. The aging process can bring loneliness simply by the reality that we lose our friends and loved ones through death. Teenagers often feel alone even in the midst of their peers. That feeling drives many of them to suicide. As busy as young housewives and mothers are, they quite often feel that others do not appreciate them, and they feel as if life is passing them by.

There is a difference between being alone and being lonely. Being alone is not only a choice, but it is healthy for us to spend some time alone. Christ spent time alone in the garden of Gethsemane, in the desert, on the mountain—alone in prayer with his Father. We too need this time alone.

He has promised he will never leave us or forsake us, and he never has, even though we have felt alone. He is a constant friend and companion.

He teaches us we need not be lonely if our attitudes are right. He teaches us how to make use of our aloneness as he did. He encourages right relationships that prevent us from being isolated and lonely. He is with us, around us and within us. We are never alone.

PRAYER:

*Loving Companion, thank you for never leaving us. Remind us that we need not be lonely if we reach out in love and acceptance. Help us to take time alone with you so that we may learn your will. Help us to reach out to others who feel lonely and share your love with them. Amen.*

Suggested for Step 12

---

# FEBRUARY 28

*"And when you stand praying, forgive, if you have anything against any, that your Father also, who is in heaven, may forgive your trespasses."*
Mark 11:25

Some of us are very prayerful people. We spend a great deal of time praying for our own needs as well as the needs of others. We desire to grow in our faith through the process of prayer. Yet our Lord cautions us that if, while we are praying, there is anything in our hearts for which we have not forgiven others, we must take care of that first. Otherwise, we will not be open to what God has to say to us. He even warns that unless we forgive, we will not be forgiven. That's pretty stern!

There have been many times in my life when I prayed even though I was hurt or angry with another person. There have also been times when I was about to receive communion and I remembered that I was asking for forgiveness although I was harboring resentment toward someone else.

Our Lord makes his desire very clear to us. Even if we have brought our gifts to the altar and remember that someone is angry with us or we with them, we are to leave the altar and go and make amends. Then he invites us to come back to him rejoicing. We cannot truly rejoice with our Lord if there is any unforgiveness in our hearts.

PRAYER:

*Lord, help us to take this verse seriously. We will experience forgiveness only if we forgive. Don't let our false pride get in the way of being loving. Help us to be willing to make amends wherever there is a need in our lives. Thank you for your forgiveness of us, which gives us the power to forgive others. Amen.*

Suggested for Steps 8 and 9

# MARCH 1

*"My Father! If it is possible, let this cup be taken away from me.*
*But I want your will, not mine."*
Matthew 26:39

The third step is a call to surrender our wills and our lives to the care of Christ even though we don't completely understand the fullness of His grace.

Our example for this is Jesus. Matthew 26 is the account of our Lord's passionate suffering and death on the cross. The month of March reminds us of this because this is the month in which we observe Lent.

Appropriately then, this should be the month in which we work on the third step. Our Lord turned his will and his life over to his Father (even to die). Now we are to do the same.

This is difficult for all of us, just as it was for Jesus. If our primary purpose is to do only what we want to do, then we will never experience the guidance of our Lord . . . and we will never know the abundant life.

I am convinced that I will never find happiness unless I want my Lord's will instead of mine.

PRAYER:

*Help me, Lord, to desire your will, not mine, so that I might know your guidance and experience the abundant life. Amen.*

Suggested for Step 3                                                   Vernon J. Bittner

---

# MARCH 2

*"From whence does my help come?*
*My help comes from the Lord, who made heaven and earth."*
Psalm 121:2

Even when our lives seem so upside down and filled with complexities we cannot solve, we are aware that he is there to help us. We give thanks for that. We give thanks that there is no difficulty beyond which he has a solution for us. We are thankful that all anxieties can be overcome if we just take the time to turn to him in trust. We need only remember the power of his love and to seek and accept his help. We are grateful for that awareness.

We are so grateful for his presence in our lives. He is there to share our joy. He laughs with us. He is there to share our sorrows. He cries with us. He is a devoted companion in our laughter and our tears. We are grateful for his constancy.

He encourages us to live our lives abundantly, to live them to the fullest. He helps us to express our faith and our love joyously. Let us always give him the praise. He is indeed the source of our help.

PRAYER:
*Help us as well as others to see the beauty and the wonder in our lives. Help us to see the beauty in one another, not just the pettiness. Help us to forgive. Help us to love unconditionally even when we are hurting. Let us remember the truth in this verse: "My help comes from the Lord!" Amen.*
Suggested for Steps 1 and 3

---

# MARCH 3

*"I will restore you to health
and heal your wounds, declares the Lord."*
Jeremiah 30:17

I have been a doubting Thomas for most of my Christian life. I doubted everything that everyone told me about healing. I really doubted that God *could* or that he *would* heal me in any way. I pretty much believed that whatever happened that was bad in my life was my fault or another person's. Likewise, I felt that if anything good was to happen, I would have to make it happen myself. I just didn't think God cared, and when times got really tough, I doubted his existence.

That was several miracles ago! Since then, things have happened to me that cannot be explained in any common-sense way. I have experienced spiritual, emotional and physical healing that is a miracle. I have had signs from God that neither I nor others can deny. Things have happened that give me goose bumps because I am forced to believe that the hand of God is present and very real. I have been cured of the doubting-Thomas attitude by healing and events that could only come from God.

PRAYER:
*Divine Healer, thank you for the miracle of healing. Thank you for showing us in the midst of our doubts how much you love us and want us to be whole. Help us to be willing to cooperate in the process of our healing. Let us willingly share your love with others and our healing with others. Amen.*
Suggested for Steps 2 and 3

---

# MARCH 4

*"Pleasant words are as a honeycomb,
sweet to the soul, and health to the bones."*
Proverbs 16:24

There has been much research on the effects of anger, resentment and unforgiveness on the body, mind and spirit. We can become physically or emotionally ill from negative thinking. We can leave ourselves wide open for serious disease unless we learn to live without anger. We can seriously hamper our immunity by harboring unforgiveness.

This verse speaks loudly to the importance of pleasant words and their effects on the soul and even bones. It has taken us centuries to learn what authors of the Bible knew so long ago. Surely our Lord encouraged love because he wanted what was best for us. He taught good emotional, spiritual and physical health through what we think and say and believe. He was the Great Physician. He has given us the most effective prescription ever prescribed: love!

PRAYER:

*Great Physician, we ask your help in living a life that is physically, emotionally and spiritually healthy for us. Help us to take seriously your teaching that "pleasant words are as a honeycomb." Let us realize the importance of filling our hearts and minds with clean thoughts. Help us to be loving and gentle with our words when dealing with others. Keep us from harboring anger. Amen.*

Suggested for Step 9

---

# MARCH 5

*"If you had faith as small as a tiny mustard seed . . .*
*nothing would be impossible."*
Matthew 17:20, *The Living Bible*

Jesus is not asking us for much: the size of a tiny mustard seed! And yet there are times in our lives when he could just as well be asking for faith the size of the tallest mountain. During barren times in our lives, it is difficult to find even a still, small glimmer of faith. During those times, we doubt our Lord. We might even question that he really cares.

But this verse gives us hope. Our faith can be so small — barely visible — and yet a tiny flicker of hot ash can start a forest fire blazing. So too can a prayer whispered in total exhaustion start the fire of faith glowing again in our hearts. He asks only that we acknowledge in some way that we still believe or even that we want to believe but are struggling.

He will take that tiny seed, that faint flicker, and ignite our spirits with his love and assurance. We need to be willing to acknowledge him. We need to be willing to let go and let God.

PRAYER:

*Loving Nurturer, we thank you for taking what we have to offer, great or small, and increasing it with the power of your love. We thank you for accepting us just as we are. We thank you for your willingness to work with us and your patience in that process. We love you, dear Lord. Amen.*

Suggested for Step 3

# MARCH 6

*"Jesus went into the temple of God,
drove out the merchants and knocked over
the money-changers' tables and the stalls
of those selling doves."*
Matthew 21:12, *The Living Bible*

Christ was human in many ways that
we are human. That should make living and doing his will much easier for
us. In this story we see Christ's anger. Too often we are taught that anger
is bad and people who get angry are bad. There is such a thing as good
anger, even healthy anger. Christ's anger was quite often directed toward
those who committed injustices against other people or toward those
who lived the life of a hypocrite.

We should recognize that there is good anger. Good anger is constructive and helps us to defend or to express a value. Or, it may force us
to make a necessary change in life style. In some situations the anger may
be lifesaving if it helps us to protect ourselves against another's violence.

Let us look at our anger and the reasons why we are angry. Is it con-
tructive or destructive anger? Is that anger helping us to get better, or is
it making us sick? Anger that results from hurt and unforgiveness is destructive anger and either makes us sicker or keeps us from getting well.

PRAYER:
*Heavenly Teacher, we thank you for your examples of good anger and
for all that you taught us when you walked among us. Help us to be willing
to take an honest look at our anger. If it is unhealthy anger, let us be willing
to turn to you for help in letting go of it. Help us to be tolerant with ourselves
and others when anger gets in the way of loving. Amen.*

Suggested for Step 4

---

# MARCH 7

*"Be kind to one another, tenderhearted,
forgiving one another, as God in Christ forgave you."*
Ephesians 4:32

It is easy to be kind to those who are
kind to us. It is easy to forgive someone who says, "I am sorry I hurt
you. Please forgive me." The true test of faith comes when we try to
apply these words with unkind, immature people who continue to hurt us
time after time. Sometimes the hurt goes so deep that it takes a long
while for it to heal. It becomes even more difficult when the people who
hurt us are the important others in our lives and are those whose love we
desire the most.

We need to turn to our Lord once again for an example of love and forgiveness. He experienced much of the same humanness that we encounter, and yet he remained kind and compassionate. He loved Judas, and Judas betrayed him for 30 pieces of silver. He loved Peter dearly, and Peter denied him. He loved Thomas, and Thomas doubted him. Many people whom Jesus loved let him down, and yet he loved them so much that he forgave them. When they were filled with despair, he gave them hope. When they were filled with sadness, he gave them joy. When they doubted, he gave them reassurance. When they were filled with sorrow, he comforted them. Christ is the greatest example of how we too must love and forgive.

PRAYER:

*Loving Lord, we thank you for the love and forgiveness that you taught us. Help us to be willing to treat others the way you treat us. Heal us when we are deeply hurt and remind us that we can love that person with your help. Remind us that you can heal our hurt. Amen.*

Suggested for Steps 8 and 9

# MARCH 8

*"The Lord your God in the midst of you is mighty;*
*he will save, he will rejoice over you with joy;*
*he will rest in his love, he will joy over you with singing."*
Zephaniah 3:17

There are many times when we feel physically, emotionally and spiritually exhausted. Far too often we rely on our own resources to renew ourselves. We might even go to a doctor, take vitamins, buy something new to cheer us up or find activities to distract ourselves. This does not always work because it has no lasting quality. We often seek solutions in the wrong places.

Another interpretation of this verse is "He will renew you in his love." He promises he will renew us. He will heal us where we need to be healed. If we are physically depleted, he will either heal us or help us to accept our situation and go on and live life the best we can. He will even help us know what we can change and what we have to accept.

He will renew us emotionally and spiritually. We have the responsibility to ask, to seek, to knock. We need to believe he can renew us with his love. We need to relax and let him fill us with his peace and calm.

PRAYER:

*Lord, Healer, Renewer, help us to trust in you enough to allow you to take over and renew us with your love. Help us to be willing to become entirely ready to have you transform our lives. Amen.*

Suggested for Step 6

# MARCH 9

*"Where two or three are gathered in my name,*
*there I am in the midst of them."*
Matthew 18:20

Our Lord wants us to know that we need not be in a large group in order to experience his presence. Where two or three of us gather *in his name,* he is in the midst of us. One important thing this tells us is that we have no excuse to fail to pray for one another. We need only invite one or two believers to pray with us in Jesus' name for ourselves and for others.

We are also assured that God's will is done in response to our prayers, whether his answer is what we specifically prayed for or not. We need to remember to pray for his will in the lives of others as well as our own. God knows what is best for us. His plan includes our long-range good, not just solutions for today's problems.

As we share the message of his love and forgiveness with others, we need to hold them up in prayer. It has been said that "prayer changes things." If we believe that God hears and answers prayers, then we are committed to praying for the needs of others. That includes praying especially for those we feel are really floundering because of their life styles. No one is lost to Christ unless a person rejects him. He died for us all.

P R A Y E R:

*Savior, we thank you that you have promised to be in our midst when we gather in prayer. Help us to leave the judgments up to you. We do not know all the circumstances in a person's life. Help us to love as you love and forgive as you forgive. Amen.*

Suggested for Step 11

# MARCH 10

*"Keep on growing in spiritual knowledge and insight,*
*for I want you always to see clearly the difference*
*between right and wrong."*
Philippians 1:10, *The Living Bible*

We are encouraged to "keep on growing in spiritual knowledge and insight." In order to do that, we need to discipline ourselves to spend more time learning about his word, more time in prayer, more time serving others and more time alone with our Lord in meditation. Our world is a busy, hectic place that pulls our time and attention in many different directions. If we do not set time aside, we will not find the time to grow.

This verse says, "for I want you always to see clearly the difference between right and wrong." We need to be able to distinguish that difference. Everyday life provides opportunity for us to choose between the two. The Bible is our rule book that tells us how we can know right from wrong. Those rules were set down by our Lord. He did not just leave us to stumble around in the darkness.

Unfortunately, even when we know the difference, we continue to do wrong. We can, for example, be unforgiving even though our Lord says very clearly that we are to forgive if we are to be forgiven. Far too often we refuse to forgive and continue to hold a grudge. We need to know that our Lord is serious about what he teaches us.

PRAYER:

*O great Teacher, thank you for giving us the opportunity to grow in spiritual knowledge. Help us to commit ourselves to grow in your love. Help us to fully understand the difference between right and wrong and let us choose right. Your way is the right way. Your way is the loving way. Thank you for your love. Help others to grow in your knowledge and love. Amen.*

Suggested for Steps 10, 11 and 12

---

# MARCH 11

*"You shall rejoice in all that you undertake,*
*in which the Lord your God has blessed you."*
Deuteronomy 12:7

We have so much to rejoice about in all that we undertake. God has truly blessed us with so much to be thankful for. Yet, we waste much of our time trying to find that magical ingredient to bring about what is called "successful living." Sometimes we miss the really important things and wonderful opportunities because success is too often incorrectly defined. In our modern-day world, far too many people judge success based on the accumulation of material possessions, but we cannot take these things with us when we die, and no amount of money can buy friends or health.

So, what is success? Maybe we seriously need to ask ourselves this question. Success is loving and being loved in return. Success is having a meaningful relationship with our Lord and with others. Success is being happy with what we have, whether much or little. Success is being satisfied as well as grateful for whatever we accomplish in life while striving to do better with the gifts he gives us. Success is having the *serenity* to accept the things we cannot change, *courage* to change the things we can and the *wisdom* to know the difference.

PRAYER:
*Thank you, Lord Jesus, for the many reasons we have to rejoice. We praise you and thank you. Help us to share that joy with others so they might know you better. Amen.*
Suggested for Steps 4 and 11

# MARCH 12

*"You also be patient."*
James 5:8

One virtue that we need to practice during the process of change in our lives is patience. Each day when we take a daily inventory of our lives, we need to be patient with ourselves. Some days we will be pleased with the progress we are making. Other days we will see old habits still in existence that we thought we had conquered. That will be disappointing, and we may feel that we have failed. We do not like setbacks or delays. We need to pray for patience and the ability to be gentle with ourselves.

Our God is a God of patience. He does not expect the perfection from us that we expect from ourselves and others. He encourages us when we stumble and fall. He gently picks us up with arms of love and assurance and says, "Keep going, my child. I wil help you and guide you."

We need patience with ourselves and others, those who struggle to change just as we do. They choose not to change their destructive life styles, but struggle much as we do in trying to keep the *status quo*. It is very frustrating to stand by and watch someone we love destroying himself with alcohol or other destructive ways. We are powerless to change him, and it hurts to observe his self-destructiveness. We need patience! We also need to turn him over to our Lord just as we do with ourselves.

PRAYER:
*Lord, we thank you for your patience. Even when we think you have abandoned us, you are right beside us. You wait patiently for us to realize the error of our ways and turn to you. Help us to be patient with ourselves and others and to wait patiently for you. Amen.*
Suggested for Step 10

# MARCH 13

*"Yes, Lord, let your constant love surround us,*
*for our hopes are in you alone."*
Psalm 33:22

Our Lord is willing to send his constant love to surround us. When our minds are weary and discouraged, he will grant new zest and enthusiasm. Where life needs renewal, he will touch us with his healing power and give our lives meaning. For those who feel too tired to go on, he will give strength and hope.

He grants us peace of mind and quietude of soul. He provides us with the wisdom that is necessary to build better lives. He will give us the courage to take an inventory of our lives and change what needs to be changed. We need to accept that we must be willing to do our part by participating in the healing process.

He will grant us patience as we struggle with destructive character traits. He will let us know that through his love, our lives can be transformed. For those of us who need a purpose for our lives, he will reassure us that he does have a purpose for us if we are willing to turn our lives over to his care. We must sincerely desire healing and be willing to listen to his will for our lives in order to be instruments of his love and forgiveness.

PRAYER:

*Precious Lord, we pray for others today who are hurting physically, emotionally or spiritually. Touch them and let them feel your presence. Fill them with the hope of your love. Ease their burdens and let them know they need not bear them alone. Help us to be willing to help others in whatever way we can to know your love and forgiveness. Amen.*

Suggested for Steps 3 and 7

# MARCH 14

*"Strengthen the weak hands, and confirm the feeble knees."*
Isaiah 35:3

This is an important reminder of the responsibility we have as Christians to do what we can to strengthen our brothers and sisters. We can share the message of his love and forgiveness with others when we find them doubting his unconditional love. We can befriend those who are new Christians as they continue to struggle with their old lives and friends of the past who are not yet Christians. We can participate with them as they meditate on God's word for the first time and dialogue with them on how it might apply in their daily lives. We need to affirm them and help whenever possible.

We may have an opportunity to minister to those who do not have Christ in their lives. They may be at a place in their lives where they are completely devastated by trials or losses. If they are not Christians, they do not have that wonderful source of power and strength that we have, Jesus Christ. Sharing with them the love and hope that Christ offers at this time could be a marvelous opportunity.

We need to be committed to witnessing to others of the love of Christ. Whether they are fellow Christians or non-Christians, we need to be available to support them. We can be friends to those who believe they have no friends. We can be wounded healers to those who are hurting. We can give hope because we have experienced hope in our despair. We can comfort the grieving and love the unlovable. All of this is possible for us because Christ has given us his strength.

PRAYER:

*Loving Father, we thank you that when we need to be strengthened, you are right there with us. Help us as wounded healers to be willingly there for others when they need your strength. Help us to love others as you love us. Amen.*

Suggested for Steps 11 and 12

# MARCH 15

*"I will instruct you and teach you the way you should go; I will counsel you with my eye upon you."*
Psalm 32:8

When we take an inventory of our strengths and weaknesses, one of the things we need to do is recognize, believe and accept our ability to learn every day. We are not only capable of learning new things and new behaviors, but we can actually "unlearn" destructive behavior and attitudes. Often we get so discouraged that we fail to see this as one of our options. We do not believe we have that potential. On our own we do not have that ability, but with the help of Christ, we know that we can do almost anything we are called upon to do. Christ is within us to teach us and guide us.

We approach this day with the assurance that whatever we encounter this day will be an opportunity for us to express the joy of life, the joy of loving God and to use our God-given talents. We know that our Lord will teach us all we need to know.

But we have a responsibility to be open to his teaching, or we may miss out on wisdom. He stands ready to teach us. We must listen and be willing to act.

PRAYER:
   *Loving Guide and Teacher, we thank you that you care enough to teach us better ways to achieve peace and serenity. Help us to be open to learn and to be willing to let go of our destructive character traits. We thank you for your patience. We thank you for the ability to understand and especially for the opportunity to know new things. We are grateful for healthy minds. Amen.*
Suggested for Step 4

# MARCH 16

*"Everyone enjoys giving good advice,
and how wonderful it is to be able to say
the right thing at the right time."*
Proverbs 15:23, *The Living Bible*

This is an important verse to listen to, particularly for those of us who love to give advice, who need to be right all of the time, and for those who do all of the talking and none of the listening. It is a blessing for us to be able to help others who seek our help or advice. It is an even greater blessing to know that some times we are right. It is also important for us to admit when we are wrong.

   It is especially important for us to understand the significance of listening as well as talking. In order to have true caring, in order to have meaningful communication, caring and communication must be two-way. We not only share ourselves and Christ when we talk, we also share when we listen, but we must listen with open hearts and open minds.

   And when we are not actively communicating with other people face-to-face, we need to communicate with our Lord on their behalf through prayer. Prayer is an important vehicle of communication. It helps us to stay in touch with what is going on in our own lives, and we can also intercede on behalf of others. That is Christlike living. Prayer also helps us to stay in tune with our Lord's will for us.

PRAYER:
   *Thank you, Divine Communicator, for opening our hearts, our minds and our spirits so that we can hear you and others. Let us be open to their needs and bless us to be a blessing for you. Help others to know that we truly care and that we will listen to them. Hear our prayer, O Lord. Amen.*
Suggested for Step 12

# MARCH 17

*"Draw near to God and he will draw near to you."*
James 4:8

There are times in our lives when we feel distant from God. We think that he has deserted us or that he doesn't care. Some times when there is pain in our lives, the noise within is so loud that all we can think of is that pain. We are so busy looking only inward toward our own suffering that we fail to look around and see God.

This verse suggests that some times we must take the first step toward God. We must acknowledge our need for him in our lives, and then he will draw near to us. He is always close at hand, but he wants an invitation to come even closer. When we decide that he has left us, we are often too angry to call out to him. We need to remember his promise never to forsake us.

Perhaps we need to practice calling on God and drawing near to him as a regular part of our Christian belief. If we only call out to him when we are in trouble, he becomes no more than an emergency God. In that case, we miss out on a lot of loving communication and fellowship with him. We need to draw near to him in good times as well as hard times.

P R A Y E R:

*Lord, we ask for your help in learning to communicate better with you. Help us to discipline ourselves so that we take more time out to draw near to you. We thank you for your constant vigil even when we are not aware of it. Bless others this day. Amen.*

Suggested for Steps 1 and 2

# MARCH 18

*"Thanks be to God, who gives us the victory."*
I Corinthians 15:57

God gives us the victory, but what does it mean to be given victory? First of all, the word *victory* means "to win"! To have victory means that we no longer need to be victims for other people to abuse. We can now break the paralysis of fear that has kept us living unfulfilled lives for so long.

We will be able to achieve victory over the poor self-image we have allowed ourselves to have. We know that God loves us and that he will give us victory over any area of our lives in which we need healing. If we are tied to the pain of the past, he will give us victory over that part of our lives by helping us to let go.

In order to claim the victory he offers us, we need to put our trust in the omnipotent God. He loves us completely. He will give us the strength to deal with any part of life that needs acceptance or change. He will give us the courage to risk new behavior and new relationships. He will help us transform our weaknesses into strengths and live victoriously in his love. He will help us to become winners and allow others to be winners, too. Together with God, we can all be winners.

PRAYER:

*Loving Father, we thank you for the victories that you make possible in our lives. Help us to be willing to trust you so that we can change our lives and be winners. Let us be willing to let go of destructive character traits so that we can live our lives in peace and serenity. Amen.*

Suggested for Steps 3 and 10

# MARCH 19

*"Make me to know thy ways, O Lord;
teach me thy paths."*
Psalm 25:4

We need to be open to God's will for our lives, to be willing to follow him where he would lead us. So many times we pray for his guidance and when he tells us what he wants of us, we reject the idea. We know his way is the right way. We need to ask forgiveness for being stubborn and wayward.

Today, let us lift our hearts and souls up to him. He will fill us with his love and light the path he would have us follow. Let us draw closer to him so that we may be used where we are needed. Let us be open to be a blessing to someone who needs to know his special love. Let us represent him in true Christian love.

At this time, some of us may be at a crossroad and unsure of the direction we should take. Pride may push us in a direction that is not the best for us, but hurt and loss whisper, "Go God's way." We need his strength. We need his guidance for important decisions.

As we pray and meditate and journal today, let us think about the decisions we make on a daily basis. If we usually choose to go our own way, why do we? If we are reluctant to follow the path he has directed us to, why are we so hesitant? Perhaps if we understand why we do what we do, we will be able to change our bad habits.

PRAYER:

*Bless others who are struggling over what to do with their lives. Lead them gently, Lord, to whatever is best for them according to your will. Thank you for your guidance and your willingness to be there for us always. Amen.*

Suggested for Steps 6 and 10

# MARCH 20

*"For freedom Christ has set us free; stand fast therefore,*
*and do not submit again to a yoke of slavery."*
Galatians 5:1

When we experience powerlessness in our lives, it is important to know that Christ has set us free from the bonds of slavery. We experience slavery in many forms in our lives. Depression is a form of slavery that keeps us from enjoying the abundant life that Christ wants for us. Some of us experience depression like a heavy, dark sack over our heads, drawn tight by a rope. It does not let light in. It does not let hope in. We cannot see the light of the love of God and others because we are in darkness. Filled with despair, we feel like we cannot breathe.

Fear is another form of slavery that causes us to waste our time worrying about things that may never happen instead of living every moment to the fullest. Fear can take over every facet of our body, mind and spirit, leaving us too paralyzed to act on our own behalf.

Guilt and anger are other forms of slavery that keep us from becoming whole. Every one of us is enslaved in some way. We need to look at our lives and face our own forms of slavery and make a decision for freedom in Christ's love. To do that, we must have faith that Christ can free us from any form of slavery regardless of how binding it is.

PRAYER:
*Dear Lord, grant us the courage to want freedom more than slavery. Help us to redirect our emotions to live healthy life styles according to your will. Give us assurance that through your love, we can live power-filled lives that are pleasing to you. We thank you for your continued care. We pray for all who struggle to be free from pain-filled lives. Free us to serve you in love and gratitude. Amen.*

Suggested for Step 2

---

# MARCH 21

*"Verily, verily, I say unto you, that you shall weep and lament . . .*
*and you shall be sorrowful, but your sorrow shall be turned into joy."*
John 16:20

It is good to know that when we go through sorrow, our sorrow will eventually be turned into joy. This verse does not promise us that we will avoid sorrow, but it does tell us that God knows our pain and assures us of his presence. He reminds us that our pain will not last forever. When we experience joy again, we will have reason to praise him.

I once heard it said that sorrows are God's winds that will blow us to his breast if we are willing to let them. Sorrows can make us better or bitter depending on how we perceive them. We must not waste our sorrows with bitterness and complaining. Disappointments, loss, loneliness and even failing health can bring us closer to God and others than can any amount of joy. Often we don't really see how much we need God until we begin to lose an important part of our lives.

One of the greatest blessings of my life was to lose my health and nearly lose my life. For the first time I had to make a priority of something other than material possessions. God's promises became more real to me, and I began to see how important it was to have the love of friends as well as God.

PRAYER:

*Merciful Lord, we thank you for the promise that our sorrows will not last forever. We are thankful for your presence during times of loss. We pray for guidance to help us through these times of sorrow. Help us to find beauty even in the most difficult times. Let us turn to you for wisdom so that we can gain from our experience. Then, help us as wounded healers to be willing to share with others all that you have done for us. Amen.*

Suggested for Step 11

# MARCH 22

*"Let us then pursue what makes for peace
and for mutual upbuilding."*
Romans 14:19

God did not create a world of war. That is the handiwork of humankind. He created us for harmony. In recreating us, he wants us to help one another in a spirit of love and understanding. Somehow we "blew it," and we continue to cause our own strife. Each of us can make a difference in the pursuit of peace, but we need to start by taking a close look at our own lives. We need to look at our hearts and realize that our motives are often mixed. Do we really want peace? Are we willing to give up pettiness and false pride in order to make peace possible? Are we willing to change our attitudes toward others in order to restore harmony?

First we need to look at the whole area of forgiveness. Is there someone to whom we need to apologize for a hurt we have caused? Is there someone whom we have refused to forgive because we want to get back at him or keep him at arm's length

We can do much to promote a spirit of love and peace if we are willing to follow Christ's example. He has given us the most powerful book there is on positive human relations. We can learn to love the unlovable, and by doing that, we are showing the path of peace. Remember, Jesus did not command us to trust everyone, but he did tell us to love everyone.

PRAYER:

*Loving God, fill us with a desire for peace. Help us to realize that we are stewards of the message of your Son, Jesus Christ, and that we teach by example, not by empty words. Let us be willing to invest our time and prayers and talents in the area of peacemaking. Help us to forgive as we are forgiven. Help us to make amends where we have caused injury. Thank you for the gift of peace. Amen.*

Suggested for Steps 8, 9 and 12

---

# MARCH 23

*"We know that in everything God works for good with those who love him, who are called according to his purpose."*
Romans 8:28

For many people, the main concern about this verse is "For what purpose am I called by God?" That is a very perplexing question and one that is not easily answered. I think we need to remember that just as our needs and our abilities change, God's purpose for us changes. Certainly a young parent with several children has less time and energy to focus on God's purpose for his life than does someone will less immediate responsibilities. Our roles differ and change with time, and so does God's purpose for our lives. He may have had one purpose of great importance when we were 25. Now he has a different but equally important purpose for us when we are 50. (Figure out your own younger and older ages here.)

The important thing is that regardless of our ages or our present circumstances, we need to be open to his purpose for our lives. The verse says, "In *everything* God works for good. . . ." That is all-inclusive! Perhaps we can serve best during times of sorrow or illness. Perhaps we can serve best when everything is "good" in our lives. We must let God choose how he can best use us.

PRAYER:

*Thank you, Divine Counselor, that you find a useful purpose for each of us. Thank you for concentrating on what is good and useful in our lives and not on what is petty and destructive. Help others to be open to your purpose for their lives. Thank you for all that you are for us. Amen.*

Suggested for Step 3

# MARCH 24

*"Yes, ask anything, using my name and I will do it."*
John 14:14

This is an easy verse for us to misinterpret because it says to ask anything! What we need to remember is that we can ask anything, but what we ask for must be in line with God's will for our lives. We ask for many things that are not the best for us, and if we got everything we asked for, it could be very destructive for us. Some times we wonder if God really loves us when he does not give us what we request. This is especially true if what we asked for was unselfish and seemingly good for us.

We need to remember what our Lord said to his Father: "If it be thy will; nevertheless, not my will but thine be done." He accepted the fact that His Father does not grant all of our wishes. He has a broader plan that we may not understand.

Certainly it was not unreasonable for Christ to ask before his crucifixion, "Let this cup pass from me." Yet if the Father had granted his Son's request, where would we be today?

P R A Y E R:

*Help us, kindly Master, to ask, understanding that what we want may not be best for us or our loved ones. Help us to accept your will for our lives and not to get discouraged even though we do not always get our way. Grant that others may be willing to pray according to your will and pray expectantly. Amen.*

Suggested for Step 11

---

# MARCH 25

*"The Lord sees not as man sees;*
*for man looks on the outward appearance,*
*but the Lord looks on the heart."*
I Samuel 16:7

Too much of our time is spent dressing up to impress other people. In the United States, we spend billions of dollars on beauty products, hair care and pills in the hope that we will impress other people. We surround ourselves with material possessions so that everyone will know how successful we really are. We want people to see us as beautiful people who have achieved much.

But God could care less about our outward appearance. He looks at our hearts and, many times, is probably saddened by what he sees. If we were to spend even a small portion of the time we use on our outward appearance to make our hearts beautiful, we would be much more loving people. If we were willing to dedicate ourselves to beautifying our hearts and our minds, beauty would also show on the outside. When we have inner beauty, when our hearts are filled with God's love, we show it on the outside. People experience us as very special when the love of God that is in us shows through us.

PRAYER:

*Heavenly Father, help us to set priorities in our lives so that we spend our time beautifying our inner spirits rather than our outward appearance. Help us to discipline ourselves so that we live to serve you and others and not just to accumulate material possessions. We thank you for all that we do have. Help us to be willing to share with others who are not as fortunate. Amen.*

Suggested for Step 4

# MARCH 26

*"Whatever you wish that men would do to you, do so to them."*
Matthew 7:12

These words are often called "The Golden Rule," and they seem so simple, and yet we find them difficult to apply in our lives. If we treated others the way we want them to treat us, life would be very pleasant because we would be loved and respected. We do not want others to treat us with cruelty, pettiness or scorn. We do not want them to be angry, resentful, hurtful or unforgiving toward us, and yet we quite often treat other people that way when we are hurt.

We want and need to be treated with love, respect and acceptance. When we are not, we feel very hurt and left out. Our egos and self-worth suffer yet another blow. If we recognize our own need to be loved and to be treated with human kindness, why do we not also realize that others have that same need?

If we give love away, it comes back multiplied. If we are kind, we usually receive kindness in return. If we are good listeners when others need someone to hear them, we will always have someone to listen to us in return. We receive in proportion to the amount we are willing to give.

PRAYER:

*Lord, we commit ourselves this day to treating others the way we would like to be treated. By doing this, we will not only be fulfilling your law of love, but we will feel your blessing upon the way we reflect you to others. Keep us ever mindful of how we treat others. Amen.*

Suggested for Steps 8 and 9

# MARCH 27

*"Let not your heart be troubled:*
*you believe in God, believe also in me.*
*Let not your heart be troubled,*
*neither let it be afraid."*
John 14:1,27

Although we hear these words often, we do not always remember them during difficult times. Although we do not mean to be so careless with our faith, we are so involved in what is happening to us that it is easy to be sidetracked. We would suffer so much less if we could only remember that even during the most painful times, he is with us. He can bring peace, hope and calm. We do not need to be afraid! He has given his word.

Sometimes we hang on for a long time before we are ready to "let go and let God." We do not easily make the decision to turn our wills and our lives over to the care of Christ. We suffer a great deal more than we would have to as a result of our stubbornness.

"Let not your heart be troubled, neither let it be afraid." If we can only practice letting go of our fears—fear of loneliness, loss, illness, failure and even death! He will give us the courage and confidence we need to face any part of our lives if we are only willing to seek him first.

PRAYER:

*O great Comforter, we are assured of your presence, and with that confidence will come the strength to live one day at a time, victoriously. Grant us the determination every new day so that we are willing to let you have our lives to direct as you see best. Help us to share our knowledge of your love with others. Amen.*

Suggested for Step 3

# MARCH 28

*"Therefore, if one is in Christ, he is a new creation;
the old has passed away, behold the new has come."*
II Corinthians 5:17

We can rejoice in the knowledge that we can become new with the help of Christ. Regardless of how destructive our past may have been, he lets us know the old can pass away and the new can begin. We may be reluctant to believe that it is truly possible to forget our past mistakes, but God has a very bad memory when it comes to our past indiscretions. Christ told the woman who was caught in adultery, "Your sins are remembered no more." Others were ready to stone her to death, and she felt she was irredeemable because of her past.

Christ paid the price for her mistakes as well as ours. Once we confess our wrong with genuine humility, he forgives us and wipes the slate clean. We can begin a new day because the old has passed away and is no longer remembered by Christ.

Then our responsibility is to accept his forgiveness unconditionally, as he wants us to, and use our energy to do better in the future. Perhaps the most difficult part for most of us is forgiving ourselves and letting go of the self-condemnation and the feeling of hopelessness that we too often carry. If we do not take this responsibility seriously, it is as though we are snubbing Christ's death on the cross and deciding that it is insufficient to deal with our terrible sins. That is a mockery of his love.

PRAYER:
*Lamb of God, who takes away the sins of the world, we thank you for your mercy. Help us to accept your forgiveness and be willing to let go of our past because we are assured by your love that we are forgiven. Help us to use the energy of your forgiveness to become the new creations you want us to be. Amen.*

Suggested for Steps 6, 8 and 9

# MARCH 29

*"Cast all your anxieties upon him, for he cares for you."*
I Peter 5:7

Many things in everyday life cause us anxieties and stress. We constantly need to be aware of our source of comfort. We need fear nothing! We need dread nothing! Our Lord is in charge. Whatever the need is, he will make sure that need is met. Whatever the problem, he will help us solve it. Nothing we come up against in our lives is greater than the power of God. That power is always present, always with us.

We need to remind ourselves that we have no need to be anxious. God is in charge. God is with us with his healing power. God is with us to supply all of our needs. God is with us with love and forgiveness. We can have peace of mind in the assurance that he is with us. Anxieties need not overwhelm us.

We can be a blessing to others who are experiencing anxieties by being available to them to share their time of stress. We can share our own experiences with them and how God's love helped us through those difficult times. There may be several ways that we can help them, and it is important that we let them know we are willing to help in whatever way they feel would be best. We must not be too pushy. We must let them choose a way for us to help. Some people have difficulty accepting help even when they desperately need it.

PRAYER:

*Lord and loving Caretaker, we thank you that you care enough for us to relieve our anxieties. We thank you for the peace and assurance you give us during times of stress. We are grateful for your presence in our lives. Help us to remember to turn to you when we are anxious. Help us to be willing to be available to others who are experiencing stress. Amen.*

Suggested for Step 1

---

# MARCH 30

*"Therefore, I tell you, whatever you ask in prayer, believe that you have received it, and it will be yours."*

Mark 11:24

When we pray, do we really pray expecting a positive answer or for that matter, any answer at all? When we pray, do we pray believing that our Lord will answer our prayers in ways best for us? This verse says, "believe that you have received it, and it will be yours." Have you ever prayed believing that you have indeed received it because you asked and he answers? Many of us will admit that we have never prayed and believed this way and that this verse is completely new to us.

What a lovely thought. What assurance! What confidence! What love! Believe you have received it, and it will be yours! That really confirms and reinforces all the other promises he has given us about asking and receiving.

PRAYER:

*Hearer of our prayers, help us to develop a new attitude toward prayer. Teach us to pray believing that we have received. Teach us to pray with a spirit of expectancy. Teach us to pray with confidence. Thank you for hearing and answering our prayers, great and small, spoken and unspoken. Help us in the area of prayer to believe that you hear and will answer. Amen.*

Suggested for Step 11

# MARCH 31

*"I will put my Spirit within you*
*so that you will obey my laws and do whatever I command."*
Ezekiel 36:27

When we are willing to allow the Spirit of God to become an active part of our lives, our lives change for the better. The Spirit of God can penetrate our fear, anxiety, doubt and insecurity. He can break down the defenses that keep us from having a loving and intimate relationship with him. His special voice within us can give us the confidence we need to make difficult decisions. He can provide shelter from the storms of life. He can direct us to a resting place where he will comfort and strengthen us. He can and does remind us that God is always with us. We need only ask, and he will make his presence known.

Think about this: If the Spirit of God is a positive influence in our lives, why do we resist giving him a place in our lives? Perhaps the answer is that old word *control*. We feel more secure if we believe that we are still in control of our lives. If we truly were to allow the Spirit of God to take over our lives, we would have to be willing to let go of the control. We would have to "let go and let God"! For some of us, that would be pretty scary!

P R A Y E R:

*Spirit of the living God, fall fresh on us. Anoint us with your love and let us learn to love your presence. Take away the fear of letting go that is so much a part of being human. Help others who struggle this same way. Amen.*

Suggested for Steps 2 and 3

# APRIL 1

*"Jesus said to her: I am the resurrection and the life.*
*Whoever believes in me will live, even though he dies. . . ."*
John 11:25

April, symbolically, is the month that reminds us of new life and the resurrection as well as spring. The fourth step invites us to look at ourselves and discover who we are, where we've come from and where we would like to go.

In order to experience more fully the significance of the resurrection of Christ, we need to open up our hearts, our souls and our lives to him. We need to know ourselves so that we can make ourselves known to him and receive the peace that comes with the reality of the resurrection.

Self-awareness is a vital part of spiritual growth. We need to become aware of our strengths and weaknesses so that we can die to that which is destructive in our lives and draw close to God's love so that we can be resurrected to new life in Christ.

The month of April symbolizes that promise. Working the fourth step makes it possible for us to rid ourselves of those things that block his love and light from entering our lives. As children of God, we have the promise of the resurrection. However, even though he has chosen us, we need to respond by choosing him as well. The resurrection, for us both now and in eternity, will only be ours if we prepare ourselves to receive his precious gift to us.

PRAYER:

*Looking at ourselves and seeing ourselves as we really are can be painful. Yet, unless we know our weaknesses, we are unable to rid ourselves of the traits that block us from receiving your most precious gift: the resurrection of our lives. Lord, help us to believe in your resurrection so that our inventory of ourselves can be fearless. Amen.*

Suggested for Step 4                                             Vernon J. Bittner

---

# APRIL 2

*"Honor your father and mother.*
*And you fathers, provoke not your children to wrath,*
*but bring them up in the nurture and admonition of the Lord."*
Ephesians 6:2,4

Many adult children remember being "pounded over the head" with the first part of this passage, "Honor your father," in such a way that they feel guilty if they do not feel that way toward their parents. Yet the truth is that many parents are not honorable. Children are threatened into "respecting" their parents even though their parents give them no reason to respect them. The only people who deserve honor and respect are those who earn that respect. The result is that when these children become adults, they are confused, angry and hurt, and they feel guilty.

But there is more to this verse than just that first part. Parents are to "provoke not [their] children to wrath," and they are to nurture and love them. That is the only way we can show the love of god to other people or to our own children. We cannot teach love through terror and brutality and then demand that our children honor us. Our actions speak louder than our words.

Those of us who were raised in homes that demanded respect but demonstrated other behavior need to make a special effort to change that for our children. We must demonstrate openness, honesty, love, patience and gentleness to our children in order to teach love. We cannot pound it into them.

PRAYER:

*Loving Father, help us to teach respect by being respectable. Help us to teach honor by living honorably. Help us to teach love by being loving. Help us to teach forgiveness by asking for and giving forgiveness. Let us be loving parents to our children as you are to us. Amen.*

Suggested for Step 12

# APRIL 3

*"God is faithful,*
*and he will not let you be tempted beyond your strength,*
*but with the temptation he will also provide the way of escape,*
*that you may be able to endure it."*
I Corinthians 10:13

There have been several times in my life when I sincerely doubted the truth of this verse. There have been times when I was so overwhelmed with grief and hurt that I sincerely doubted that God knew the capacity of my strength. I kept reminding him that he was leaving things on the wrong doorstep and that he had miscalculated my coping ability.

I also believed that he had deserted me in my hour of greatest need, and I was angry with him. I couldn't see him. I couldn't feel him. I couldn't hear him. I felt abandoned by the very one who was always supposed to be there for me. In my grief and loneliness, I turned away from him and decided he was unreliable. Of course that made my situation a lot worse.

And yet, each time I look back in retrospect, I realize that he had never left me. He was right with me in every moment of physical, emotional and spiritual peril. If he was willing to die on the cross for me, how could he leave me in my hour of need?" The answer was always "No, he loves me too much to leave me alone." I realize now that at those points of exhaustion, I needed to admit my powerlessness and turn to him for help.

PRAYER:

*Almighty Father, thank you for your protection in times of trial. Thank you for knowing our capabilities better than we know them ourselves. Help us to use all that you have provided for us, including the Word and Sacrament, to renew ourselves when we are exhausted. Be with those who doubt you during the times of their powerlessness and give them confidence to turn to you. Amen.*

Suggested for Steps 2 and 3

# APRIL 4

*"Faith comes from hearing,*
*and hearing by the word of God."*
Romans 10:17

If, indeed, faith does come from hearing, then we must be sure that we listen intently. We can be so distracted at times that it is possible to attend a worship service and listen to the word of God without ever actually "hearing" it. We can discipline ourselves to take the time out for prayer and then have our minds so cluttered that we neither "hear" nor "feel" the presence of God. We may be aware of the distraction and try to bring ourselves back to a committed state of awareness in the prayer process but soon drift off again.

We need to ask ourselves if we really hear the word of God. Do we hear our Lord when he speaks to us through the needs of other people? Do we really concentrate when we are in the presence of our Lord?

Since faith comes by hearing and hearing by the word of God, we need to make a fresh commitment every morning to listen intently. Otherwise we might not hear the important message our Lord has for us.

P R A Y E R:

*Gracious Lord, help us to improve our listening skills so that we may learn more about you and your will for our lives. Help us to listen more clearly to other people so that we can really be available to them. Teach us the discipline we need to commit ourselves to being better listeners. Amen.*

Suggested for Step 11

# APRIL 5

*"So neither he who plants nor he who waters is anything,*
*but only God who gives the growth."*
I Corinthians 3:7

We are reminded here that we can do nothing about our powerlessness. The verse also reminds us that only Christ can transform our weaknesses into strengths. We have available to us the potential power of the Triune God if we are willing to seek him. We can do many things to change our lives, but if we do not have Christ as a part of our lives, we will fail. It is like taking a hybrid seed, planting it in perfect soil, watering it regularly, but giving it no light to grow. Without light of some kind, no growth will take place. Christ is that light, and he also helps in the weeding process.

This verse is humbling for those of us who believe we can take care of ourselves. In fact, we may struggle for quite some time, believing there is some other way we can get the same results. The problem is that we never reach a point of harvest. We struggle to grow on our own, but we fail because we exist in total darkness. We cannot live our lives without the source of light. We cannot grow without the touch of the Master's hand.

PRAYER:

*Lord, Giver of life, we acknowledge that we cannot change our lives without your influence. We are only stumbling in the darkness. We cannot grow unless we involve you in the growth process. Help us to let go of our false pride and invite you into our lives. Make us willing to let go sooner so that we can be available to others who struggle as we do toward wholeness. Amen.*

Suggested for Step 7

# APRIL 6

*"As thy day is so shall thy strength be."*
Deuteronomy 33:25

We may wonder about the truth this verse promises some days. On those days when our lives seem to be filled with strife and pain, we may really question that we have the strength for that day. Our struggles often seem so intense that we are worn out just trying to get through the day. Every new day brings a different set of circumstances into our lives. Some days our needs are great, and some day our needs are small. But in his infinite wisdom, God knows our every need, great or small, and he provides it even before we ask.

We have no need to worry, for in the goodness of his heart, God supplies all of our needs beyond all measure. Lovingly as our lives change amid pain and pleasure, he showers us with peace and rest. We can take his hand trustingly, believing his promise, "As thy day is so shall thy strength be." He has never failed us, and he never will. We have failed him and ourselves, and he still loves us.

PRAYER:

*Heavenly Fahter, you are near every hour of every day with your special mercy. You cheer us on and give us the confidence to keep going. Thank you for your presence every day. Thank you for the touch of your hand and the smile on your face. Grant that we may help others whose days are filled with stress and share the promise of your love with them. Amen.*

Suggested for Steps 4 and 10

# APRIL 7

*"Rest in the Lord;*
*wait patiently for him to act."*
Psalm 37:7, *The Living Bible*

Hopefully we all know what it is like to rest in the Lord. When we experience difficult times such as a loss, anxiety and fear, we can become very exhausted by trying to handle things completely on our own. We may struggle along for quite some time before we finally admit our powerlessness. Until we admit our powerlessness, no one, including God, can help us. We are, in reality, trying to be our own gods, and it never works out.

This verse also says we need to "wait patiently for him to act." It is difficult to have patience when we—or someone we love—are experiencing great pain. We want the pain to stop *now*! We want things to be better *now*! We want healing *now*! We almost demand that God will give us the solution we want.

When we finally acknowledge our powerlessness and admit that only God can help, a feeling of peace settles over us. We begin to feel rested. We begin to feel at peace. But first we need to recognize that all of our bargaining is to no avail. God cannot be compromised. We cannot trade favors. We cannot dictate the terms of surrender. We will not get help until we recognize that reality.

P R A Y E R :

*Lord of peace and rest, we thank you that we can rest in you and feel sure that all is well. We thank you for that rest. We thank you for the many lessons you teach about patience. Help us to be more patient with you and with others. Amen.*

Suggested for Step 3

---

# APRIL 8

*"Be ye steadfast, unmovable,*
*always abounding in the work of the Lord,*
*forasmuch as ye know that your labor is not in vain*
*in the Lord."*
I Corinthians 15:58

Is there any reward, any payoff for taking a serious look at our lives to see what needs to be changed? It takes a lot of self-discipline to take a daily inventory and then take action when we need to make changes. Is it really worth it? Old ways are predictable ways. It is easier to do what we already know than to venture out and try new ways.

Most of the time we are unable to achieve serenity unless we are willing to part with the old ways. A healthy pride and a positive self image can only be achieved if we are willing to change those destructive character traits. We can con ourselves into believing that our lives are satisfying, but chances are we will continually be reminded that it is not as we would like it to be.

This verse promises that our efforts will not be in vain. If you have ever successfully broken a bad habit such as smoking or nail biting, you know the good feeling that comes with that success. Christ wants us to feel good, and he is willing to help us through the process of change.

PRAYER:

*Eternal God, grant that we may remain steadfast, pursuing your will. We know we continually need to work on our lives so that happiness can be ours. Give us the desire to find our true selves in you. When we truly love you, we are able to lose ourselves in genuine helpfulness to others. Help us to be fully committed to the necessary changes in our lives. Amen.*

Suggested for Step 10

# APRIL 9

*"It is the spirit in a man, the breath of the Almighty, that makes him understand."*

Job 32:8

The second step requires us to be willing to believe in the power of the Holy Spirit so that Christ can transform our weaknesses into strengths. This Spirit of God within us gives us the understanding we need in order to change. This Spirit can give us love for, and understanding of, ourselves and others. If our hearts are filled with love and understanding, we can release the past and set new goals for our lives. If we listen to the voice of the Holy Spirit, past hurts will no longer have power over us. We can change our lives if we are willing to let go of destructive character traits and live one day at a time. The Holy Spirit can give us the courage to let go of the past, stop worrying about the future and live for today.

But there is a requirement: we must believe in the power of the Holy Spirit, and we must be open and willing to have our lives transformed. That requires faith and trust. That requires taking a risk. That requires action, not reaction.

PRAYER:

*Holy Spirit, Divine presence, we freely acknowledge our need of you in our lives. Help us to take the time to become better acquainted with you. Help us to trust enough to let go willingly because we believe in your power.*

*Help others who struggle and give them the assurance that if they just let go, they will be led by you. Teach us to trust. Amen.*
Suggested for Step 2

---

# APRIL 10

*"God did not give us a spirit of timidity, but a spirit of power and love and self-control."*
II Timothy 1:7

We need to be thankful for the spirit of power and love and self-control that we have been given by our Lord. We need to use that spirit wisely and unselfishly. Let us refrain from abusing any destructive power that we have. We need to practice an inner strength to love others patiently, calmly and with true Christian love. We need a love that accepts others just as they are. God can help us to use our self-control to keep us from trying to change them our way. Changing others is Christ's responsibility. Ours is only to love them unconditionally.

Our Lord can help us to refrain from becoming angry or irritable with people about unimportant things just because we want control. Through Christ, we can remain in control of ourselves and be loving. He will help us to encourage others to grow and change in the way they need to and not as we see their needs. Our responsibility is to support them in love and show them we really care. We also need to show them that at times, we care enough to confront them with tough love.

PRAYER:

*Thank you, Lord, for your investment of love in us. Thank you for trusting us to serve others in whatever way you choose. Let us be open so that if someone needs friends, they will feel that they can turn to us. Let us love as you love us. Thank you for teaching us self-control. Amen.*
Suggested for Steps 6, 7 and 10

---

# APRIL 11

*"And when he had thus spoken, he showed them his hands and his feet."*
Luke 24:40

Christ's disciples needed to see his nail-pierced hands to be assured that this was indeed their Lord. They needed proof positive. They did not trust his word. We are not much different from them today. There are times when it is difficult for us to trust Christ just on his word. It would be so much easier if we could see his nail-pierced hands and put our fingers in the wounds in his side. But how much more wonderful it would be if only we could trust him completely without having visible proof!

There is much more in the hands of Jesus than the scars of a cruel crucifixion. His hands reach out in healing to those who will believe. His hands reach out in comfort to those who grieve. His hands reach out in cleansing to those who will receive from him.

His hands are gentle, loving hands that reach out to welcome us into his open arms. His hands are secure hands that assure us of eternal life when we accept him as our Lord. His hands touch people of all classes, races, ages and religious beliefs. There is no bigotry in his ministry. His hands still reach out to any and all who will believe in him and receive him as their Lord.

P R A Y E R:

*Gentle, loving Savior, we thank you that your hands reach out and touch each of us at our point of need. We thank you for all you offer us. Help us to reach forth boldly and take your hands in trust. Walk with us, gentle Savior, and lead us to the service you would have us do. Let us extend our hands to others in love as you have love for us. Amen.*

Suggested for Steps 2 and 12

---

# APRIL 12

*"It came to pass that Jesus went out into a mountain to pray and continued all night in prayer to God."*
Luke 6:12

We need to take a lesson from our Lord. He took the time to be alone so that he could meditate and pray. He knew the importance of spending time apart from others and alone with God. Certainly we must not isolate ourselves by being alone, but we need to spend some private time with God and his creation. There is an important difference between solitude and isolation. One brings peace, the other only loneliness.

Our Lord also taught us much about nature. Many of his sermons were preached by the seaside, in the fields, on the hillside, in a boat on a lake. Many of his illustrations were about things of nature: the birds and foxes, the harvest, the furrow, the clouds and wind, lightning, a grain of mustard seed and many more. He must have loved nature and shared that love when he spoke to others.

For many of us, it is not possible to go out into the country to be alone with God. We are prisoners in a cement jungle. Nevertheless, it is important for us to find a special place to be alone to meditate and pray. It need not be elaborate or costly. We only need some uninterrupted time and space to be with God

PRAYER:

*Divine Creator of the earth and all its wonders, help us to appreciate the beauty of your creation. Help us to take time to enjoy the loveliness of flowers, the singing of birds, the ripple of streams, the beauty of sunshine and all you have given us. Help us to respect these wondrous gifts and teach others to preserve your creation. Amen.*

Suggested for Step 11

# APRIL 13

*"By this all men will know that you are my disciples,*
*if you have love for one another."*

John 13:35

How can we find a better way to show the love of Christ in us than through the practice of love? Whatever we may be doing, we can do it better with love. If we need to make amends, we must first love. Love heals hurt feelings. Love forgives mistakes. Love sees good and beauty in others, not just their faults. Love conquers fear and loneliness. Love unites us with one another and with God. Love changes ugliness into beauty in our lives, if we are willing to seek it. Love allows us to experience the best in other people. Love teaches us patience and tolerance toward those who seem incapable of giving or receiving love.

We can show our love for one another in many ways. Today we make a commitment to love in as many ways as we possibly can. We will love and protect the gifts of nature that God gives us. We will love and affirm our love to as many people as we encounter today. We will love the unlovable by remembering them in our prayers of intercession. We will love ourselves unconditionally, for we too are gifts of God to all people. We will love and appreciate our Lord by showing that we love one another.

PRAYER:

*O Divine Lover, Creator, we thank you for love and for all that you teach us about love in the Bible. We thank you for your example of love when you walked this earth and for you love of each of us as special and unique to you. We are grateful that you loved us so much that you gave your life that we might be forgiven and have abundant life. Amen.*

Suggested for Steps 8 and 9

# APRIL 14

*"But now is the time. Never forget the warning,*
*'Today if you hear God's voice speaking to you,*
*do not harden your hearts against him.'"*
Hebrews 3:15

Now is the time to let go. Now is the time to turn our wills and our lives over to the care of Christ. Yesterday is gone, and tomorrow is not yet given. We need to start living in the present if we are going to find meaning in our lives. One of the important responsibilities of living in the present is to do as this verse suggests: "Today if you hear God's voice speaking to you, do not harden your hearts against him."

First, we need to listen for God's voice. At times, we get so involved in the noise of our lives that we tune out the voice of God. We need to quiet ourselves so that we can hear God speaking to us. We need to be "be still" so we can know God.

Next, we need to open our eyes so that we can "see" God speaking to us. He does not always speak to us in words, but many times in pictures. He speaks to us through joy and sorrow. He speaks to us during moments of quiet meditation and during loud, boisterous confusion. Whether or not we hear him may depend on how sincerely we want to hear him.

PRAYER:
*Precious Lord, help us to quiet ourselves so that we can hear you when you speak. We need to let go of the turmoil of our lives, but that is not easy. Give us trust so that we feel safe in letting go. Give us patience so that we understand that change takes time. We acknowledge our powerlessness to change on our own. Help us! Amen.*
Suggested for Steps 2, 3 and 11

---

# APRIL 15

*"When you pass through the waters, I will be with you.*
*They shall not overflow you."*
Isaiah 43:2

Often during stressful times, we feel like we are "in over our heads." We may be so burdened that we feel like we are drowning, like we are going down for the last time. It is a frightening experience, and at the same time we also become aware of just how powerless we are to change our circumstances. But we can be comforted in the reality that God knows that we are in deep waters and will not allow those waters to overtake us. He measures them out in such a way that we can grow from the experience but not be overwhelmed by it.

In our time of grief, our time of deep waters, we are never without his abiding presence and constant help. We may not always be aware of his presence, but he is always there to walk beside us. He guides us through the deep waters and onto the higher ground. He makes sure that our feet do not slip, plunging us into the depths of darkness. He is our life preserver.

If only we could have the presence of mind to remember that he will not let us down, we could go through our deep waters more easily. We need to call out to our preserver of life and hope and acknowledge his presence. He is always with us, waiting to help.

P R A Y E R:

*Great Comforter, we thank you for your presence in our lives. We thank you for guiding us through the deep waters. We thank you for your strength, comfort and assurance every day of our lives. We thank you that you know when we need your help even though we do not always acknowledge our need. Amen.*

Suggested for Step 1

# APRIL 16

*"You hypocrite, first take the log out of your own eye,*
*and then you will see clearly to take the speck out of your brother's eye."*
Matthew 7:5

Let us think together today about how we treat other people, those we are close to and those who are strangers. How easy it is to find fault in others for the same things we do ourselves. We often require higher standards of others than we do of ourselves. We are quite often more loving with ourselves than we are with others. We may excuse in ourselves the very thing we condemn in others. Our eyes are wide open to the faults of others and blind to our own shortcomings. Far too often we take for granted all that other people do for us and fail to realize just how much we demand of them.

People, and the way in which they care for us, are genuine blessings from God. But, we must remember that the blessing is is a two-way street. We receive in proportion to the amount that we give. Our blessing is dependent upon how much time and energy we are willing to spend in being a blessing to others. We learn even as we teach. We receive even as we give. We are blessed even as we bless. As we empty ourselves in service to our Lord and others, we are filled. Praise God from whom all blessings flow!

PRAYER:

*Lord and lover of our very beings, we ask you to help us to be aware of how we treat others. We ask that our lives might exemplify Christlike love, Christlike living. Help us to fulfill your law and your commandment to "love one another." This we ask for your love's sake. Amen.*

Suggested for Step 12

# APRIL 17

*"So will I comfort you."*

Isaiah 66:13

After my brother committed suicide, I felt so alone. He had been a very special person in my life, and when he died, I felt such a profound sense of loss that I felt as if I were in a fog. Nothing seemed to hold much interest for me in life anymore. Even though my brother was often a violent, cruel and terrifying person, and even though he had caused me severe physical injuries the week he killed himself, I loved him. I saw a good person in him. He had given me a great deal of the self-worth that I had.

God not only comforted me in my loss, but his love taught me to forgive my brother and to confirm my love and forgiveness to him before he died. God helped me to reach the point where I was able to commit my brother completely into his hands the last years of his life. There was little I or anyone else could do for him, and I felt so powerless. I loved him very much, and I missed him so terribly. For a while, I just avoided any other relationships because I didn't want to get close to someone else again and then just lose him.

We need not suffer alone in our grief. No matter how profound the loss or how special the grief may be in our lives, God makes it possible for us to recover from any loss and come out better persons. We must trust him to know what is best for us and believe that he can heal our brokenness. We must be willing to "let go and let God."

PRAYER:

*Loving God, thank you for your love and comfort. Thank you for others you send to us to fill a part of the void when we suffer a loss. Thank you for giving us new ways to serve you through other hurting people. It keeps our minds on useful work rather than on destructive grief. Amen.*

Suggested for Steps 1 and 3

# APRIL 18

*"It is more blessed to give than to receive."*
Acts 20:35

It is difficult for many to receive from others. Some of us practice the words of Christ, "It is more blessed to give than to receive," with a genuine flare. We get a great deal of self-satisfaction from giving to other people. Some of us feel better when we give than when we receive. We believe we do not have to receive from another person. We see ourselves as generous, not selfish.

But to always be the giver is not the will of God. We must be willing to be served as well as to do the serving. We must be willing not only to bear the burdens of other people, but to let others bear our burdens with us. We need to be willing to be ministered to as well as to minister. We need the prayers of others as well as we need to pray for others.

We know how good it feels to be a giver. We must be willing to let others experience the joy of giving to us. Christ allowed John to baptize him. He allowed others to minister to his needs even though he was the Lord of all creation, the Master. Can we do less? We need to humble ourselves so that we are willing to be receivers as well as givers.

PRAYER:

*Thank you, Lord, for teaching us how to receive. Thank you for being our conscience so that we are willing to be ministered to by others. Keep us humble. Let us be grateful that others are willing to give as well as receive. Amen.*

Suggested for Step 12

# APRIL 19

*"Now the God of hope fill you with all joy and peace in believing, that you may abound in hope, through the power of the Holy Ghost."*
Romans 15:13

Being full of hope, joy and peace is not easy, especially during the difficult times in our lives. Too often we grieve over what we have lost or what we don't have and forget to see our blessings. If only we would take time to reflect on the positive aspects of our lives, we might find the energy to be motivated to transform the destructive parts of our lives. If we concentrate on our blessings more than on our disappointments, our whole attitude toward life will change. Emphasizing the positive allows us to experience more fully the joy and peace that only the God of hope can give.

Hope comes from God, and we can hope in God because he has given us the example of his Son, Jesus Christ. It is because of the life, death and resurrection of Christ that we, too, can have hope. Instead of wishing we were somewhere else or someone else, we need to pray for hope so that we can accept who we are and where we are in life. When we experience this God of hope, we will also know the joy and peace of believing and trust him. Then we will also know the joy and peace of being okay with our station in life because we have allowed the power of the Holy Spirit to transform our discontent into hope.

PRAYER:

*God of hope, we thank you for all that you do for us. We thank you for giving us hope even when our lives seem hopeless. We are grateful for the joy and peace we receive when we believe and put our trust in you. Thank you for breaking in upon us with your Spirit of hope so that we are able to know the joy and peace of believing. Amen.*

Suggested for Steps 2, 4 and 6

---

# EASTER

*"And they said among themselves,
who shall roll away the stone from the door of the sepulchre?"*

Mark 16:3

This is the Easter season! It is the time when we commemorate the victory of our *Risen Lord*! It is a wondrously beautiful season as spring opens up before us and the bleak winter months fall behind us. The miracle of the touch of God's hand is seen in the singing of birds, the budding of trees and flowers, and all things are waking into new life.

All around us there is this newness of life. The caterpillar that has been locked into a cocoon springs forth into a beautiful butterfly. God's creatures are bringing forth life, and baby animals are flourishing. God's beauty surrounds us as never before, and we stand in awe of all he has given us. With this newness of life comes newness of hope!

But Easter is not just beauty, new life, hope and promise. We remember the cruel crucifixion of a Man who had committed no crime! We remember our Lord's pain and sacrifice, and we give thanks.

To me, the final message of Easter is the resurrection. We are given hope because of the resurrection. "The stone was rolled away" (Luke 16:4). The message is *he lives!* We can share in this resurrection. We can have the stone rolled away, and we can be free. Let us journal about what Easter means to us. Take time to read and reflect on the entire 16th chapter of Luke.

PRAYER:

*Lamb of God, who takes away the sin of the world, have mercy on us. Thank you for your sacrifice. Thank you for letting us share in the resurrection. Help us to be willing to have the stone rolled away and set us free to love. Amen.*

Suggested for Step 2

# APRIL 20

*"Blessed are you that hunger now, for you shall be filled. Blessed are you that weep now, for you shall laugh."*
Luke 6:21

One of the unfortunate things about the kind of Christianity some people practice is the belief that it is sinful to laugh and be happy. They honestly believe that in order to be good Christians, they have to be very somber and strict. What a drab life style that would be! It would be a poor advertisement for new recruits. I personally would not qualify because I have a great sense of humor, and I enjoy laughter.

Those who have been serious most of their lives will have to work hard at learning to laugh, to relax and be joyful. The Christian life should be one of joy and laughter. There is enough in life for us to be serious about. We really need to learn how to laugh and to have fun. In addition to having more fun when we put laughter into our lives, our bodies, minds and spirits become healthier. It took a serious illness to show me how important laughter and joy can be.

PRAYER:

*Loving Father, we thank you this day for laughter. Thank you that many times when life seems too serious, there is a sense of humor that has cleansing power to wash away sadness. We are so grateful for those times when we are even able to laugh at ourselves although it seems there is nothing to smile about.*

*Thank you for joy and pleasure and the optimism it brings to us. You have given us a quick wit and the ability to see and experience humor. Thank you for so many people—and creatures—who give us reasons to smile and laugh. Help us to share the gift of laughter with others so that they, too, may learn to know and love you as a joyful and humorous God. Amen.*

Suggested for Steps 1 and 4

# APRIL 21

*"The steps of a good man are ordered by the Lord,*
*and he delights in his ways."*
Psalm 37:23

As we take a daily inventory of our lives, sometimes we become discouraged. We thought we were rid of some of the old ways, and yet we seem to fall back into them. We had such a feeling of triumph when we first began to change destructive life styles. But when we slip back, we become very negative and hard on ourselves. We need to be patient with ourselves and others who struggle through change. We need to remember we will never achieve perfection while we are on this earth.

We also need to claim the promise in this verse. When we are willing to let God guide us, he will direct our steps. Even when we falter or misstep, he is there to get us going in the right direction if we seek him.

False pride often gets in our way, and we are so convinced we can take care of things ourselves that we fail to seek his guidance. The result is usually the same: confusion, frustration and failure. He wants us to let go of our false pride and rely completely on him.

P R A Y E R:
*Lord and loving Leader, we thank you for guiding our steps and keeping us on the right path. We thank you for your patience when we slip away from you and go our own ways. Thank you for welcoming us back with open arms. Bless others and direct their lives. Amen.*

Suggested for Step 10

# APRIL 22

*"Commit your work to the Lord, and then it will succeed."*
Proverbs 16:3

Whenever we commit our work to the Lord, we succeed. Whenever we trust him to guide and direct us, our work goes well. No matter what the project is or how difficult it may be, when he is involved, all goes well. We are grateful for his involvement. We must work on trusting him so that we do not waste our time stumbling around in the dark. Let us ask for and utilize his power in all we do.

Many times we fail because we want to do something our way even though we know it is not his way. Often when it fails, we blame him because we dislike failing. It is much easier to blame God and others for our failures than it is to take an honest look at ourselves and be willing to change what we need to change. Unfortunately, when we blame others, our lives remain the same and we continue to make the same mistakes over again.

PRAYER:

*Thank you for all the help you give us in all the things we do. We are truly grateful, Father. We want to learn to do things according to your will, for then we know that whatever the outcome, all will be well. Give us patience and vision. Disappoint us, if necessary, if that is the only way we are willing to learn.*

*Help others to trust in you and to have the assurance that if they commit their work to you, they will succeed. We need you as our Teacher. Thank you, Lord, for teaching us. Amen.*

Suggested for Steps 7, 10 and 11

# APRIL 23

*"I pray for them; I pray not for the world, but for them which thou hast given me; for they are thine."*
John 17:9

The most loving thing we can do for others is to pray for them. No matter how far away they may be, no matter what the circumstances of their lives, we can reach them and touch them through our prayers. We need to reach out and enfold others with our loving thoughts and prayers. We can help them and be a part of their healing process by taking them to our Lord in prayer. We can be assured that even as we pray for them, God is touching them right then. Our positive thoughts and faith-filled prayers can have an impact on us as well as on others.

Have you prayed for someone else today? Is there someone that you can send a card to today? Is there someone you can visit or call on the telephone today? Tell that person you are thinking of him in a special way. Tell him you are praying especially for him today. Ask if there is anything you can do to help him. Let him see the love of Christ in you!

PRAYER:

*Loving Creator and Friend, we ask that you will touch the lives of others today, especially those we name here. (Name them individually.) Let them feel your love and your presence. Help us to let them know that we care. Help us to be available to them whenever we are needed. We thank you for hearing our prayers and answering in the way you see best for each of us. Amen.*

Suggested for Step 11

# APRIL 24

*"He reveals the deep and secret things;*
*he knows what is in the darkness, and the light dwells with him."*
Daniel 2:22

Most of us have a skeleton or two that we choose to keep hidden in a closet. Some have deep secrets such as incest, violence, rape or infidelity. We have allowed these secrets to deteriorate our self-worth to the point that it becomes self-destructive. We convince ourselves that because of these dark areas, no one could possibly love us. Some even seek freedom from pain through amnesia!

We also convince ourselves that God apparently does not care about our pain or he would not have allowed it to happen. We hide behind our darkness and turn away from God. That part of us hates everyone, including God. We refuse to let people into our lives because we have not be able to trust them in the past. We sit alone and do not get the help we need.

Yet, God knows everything about us. We cannot hide anything from him. He accepts us even in our darkness. He did not cause the pain in our lives, and he desires to heal us. He wants to teach us to love and trust so that we can be whole. His love can bring light into the darkest areas. There is nothing too terrible for him. He forgives us for hanging onto our failures. We need to accept his forgiveness of us so that we can forgive those who have caused the pain in our lives.

P R A Y E R:
*Loving God, beloved Son, help us to let go of the darkness in our lives. We have allowed it to harm us long enough. Transform our sorrow into joy. Heal our brokenness and let us be willing to share our healing with others. Amen.*

Suggested for Steps 4, 6 and 10

---

# APRIL 25

*"Let your light so shine before all,*
*that they will see your good works and glorify your*
*Father which is in heaven."*
Matthew 5:16

The 12th step requires that we be willing to share the message of his love and forgiveness with others. We can only do that if we are truly committed to the principles that Christ teaches. We cannot teach love if we are not loving. We cannot truly represent Christ unless we forgive unconditionally. We cannot spend our time trying to change others and be ignorant of the changes that need to be made in our own lives. If we are going to represent the love of Christ, we must do it in all things and not just in the areas we choose. We cannot choose those commandments that we like and agree with and ignore those that require more than we want to give.

Christ requires a total commitment, and although he allows for the fact that we are imperfect, he still wants us to do our best.

P R A Y E R:

*Heavenly Father, give us the insights of Christian fellowship as we seek to share it with relatives, friends and strangers. Let your love abide in us so completely that it radiates to others. Fill our hearts and our minds with openness, with unreserved willingness to be used by you in the work of each new day. Bless us to be a blessing in your name. Amen.*

Suggested for Step 12

---

# APRIL 26

*"The apostles said to the Lord, 'We need more faith; tell us how to get it.'"*

Luke 17:5

Our Lord's disciples spoke these words on more than one occasion. Sometimes it was difficult for them to believe. In the story of the five loaves and two fishes, it seemed inconceivable, if not impossible, that the masses could be fed at all, let alone with so little. They tried to dismiss the small boy with his seemingly inadequate offering. They were perhaps even a bit upset by our Lord's confidence.

But as often happens, our Lord met the people at their point of need, as he does for us every day. They greatly needed to hear him speak and to experience his presence that day, but as the day grew late, they also needed bodily nourishment. Their minds and spirits had been fed, but they were physically hungry.

Like his disciples, we too doubt our Lord's ability to meet us at our point of need. We may not even realize that what we perceive as our point of need may not be what our Lord sees as our greatest need. When I was seriously ill, I saw my greatest need as physical healing. My Lord knew that my first need was spiritual and emotional healing. That made physical healing possible. I also learned that even though total healing was not to be (up to this point), spiritual healing made it possible for me to accept my life even with some limitations.

P R A Y E R:

*Loving Lord, we admit that we do not always have the faith we need. Help us to trust you to meet us at our point of need so that we can turn our wills and our lives over to you in confidence. Remind us, when we need it, that nothing is impossible for you. Bless us to be a blessing to others and remind us that total healing is possible for us only in eternity. Amen.*

Suggested for Step 3

# APRIL 27

*"These things I have spoken to you, that my joy may be in you,*
*and that your joy may be full."*
John 15:11

Joy is a wonderful, uplifting feeling that makes us glad we are alive. Joy in our hearts gives us a positive attitude toward life. Joy—and all the wonderful emotions that go with it—has great healing power for our bodies, minds and spirits. When we practice the presence of Christ, we experience joy at its fullest. The experience of joy gives us the desire to continue on in spite of our difficulties.

It is not always easy to tap into memories of joy-filled experiences. When we struggle with trials, we are likely to forget the joys we have had. Yet, joy can help us overcome the obstacles in our lives.

We need to remember joyful events in our lives. Happy occasions such as a special childhood Christmas, marriages, births of children and successes are important to remember. It is so easy to remember the pain in our lives. We need to take time to remember the joy and the laughter and be open to joyful experiences in the present. Past joys are often inadequate to fill the present with meaning, and this may even cause us to live in the past rather than the present. John reminds us in the preceding verses that if we keep the commandments that Jesus taught us and love God and our neighbors as ourselves, we will have joy. The joy that lasts and makes our lives full is a meaningful relationship with God and the important others in our lives.

P R A Y E R :
*Lord, teach us to say and to practice these words: "The joy of the Lord is my strength." Help us to find reasons to be joyful and be willing to celebrate that joy with others. Teach us to claim the joy and gladness that can come from within our hearts and minds when our lives are in your hands and we are in harmony with one another. May we daily take the time to discern those things that give us true joy. Amen.*

Suggested for Step 10

---

# APRIL 28

*"The God of peace be with you all."*
Romans 15:33

"Let there be peace on earth and let it begin with me." The words of that song are beautiful but certainly not easy to make our own. Perhaps at this time you are at war with several people or with someone special in your life. They may be people you trusted to love and stand by you. They may be people who preach Christianity and expound his love as a way of life. And yet, they have made judgments about you, and decisions based on those judgments, which have profoundly affected your life. Perhaps they lived and spoke deception and cruelty and yet pretended to be wonderful, loving Christians.

They did not leave judgments up to our Lord, but made them all on their own. What they did was contrary to everything they preached to so many people. They talked one way and lived another. We expect Christians to be perfect, and when they are not, we become angry and lose faith.

You may have a difficult time believing that you could ever trust them again. Somehow the hurt is worse when they supposedly commit their acts in the name of Christianity. They hurt the cause of Christianity by their actions and words, but we must remember that it is still important to love and forgive them.

PRAYER:

*Dear Lord, help us to forgive these people and give up our expectations that they will ever be able to represent your love to us through their destructive actions. Help them to see the harm they do to other people and be willing to change. Amen.*

Suggested for Steps 8 and 9

# APRIL 29

*"He who trusts in the Lord is safe."*
Proverbs 29:25

We are assured that we may confidently let go and become entirely ready to let Christ transform our weaknesses into strengths. The key word in this verse is *trust*. We are assured that no matter what our difficulty may be, we can trust in him and he will keep us safe. We need not continue to hold onto those areas of our lives that weigh us down and keep us from being whole. We can release every care into his capable hands and know that all is well.

It is a great blessing to know that God's loving, protecting presence is with us wherever we go. We cannot wander away so far that he is not there. He is always with us to protect and support us. Though our circumstances may change, he never does, and his promise is real.

We can approach life with courage, knowing that we are never alone. He will guide us and keep us safe. The more we risk trusting him, the more confident we will become. Success breeds success, and the more we trust, the more we will believe his promise that he will keep us safe.

PRAYER:

*O God our Father, help us to turn to you in absolute trust, believing that you can help us help ourselves. We are thankful for your constant presence. We are grateful that you love us with the patience of a heavenly Father who loves his children unconditionally. Help us to continue to risk believing in you. Amen.*

Suggested for Steps 2 and 6

# APRIL 30

*"When I am afraid, I will trust in thee."*
Psalm 56:3

We can find so many things in life to fear, and we waste so much time and energy fearing things that never happen. Fear can only thrive where faith is absent or substantially diminished. Since we know that at least intellectually, we need to work to change our lives so that we practice faith instead of fear. We need to turn to our Lord and trust him completely to help us relinquish our fears into his hands. We need to practice an active faith. We need to read his word, to meditate and to pray. We need to find a trusted friend or counselor with whom we may share our fears and feelings. Talking about our fears with this friend helps us to get in touch with many feelings that we were unaware of before this sharing. Sometimes we need to hear ourselves say something to another person and solicit his feedback.

We need to journal about our fears on a daily basis so that we can understand them more fully. As we journal, we are able to get in touch with many things from the subconscious. The more we journal, the more we get in touch. Once what was hidden is out in the open, we can deal with it honestly. Then healing can begin.

PRAYER:

*Lord, our Protector and Defender, we ask that you help us with our fears. Help us to replace those fears with faith in you. We turn to you for our strength and comfort. Bless others who struggle with fear and let them turn to you. Let us be available to one another during fearful times. Amen.*

Suggested for Step 11

## MAY 1

*"Therefore, confess your sins to one another,*
*and pray for one another that you may be healed."*
James 5:16

Step 5 speaks of the importance of confession in the whole process of spiritual growth. Unless we admit to the sins of the past and experience forgiveness, we will have difficulty growing spiritually. Not only will we be tempted to continue destructive behavior, but the guilt of the past will continue to control our lives. Through the process of naming our faults (confession), we are in a better position to control our future behavior. By admitting our shortcomings, we are taking the first step toward becoming entirely ready to have Christ heal us, especially when we confess to someone we trust.

The month of May is the time when we observe Pentecost and the coming of the Holy Spirit. Evidence of his coming was that Christians began to speak in foreign languages, and this seemed to be the only logical explanation for the rapid spread of Christianity to other countries. The followers of Christ were also filled with a strength to believe and even to confess their sins to one another. The ability to share all of who we are with others whom we trust takes courage. The month of May reminds us of Pentecost and that this power came to us through the Holy Spirit to enable us to confess our sins to one another and pray for one another that we all might be healed.

P R A Y E R:

*Spirit of God, fill us with your power that we might have the courage to share all of ourselves—both our strengths and weaknesses—with one another and pray with one another so that healing might come to us all. Amen.*

Suggested for Step 5                                          Vernon J. Bittner

---

## MAY 2

*"Not that I speak in respect of want;*
*for I have learned, in whatsoever state I am,*
*therewith to be content."*
Philippians 4:11

The most important lesson I have learned from serious illness is the truth in this verse. With God's help, I was able to endure and survive numerous surgeries, chronic bone pain, consistent high fever and nausea. At that time, I could do very little for myself. Food and medication ran into my body to nourish me, and a catheter took care of bodily eliminations. Held captive in a small hospital isolation room, I was forced to learn to be content with only myself and my

God. Staff very seldom came in. Visitors became even more scarce as the disease dragged into years. My appearance became emaciated, and that frightened a lot of people.

Everything I had valued and enjoyed before the disease was unreachable. I had to find value in solitude. I had to find serenity in aloneness. I had to find companionship in my Lord. Most of all, I learned the wonderful opportunity that illness and pain can bring. I learned valuable lessons that I would have passed by if I had not become desperately ill. I learned that even in the most desperate of circumstances there is still hope for healing.

PRAYER:

*Lord, the precious Presence, this present moment is the moment we must live to the fullest. Help us to learn all that we can from our experiences and be willing to share them with others. Thank you, Lord, for all of our blessings, even those that come in the form of illness or loss. Thank you for healing us where you see best. Amen.*

Suggested for Step 1

---

# MAY 3

*"Whosoever shall give you a cup of water to drink in my name, because you belong to Christ, verily, I say unto you, he shall not lose his reward."*

Mark 9:41

It does not sound so difficult to give a cup of cold water to someone in need. Christ says it is important for us as Christians to do this. That cup of cold water represents love given in his name to anyone who is in need, whether they ask or not. That cup of cold water may be comfort to a sorrowing soul, assurance in the face of fear, our presence in the midst of loneliness, our prayers during difficult times. It may be the simple act of giving someone permission to cry or even crying with them. It may be a hug or a smile, or some food or clothing.

We are called in so many ways to give a cup of cold water, thereby witnessing to the love of Christ alive in us. Our kindness, even our little acts of love, should be a perpetual proclamation to everyone, wherever we go, of his love for all. This is the way we share the message of his love and forgiveness with others.

PRAYER:

*Kindly Shepherd, touch each of us in such a way that we willingly share a cup of cold water in your name. Let our lives be mirrors of your love. Bless others this day who thirst and fill them with your love. We love you. Amen.*

Suggested for Step 12

# MAY 4

*"We have the mind of Christ."*
I Corinthians 2:16

If we believe in Christ and turn our wills and our lives over to him, we can have the mind of Christ. When we have the mind of Christ, we will have the spiritual qualities of wisdom and good judgment, which are inherent in every one of us. Christ gives these qualities to us as a part of our spiritual nature. At any time, whether our needs are great or small, we can turn within and receive the answers we seek. With this new wisdom, we seek guidance in the following areas. Let us ask the Lord that we may have:

- a loving heart not hardened by anger and resentment.
- a tongue that speaks loving words and assurances to others.
- a pleasant disposition with a ready smile.
- a willingness to bear the burdens of others.
- a friendly face that invites others' involvement.
- the courage to accept the opportunities that come our way.
- the grace to appreciate love and beauty all around us
  and to acknowledge all of our blessings.

PRAYER:
*We thank you, Lord, that you are an intimate part of our very beings. We are grateful that you not only give us wisdom and good judgment, but that you are willing to guide us in the many areas of life. We often stumble and fall because we do not seek your wisdom for our lives. Help us to turn to you sooner so that we do not become so discouraged. We love you. Amen.*
Suggested for Step 6

# MAY 5

*"Forgetting what lies behind
and straining forward to what lies ahead,
I press on toward the goal for the prize
of the upward call of God in Christ Jesus."*
I Corinthians 2:16

We need to make this our goal: to be able to forget about what lies behind us and just press on, believing. We want to be able to let go of the past and not worry about the future and spend our time living one day at a time.

That is not easy. There have been so many hurts and other losses for many of us that we just expect more tragedy. Sometimes we wonder if we even believe in goodness, kindness, mercy or joy anymore. We feel like most of life is a "vale of tears" and there is not enough time to heal after one loss before another loss occurs.

We have to work at getting rid of that losing attitude. What we believe has a great deal to do with what we become. If we believe that no matter how hard we try we will continue to come out on the losing side, we may help that very thing to happen. We need to believe that with the help of God, we can come out of any situation victoriously.

P R A Y E R:

*Help us, Lord, to let go of our despair. Give us hope for today and help us to have faith and determination in what we do. Rekindle that creative, capable spirit in us that used to be willing to see visions of beauty rather than obstacles and ugliness.*

*We ask your blessing on others who need help in this area. Remind them that you have promised you will never forsake those who love you. Thank you, heavenly Father. Amen.*

Suggested for Step 3

# MAY 6

*"Lo, I am with you always, even unto the end of the world."*
Matthew 28:20

Many times we are so alone and lonely that we feel overwhelmed. Far too often we isolate ourselves and hold off people who love us because of fear of rejection. It is difficult for us to trust other people because of past hurts.

Yet, we never need to be alone if only we are willing to claim God's promise. If we love him as we should, we will also be more open to other people. We will trust them to love us, to get close to us. We will give our love to them and accept their love in return. And even though we may be hurt again, we will continue to trust because we need relationships in order to be happy, healthy individuals. There will be times when it will be difficult for us to maintain relationships, but we must do our best to relate meaningfully to others. We need to pray for ourselves and others on a continuing basis. We need to pray especially for those who are difficult to get along with.

P R A Y E R:

*Help us, Lord, to refrain from isolating ourselves so that we can enjoy this blessing you have given us, the blessing of other people in our lives. Thanks for your presence. Thank you for the assurance that you will never leave us alone. Thank you for reminding us that we need not be lonely.*

*Bless others whose paths we cross in life. Help us to be a blessing to one another. Help us mutually to risk being loved. Teach us to hug, Lord, with arms as well as words. Amen.*
Suggested for Step 12

## MAY 7

*"Thou dost show me the path of life."*
Psalm 16:11

When I was young, I was afraid to walk home after dark. The road from town to our farm passed a long stretch of woods that seemed ominous and terrifying to me. I had to walk home several times, usually when my older brother dropped me off in town for a movie and promised to pick me up after his date. He seldom returned for me, and I would stay at the theater until it closed, wait in the restaurant until it closed and finally accept the fact that I had to walk home.

The only way I could survive that stretch by the woods was to whistle as loud as I could and half-walk, half-run toward home. I was so scared that some times it was difficult to keep my lips wet enough to whistle. I wildly imagined all kinds of things that might happen to me, and I was terribly insecure.

Even now when I am afraid or anxious, I am reminded of those days. Instead of remembering that my heavenly Father cares for me and protects me, I try to solve my problems my way. I whistle in the dark instead of quietly turning to the source of my strength.

PRAYER:

*Loving Protector, we thank you that when we quiet ourselves and allow the Holy Spirit to fill us, you still our fears. You show us the path of life. Help us to refrain from whistling in the dark to solve our own problems. Let us turn to you sooner. Amen.*
Suggested for Step 2

## MAY 8

*"Rejoice always, pray constantly."*
I Thessalonians 5:16,17

We want to give thanks in all circumstances as Paul urges. We want to rejoice and praise God at all times, not just when things are going well in our lives. We want to thank him in the midst of pain and loss. We want to sing through our tears and be grateful for the freedom to cry. We want to praise him when we hurt. We want to be able to say, "Thank you, Lord, for feelings and the vision to understand them." We want to say, "Thank you, Lord, for your comfort and for your strength to keep on keeping on."

We rejoice for the many good things in our lives that we do not always acknowledge because pain gets in our way. He has blessed us with much to be thankful for. If we can remember to turn to God in times of sorrow as well as in times of joy, we will be richly blessed with a closer walk with him. We will be better able to understand his will for our lives if we stay in contact with him through prayer and meditation.

PRAYER:

*Help us, Father, to be more fully aware of all of our blessings, even the blessings of trials. Thank you for trials that challenge us to grow and stay closer to you.*

*Bless others so that they, too, may see the many reasons they have to rejoice. Help them to turn to you in their sorrow so that they may rejoice in your healing love. Amen.*

Suggested for Step 11

---

# MAY 9

*"He will wipe away all tears from their eyes,*
*and there shall be no more death, nor sorrow, nor crying, nor pain.*
*All of that has gone forever."*
Revelation 21:4

Some of us experience multiple losses in a short span of time. We do not have time to recover from one loss before another hits us. We wonder if we will ever get through this vale of tears called life. We experience a death in ourselves and others. We are afflicted with sorrow and pain.

Our Lord has promised us that one day he will wipe away all the tears from our eyes. He assures us that there will be no more death, nor sorrow, nor crying, nor pain. He promises us life and beauty and serenity.

Our Lord not only promises us these things by giving us heaven when we have completed his purpose for our lives on this earth, but he offers us much while we are still here. He will comfort and strengthen us during our most difficult times. We need only turn to our Lord in prayer, and he will answer in the way best for us.

PRAYER:

*Divine Comforter, we thank you for your love. We thank you for your presence in our lives during times of loss. We thank you for the promise that there will be an end to sorrow, pain and death. Thank you for your companionship. Amen.*

Suggested for Step 3

# MAY 10

*"Therefore, if any one is in Christ, he is a new creation; the old has passed away, behold the new has come."*
II Corinthians 5:17

We want very much to become new creations. We want to take a fearless inventory of our lives and change our self-destructive character traits. Some old habits die hard because they are familiar and comfortable. We do not have to work hard to stay the way we are, but it will take discipline to change. We need our Friend more than ever before in our lives. He has helped us all of our lives to endure the pain that was often caused by our own destructive life styles. Many times we were out of control because we refused to let go. We wanted and needed to be in control. We felt we could take care of ourselves without any help.

We need to let go of our foolish pride. We must stop denying that we need God's help to change. He is the God of might and miracles, and that is what it will take to change us into new creations. We know he loves us. We know he wants what is best for us. We need his help to be willing to surrender completely so that we can be healed.

PRAYER:

*Help us to take an honest inventory of both our strengths and weaknesses. We are at a point, Lord, where we are willing to trust you in this process. Thank you for your willingness to help us. Bless others who are working on this same process. Give them the courage to change. Amen.*

Suggested for Step 4

# MAY 11

*"These things I have spoken unto you,*
*that in me you might have peace.*
*In the world you shall have tribulation;*
*but be of good cheer; I have overcome the world."*
John 16:33

It is not always easy to "be of good cheer." No matter what happens to us, we still have reason to rejoice. We need only remember the experience of our Lord when he was on earth. He went through much pain and disappointment, yet he possessed a positive attitude.

Our Lord does not cause our grief or losses. He is always there to walk with us and help us through our tragedies, but he does not desire pain for our lives. He desires the abundant life for us. With his own life he provided for a resurrection in which we can all share. He gave us hope. He gave us life, even eternal life.

With his help, we can turn even the darkest tragedy into a splendor-filled triumph. We can learn and grow from every experience in life, whether it is filled with joy or sorrow. As his children, we can be certain of the presence of our living Lord. He quietly encourages us to "be of good cheer," even on the darkest days.

PRAYER:
*Loving Father, grant us a cheerful countenance as we go about our responsibilities this day. Help us to remember that nothing need overwhelm us as long as we trust in you and let you direct our lives. Keep us from the fears of unbelief. Grant that we may know and love you more fully. give us poise in the face of disappointment and a quiet confidence during times of tragedy. Help us to share that confidence with others so they, too, will want to know you better. Thank you for all you do for us and for those we love. Amen.*

Suggested for Steps 6 and 7

---

# MAY 12

*"As sorrowful, yet always rejoicing;*
*as poor, yet making men rich;*
*as having nothing, and yet possessing all things."*
II Corinthians 6:10

For the first time in my life, I believe I understand the true meaning of this verse. After seven years of devastating, nearly fatal illness, I know what it means to be "sorrowful, yet always rejoicing." I experienced severe depression as a result of what happened to me. Yet the more I lost, the more I realized how many reasons I had to rejoice. Sorrows had exhausted me so totally that I had to recover from emotional exhaustion before I had enough energy to cope with my physical disease.

I also discovered what it means to be poor and yet very rich. The cost of my illness, the loss of my career, the loss of all health insurance when I was divorced, left me financially and emotionally depleted. But once again, the more I lost, the more I found. I had to reach the deepest pit of my life before I could experience the heights of joy that God's love can bring when we are open to him. My life had to be completely rebuilt and founded on things far more important than material possessions. I thought I had nothing, only to find that I had everything! That is a miracle of God's love.

PRAYER:

*Loving Lord, thank you that out of the ashes of our lives come beauty and joy greater than we could ever imagine. Thank you for courage to get through difficult times. Thank you for teaching us that even when we think we have nothing, we still have reasons to rejoice. We are grateful for your patience with us when we give up on you so easily. Grant us the gift to discern what really makes us rich. Amen.*

Suggested for Steps 1 and 3

# MAY 13

*"Wisely spoken words can heal."*
Proverbs 12:18

The words from Scripture give insight into our role as people who are in relationships with others. It is especially important for us as parents to be aware of the words we use when we speak to our children. What we say and how we say it can determine whether our children grow up with healthy self-images or damaged inner selves from the experiences of childhood. Some people never recover from the trauma of childhood. They are seriously affected, not only by the unkind words used against them, but also by the absence of kind and loving words they deserved to hear.

What the people who are supposed to love us say to us, especially in childhood, is intensely important. Words can hurt deeply and leave a lasting impression that only professional help and the power of our Lord can heal. If we realize the significance of the words we use and how we use them, we will think before we speak.

Words can also heal, as this verse indicates. Words are powerful motivators. If we feel good about ourselves, we will have self-confidence to try even greater things. We will trust other people more easily if we are not continually hurt by their unkind words.

**P R A Y E R:**

*Lord, you taught us in your ministry how important words are. Help us to follow your example so that our words are more helpful than hurtful, more praising than critical, more loving than hateful. Teach us to speak our words wisely in all of our relationships, and may you be glorified in what we say. Amen.*

Suggested for Step 12

# MAY 14

*"Let every person learn to assess properly the value of their work and they can then be glad when they have done something worth doing without depending on the approval of others."*

Galatians 6:4

There are many books, sermons and seminars on how to acquire or enhance our self-worth. But the Bible is the greatest learning resource for self-worth, self-confidence, success and happiness. If only we would take seriously the teachings of Christ and all the others in the Bible, we could save a lot of time and money. We spend billions on drugs, liquor, the medical world, the psychiatric world, healers and gurus, trying to find that elusive self-worth.

This verse reminds us that we must find value in ourselves rather than depending on the approval of others. If we do not love and accept ourselves, why should anyone else? If we cannot find value, we will probably not make a favorable appearance to others, either. We can believe we are valuable . . . because God does not make *junk*! We are lovable because God sees us as lovable, and he loves us totally. God chose us. He considered us worth the death of his Son on our behalf.

If we love God, we should reflect that love in every aspect of our lives. Love should show in our face, be heard in our speech and be seen in our actions.

**P R A Y E R:**

*Thank you, loving Counselor, that you consider us worthwhile, valuable people. Thank you for seeing our potential and encouraging us to develop it. Give us courage to take an honest inventory and be willing to change those parts of our lives that are unpleasing to you. Help us not to be destructive either to ourselves or to others. Amen.*

Suggested for Step 4

# MAY 15

*"Wherefore have you not fulfilled your task?"*
Exodus 5:14

Although these words were spoken to the children of Israel because they had not produced their quota of bricks for the pharaoh's taskmasters, the same words could just as easily be asked of us today. Why have we not fulfilled our tasks? There may be many things that we have promised to do and not fulfilled. Even though we have good reasons for not fulfilling our commitment, the result is the same.

What tasks have we left undone? Have we refused to share the gift of God's love with others? Do we continue to carry the grief and pain of the past because we don't trust God to heal us? Have we neglected to forgive someone for a hurt he caused us long ago? Do we continue to refrain from becoming involved with others because we fear being rejected or hurt again?

As we work on the tenth step and take a daily inventory, we need to be honest about the tasks we have not fulfilled. It may even require that we go back to our fourth-step inventory and see if there is any pain of the past that needs to be healed. If we have unfinished business that gets in the way of our being whole, we need to deal with it now! We need to ask for healing today and leave the past in the past. Let's journal about our uncompleted tasks and see if we can understand why we avoid them.

PRAYER:
*Eternal God, thank you for encouraging us to take a daily inventory of our lives. Give us the courage to do an honest inventory and help us to commit ourselves to making the changes that are necessary as we work toward wholeness. Thank you, too, for your continued presence and guidance in this process. Amen.*

Suggested for Step 10

# MAY 16

*"Who told you that you were naked?*
*Have you eaten of the tree that I commanded you that you should not eat?"*
Genesis 3:11

This is the story of Adam and Eve after they broke God's law. They, as we do sometimes, believed that they could do whatever they pleased. Then they tried to hide what they had done. We fool ourselves into believing that no one will know, not even God. Some times we rationalize that what we are doing is not really wrong, anyway, so that makes it okay. Or, we reason that we can do it as long as we confess it.

First of all, we cannot hide anything from God. He knows everything about us. We cannot make a wrong into a right no matter how much we rationalize. If God's word says something is wrong, it is wrong and cannot be whitewashed.

We really don't fool other people, either, and we pay a heavy personal toll in trying to fool ourselves. We may think we are fooling others, but we are not the people God intends us to be when we keep secrets. We are phony! We do not have God's peace because we know we are being dishonest in our life styles. We need to confess our wrongs and do better from that moment on. Once we know that we are breaking spiritual and moral laws, we must not continue to break them.

P R A Y E R:

*Loving God, thank you for being so patient with us. Some times we do wrong even when we know we shouldn't do it. We try to hide from you and then feel guilty about it. Help us to be willing to refrain from knowingly doing wrong and be willing to admit it. When we do so, we are in a position to change our destructive behavior. Amen.*

Suggested for Step 5

---

# MAY 17

*"I am not aware of anything against me,*
*but I am not thereby acquitted.*
*It is the Lord who judges me."*
I Corinthians 4:4

This verse both challenges and consoles us. It is a challenge because it tells us that everything we think or say or do is judged by our Lord. If we do not love others, he will judge us. If we do not forgive others, he will judge us. If we do not live lives that are pleasing to him, once again, he will judge us.

This scripture is also a consolation because it says that God alone is our Judge. A lot of people love to judge us unfairly. Quite often they do not have adequate information to make judgments about us, but they do it anyway. Fortunately, God not only judges us, but he forgives us, too.

This verse makes a statement to those of us who like to judge others. Regardless of what we think about others or how inadequately we may judge them, what they do is really none of our business. Critical judgments that accomplish nothing more than putting a person down are wrong. "Judge not lest you too be judged" is a good verse to remember (Matthew 7:1).

PRAYER:
*Lord and Judge, thank you for your mercy in your judgment of us. We thank you for forgiving us and allowing us to try again. Help us to be loving in dealing with other people so that we will refrain from being judgmental. Amen.*
Suggested for Steps 8 and 9

# MAY 18

*"When you lie down, you will not be afraid; when you lie down, your sleep will be sweet."*
Proverbs 3:24

A peaceful, restful night's sleep is important for our well-being. And yet, many of us take all of our anxieties and sorrows to bed with us. We toss and turn and get little rest. By nature we are worriers, and we have not learned to turn our cares over to our Lord. Although he has invited us to "cast our cares on him," we hesitate.

Most of our worries are useless. We often worry about things that never happen! The rest of the time we worry about things that we cannot do anything about. We are powerless to change other people, and we are powerless to change many circumstances, but we still hang onto our habit of worrying and live unsettled lives.

If only we would be willing to admit our powerlessness and turn our lives over to God's care, we would achieve peace and serenity. We would sleep better at night. Our Lord encourage us to give our cares to him so that we can live more serenely.

PRAYER:
*Loving Father, help us to recognize our powerlessness. Help us to turn our wills and lives over to you. We need to be reminded that regardless of how much we try to manipulate our lives so that they become more manageable, we will only achieve self-control through surrender to you. Our lives will have meaning and manageability when we live them according to your will.*

*Grant us periods of rest and sleep that are peaceful and without fear. Touch others' lives in a special way. Amen.*
Suggested for Steps 1, 2 and 3

# MAY 19

*"Bless the Lord, O my soul, and forget not all his benefits:*
*he forgives all your iniquities; he heals all your diseases."*
Psalm 103:2,3

It is human nature to be hard on ourselves and to see ourselves as terrible, unforgivable people. Many times we are willing to forgive others but not ourselves. Scripture says that "he forgives *all* my sins"! If we choose not to accept his forgiveness, we mock Christ's death on the cross. In essence we say, "That was not enough for what I have done." It is like slapping God in the face, because he gave his only Son for our forgiveness.

This scripture also says that the Lord heals us, yet many of us do not believe it or do not accept it. We have become our own gods. We have appointed ourselves as judge, jury and executioner. We do not turn to our Lord because we intend to decide what is best for us.

That behavior is as foolish as a physician attempting to remove his own appendix. When we try to be our own saviors, we close the channels to healing and wholeness.

PRAYER:

*Help us, Lord, to accept your forgiveness. Then we can forgive ourselves and others. Help us to be willing to be healed. In order to believe healing will happen, we need to let go and trust your will for our lives. Thank you for your forgiveness and power to heal. Amen.*

Suggested for Steps 8 and 9

# MAY 20

*"For thou hast made him a little lower than the angels,*
*and hast crowned him with glory and honor."*
Psalm 8:5

Our Lord offers us a crown. He treats us as royalty, as heirs to a throne. He makes us feel loved, accepted, important and especially, needed. He says to us, "I have a special place for you in my kingdom." None other is more important to him. No one else can take your place. No one else is more needed. He has chosen us, and we are filled with gratitude.

Our Lord asks only that we share his love and his life with others. He asks us to be those special selves that he created us to be. He asks that we be willing to express the love of God, the peace of God, the understanding of God, in the best way we know how with his help.

As we look around us, we are reminded of how much he loves us, and we need to be thankful. We need to appreciate all that we have and be willing to share our gifts and blessings with others. Take some time today to journal about the many blessings you have. You might be surprised how many you have.

P R A Y E R:

*Loving God, our prayer is that we can repay your love and confirm the confidence you have placed in us by serving you and other people in whatever ways are possible. Help us, Lord, to share your love in order to make someone a little happier, to make life a little less painful for someone who is hurting. We pray that we might help to make this world a brighter and better place to live.*

*Be with those today who are hurting and touch them with your healing hands. Be with those who are joyful and help them to be willing to share that joy with others. Amen.*

Suggested for Step 12

# MAY 21

*"In all your ways acknowledge him,
and he shall make straight your paths."*
Proverbs 3:6

This is a challenging verse on which to meditate. Do we truly acknowledge God in all our ways? Do we acknowledge him when our lives are going well and filled with joy? Or, do we just take the verse for granted and believe that we cause all good things to happen? Do we acknowledge God in trust and gratitude when things go wrong? Or, do we blame God for our problems and decide we need to find our own way out? Are we grateful for trials because we understand they are opportunities for growth in his love? Or, do we complain about our situations and refuse to see beauty in sorrow?

It is important to consider this aspect of our lives. We get out of life what we put into it. We can become better Christians from life experiences, or we can become bitter. Which will we be this day? Will we acknowledge God in all our ways? Will we grow stronger in our faith as the result of testing or more cynical? The choice is ours. We can be better!

P R A Y E R:

*Lord, help us to acknowledge you in all our ways. Help us to be willing to confess our feelings of fear and inadequacy to you and accept the healing you offer. Bless us to be blessings to others so they, too, will acknowledge you as Lord and Savior. Amen.*

Suggested for Steps 3 and 5

# MAY 22

*"Go now and remember that I am sending you out
as lambs among wolves."*
Luke 10:3

This verse certainly does not sound like an advertisement to lure people into Christianity. In fact, it sounds a little scary. Yet, our Lord does not say, *"Would* you like to go?" He commands, "Go now." Then he lets us know that the way will not be easy. There will be times when we will be hurt and feel angry, betrayed or even guilty. There will be times when we fail and all seems lost.

We are never lost or hopeless! When he refers to us as lambs, we need to remember that he is our Shepherd and he will not abandon us. Even if he loses one out of a hundred, he will leave the 99 and seek the lost one. Each one of us is of special value to him.

God has promised that we will not have to endure more than we are capable of enduring. He has promised to find a way. He is not sending his lambs to the slaughter, although we may feel like that is exactly where we are going at times. He is sending us out to learning experiences so that we can grow in faith, trust and acceptance.

PRAYER:
*Gentle, loving Shepherd, thank you for guiding our footsteps along the right paths. We thank you for your presence and assurance in our lives. We pray that we might be worthy to be your lambs. Help us to share our journeys with others. Help us to show them that you are the loving Shepherd who cares for each of his lambs. Amen.*

Suggested for Steps 1 and 2

---

# MAY 23

*"Let us get away from the crowds for a while and rest."*
Mark 6:31

Jesus spoke these words to his disciples when they were going about the countryside preaching. As we take the time to do a fourth-step inventory, we need to discipline ourselves to get away for a while and rest. It takes energy to do this inventory honestly. We need to meditate and pray, to become relaxed and concentrate on what we are doing. Getting away helps us to shut out the noise and clutter around and within us.

It is especially important for us to take time for journaling. One way to get in touch with what is going on in our lives is to write about it. Journaling enables us to examine areas of our lives that need healing. This is an effective way to discover our hidden selves.

We should write our dreams down, too. This requires the discipline of waking up to journal in the middle of the night if need be. If we do not make the effort, the dreams will be forgotten by morning. Not only do we become aware of our inner thoughts this way, but occasionally God speaks to us in our dreams.

PRAYER:

*Loving Lord, help us to set time aside to take an honest inventory of ourselves, our strengths and our weaknesses. Help us to be committed to journaling and to make an effort to learn from our dreams. Thank you for speaking to us in the quiet times. Amen.*

Suggested for Steps 4 and 10

---

# MAY 24

*"My son, attend to my words; incline thine ear unto my sayings. Let them not depart from thine eyes. Keep them in the midst of thine heart. For they are life unto those that find them, and health to all their flesh."*
Proverbs 4:20-22

As we work on Step 6, we have to ask ourselves if we are really willing to "become entirely ready to have Christ heal these defects of character." In today's verse we are reminded that we need to listen to what God says and keep his words in our hearts. If we are sincere about loving and serving him, we must pay attention to his will for our lives. Part of his will we may not know, but we will discover it if we take time to read his word and practice his presence through prayer and meditation.

God wants us to love one another! We do not love one another by hurting one another. We cannot excuse our inappropriate behavior simply by saying, "I couldn't help myself." It doesn't matter whether we are talking about adultery, drunk driving or telling lies. We are responsible for our behavior. We can choose to do things that hurt ourselves and others, or we can choose to be good examples of the Christian life. We can choose to live lives of love, acceptance and forgiveness or lives of lust, greed and deceit.

God's word is clear. Whatever we choose, there are three questions to consider: Would Christ do what I am doing? Does my behavior reflect the love and will of God? What are the consequences to myself, others and my Christian witness?

PRAYER:

*Lord, we don't always do what you would have us do. We don't always love as you would have us love. We know what the word of God says, but we don't always practice it. Help us to be committed to living and loving the way you would have us do. Let us set aside rationalizations and stop excusing*

*our destructive behavior. Help us to be true examples of your love to others. If there are those who struggle with this area of their lives, touch them so that they, too, might be examples of your love. Amen.*
Suggested for Steps 6 and 11

# MAY 25

*"These things I have spoken to you, that in me you might have peace.
In the world you shall have tribulation:
but be of good cheer; I have overcome the world."*
John 16:33

As humans we are not always filled with good cheer. Trials overwhelm us to the extent that we forget the help available to us. Some times our pain or our anger is so overpowering that we forget the resource of comfort we have in prayer. We need to slow down and think about the example of our Lord when he was on this earth.

He had many reasons to be sad, not cheerful. People he loved denied him, betrayed him, scorned him and finally crucified him. He was given tests of human and Divine love, and he remained faithful to his beliefs. He fulfilled his commitment to his Father and to us even though it meant a cruel, terrible death. He overcame the world, and that should be the supreme example to all of us. Love can conquer in even the most adverse situation.

He does not promise that we will be free of tribulations, but he assures us that we can have peace and be cheerful in spite of trials. He reminds us of the difficulty of his own ministry and wants us to know that we, too, can overcome as he did.

PRAYER:
*Thank you, Holy Comforter, for your example when you walked among us. Thank you for your total commitment. Thank you for your ultimate sacrifice. You overcame the world, and your victory offers us hope. Be with us as we struggle in this world. Give us the courage to go on. Let us be thankful for all you have done. Bless others and help them to feel the assurance of your love. Amen.*
Suggested for Steps 1 and 11

## MAY 26

*"They were filled with the Holy Spirit
and spoke the word of God with boldness."*
Acts 4:31

What does it mean to speak the word of God with boldness? The dictionary defines the word *bold* as "courageous and daring." When we witness to others of our love for our Lord and his love for us, how do we do it? It is especially important to ask ourselves this question when dealing with those who are new to Christianity or not yet committed to Christ.

Many people use intellectual methods to talk about Christianity. They can repeat any scripture, who wrote it, the scholarly meaning of the verses and much more. They can repeat church doctrine verbatim. But the question is, do they convince anyone through their intellectual interpretations?

New Christians, or those looking at Christians for the first time, are more impressed by a personal witness presented with a warm, loving Christian attitude. If we share what the love of Christ has done for us, they will be able to relate on a personal level. They will know, by observing our life styles and by listening to what we say, whether or not being a Christian is really worthwhile.

PRAYER:

*Loving Savior, help us to take the risk of telling others about your love for them. Help us to do it with courage and daring. Help us to let our light so shine before others that they will see our Father in heaven. Amen.*

Suggested for Step 12

---

## MAY 27

*"Beloved, we are God's children now;
it does not appear what we shall be, but . . .
we shall be like him."*
I John 3:2

How we see ourselves, our self-image, is very important. It will affect our feelings about life, whether we feel adequate or inadequate, whether we see ourselves as successful or as failures and even determine our health physically, emotionally and spiritually. Too often we concentrate on what we feel we lack, our weaknesses, rather than what we have, our strengths. We may be concentrating on what we are *not* rather than on what we *are.* Many of us have pictures of ourselves, painted by other people, that continue to influence us. We give people too much power over our lives. We give them too much power to decide who or what we are. That subservience almost always leaves us feeling inadequate, with a poor self-image.

We need to be careful when we take a personal inventory that we look at our assets and not just our liabilities. We need to see ourselves as God sees us, created for good. He sees us with the ability to grow and change and become. Most important, he is willing to help us through those changes.

PRAYER:

*Creator, Father, we thank you for the promise in this verse. Help us to be open to your will for our lives. Help us to share a healthy self-image with the people around us and let us give you the credit. We need to concentrate on the many good things in our lives and forgive and let go of our mistakes. Amen.*

Suggested for Step 10

# MAY 28

*"My soul, wait thou only upon God; for my expectation is from him."*
Psalm 62:5

Unfortunately, I did not learn how to wait upon God until my health was gone and I found myself near death. Like so many others, I kept so busy with business and personal life that I didn't take time to "be still and know that [he] is God" (Psalm 46:10). I was a full-fledged workaholic. Oh, I made my excuses, and I made my apologies to my Lord. I was going to take time . . . *tomorrow*. There were not enough hours in a day.

Then tragedy struck, and I was overwhelmed with a series of losses. The most devastating loss was that of my health because it brought about so many other losses. Then days and months became so long that I didn't know how I could stand to live through 24 more interminable hours. Time became my greatest enemy, an almost fatal enemy.

When I had my health and everything else, I did not think about the expectations I might have had from God. Suddenly I needed so many things that my expectations became endless. I wanted God to end my pain by meeting all of my needs. I could not wait. I wanted everything *now*. I had to learn how to wait. I had to relearn what my expectations from God could be. I learned patience. I learned trust. I learned gratitude. I learned acceptance of what *was*, not what I wanted. Most important, I learned what my real priorities were.

PRAYER:
*Loving Healer, precious Lord, thank you for those experiences that teach us how to wait upon you. Thank you for fulfilling our expectations for us when we are willing to seek your will. We are grateful that you are with us as we work on the changes in our lives. Amen.*
Suggested for Steps 1, 2 and 4

---

# MAY 29

*"The Lord has heard the voice of my weeping.*
*The Lord has heard my supplication;*
*the Lord will receive my prayer."*
Psalm 6:8,9

There may be times when we wonder if our Lord really hears the voice of our weeping. Some times when we experience trials, we feel as if we are completely alone in the hour of need. We may even feel that he has deserted us, and so we turn away from him in anger. Yet, our Lord promises that he will always be with us. He knows our pain even before we cry out.

This verse says he not only hears, but he will receive our prayers. Our faith can be very small, very weak, and yet as long as we have enough faith left to call out to him, he will answer. We need only speak his name in silent prayer, and he will respond.

He may not respond the way we want him to or the way we think he should. Perhaps we want all pain to cease immediately. Perhaps we want something—or someone—that is unavailable to us or even what is not in our best interest. we need to discipline ourselves to trust him completely and to accept that his answer is best for us.

PRAYER:
*Loving Lord, we thank you that you hear us when we weep and you receive our prayers. Help us to trust that your judgment is best for us. Let us turn to you early rather than suffer in our powerlessness. Thank you for your presence. Amen.*
Suggested for Step 11

# MAY 30

*"If a house be divided against itself,*
*that house cannot stand."*
Mark 3:25

We live in a world of conflict. An example of this is the divorce rate, which is higher than it has ever been. Spouses turn against each other, parents against children, children against parents, friends against friends and nations against nations. It is difficult to experience love in some homes, the homes of despair, hurt and anger. Households are divided against themselves, so they "cannot stand." They break apart and become separate individuals seeking their own ends instead of loving families unified in Christ. When they meet, they are like "ships passing in the night." Children of these households are insecure and feel torn because they have to divide their love and loyalty between warring parents.

How often are we overcome by our unwillingness to forgive one another? Even though we may fail one another on occasion, we need to forgive those hurts and keep open minds. That is more easily said than done and requires maturity, humility and commitment. We need to turn to our Lord for help.

PRAYER:

*Lord, help us to be more loving and forgiving toward the important people in our lives. Keep us from pettiness and help us to refrain from getting even with others. Give us the grace to apologize when we are wrong and to ask the forgiveness of those we have hurt. Help us to forgive willingly and let the hurt be in the past so that we might know the serenity of being one in Christ. Amen.*

Suggested for Steps 8 and 9

# MAY 31

*"And the Lord shall guide you continually,*
*and satisfy your soul in drought, and make fat your bones;*
*and you shall be like a watered garden,*
*and like a spring of water, whose waters fail not."*
Isaiah 58:11

As Christians, we believe that the Lord will guide us, but there are times when believing is difficult. Times get tough, and we think he does not care. We become discouraged and fear that he has abandoned us in the hour of greatest need. We lose sight of him, and instead of realizing that we have turned away from him, we believe that he has forgotten us. Nothing could be farther from the truth.

This verse says God guides us continually. He does not always allow us to see far down the path. *He* knows what lies ahead, and he also knows whether we can better cope with the challenges now or in the future. As long as we trust him, he will never allow us more than we can endure.

Frightening times when we cannot see our way are times of opportunity. The bends and blind spots in the road discipline our faith, teach us patience to walk step by step and prepare us for the special blessings God has in store for us. When our vision of what lies ahead is limited, we are more likely to seek his guidance and trust him. In fact, trusting may be all we can do at the time.

P R A Y E R:

*Triune God, thank you that when we believe in you, all things work together for good because we love you and you love us. We are grateful for your continual guidance. Help us to be willing to walk with others when their paths seem uncertain. Touch them with your healing. Amen.*

Suggested for Steps 2 and 3

# JUNE 1

*"Go and do not sin again."*

John 8:11

Summer is a time for growth, and significantly, Step 6 calls us to change and grow in new and different ways. We are asked to "become entirely ready to have Christ heal all of these defects of character."

I am continually struck by how patient God is for me to repent, turn about and change the destructive aspects of my life. Often I am aware that he has patience enough to wait until I am ready to be healed. Many times this is only when the pain is serious enough to motivate me to want something better. I also believe that at times he knows I am not ready to receive the healing he wants to give me because I would not handle it properly . . . so he waits.

Growth takes time. We need to be nurtured and prepared. The words quoted from John 8:11 are those Jesus spoke to the woman involved in adultery. First he loved her, and then he told her not to sin again.

Perhaps many of us think that we must change before God will love us, but that is not the way it happens. God does not love us because we repent and believe. Rather, we are able to become entirely ready because we have been loved by God, even in our state of unreadiness and disbelief that he can heal.

P R A Y E R:
*Thank you, Jesus, for loving us just as you loved this woman who was taken in adultery. Your unconditional love enables us to "become entirely ready." May we all use this summer as time to experience the miracle of growth because we have been loved into readiness. Amen.*
Suggested for Step 6                                             Vernon J. Bittner

# JUNE 2

*"And you shall know the truth,
and the truth shall set you free."*
John 8:32

There is wisdom in this verse, but finding the truth and accepting the truth are not the same action. For those of us who are truly seeking wholeness, an essential step is learning the truth about ourselves. We must be willing to be honest about *who* we are and *what* we are if we intend to allow Christ to transform our lives.

We don't always like the truth we learn about ourselves. We may find self-destructive things that have been in our lives for a long time. Eliminating those destructive character traits may cause us pain as well as time and energy. We must not underestimate how sincere our commitment will have to be in order to see the truth and really do something about it.

We will need to want Christ's help to change our lives more than we want anything else. Otherwise, we will not be committed enough to succeed and we will feel even more negative about our lives. Those who have had intense counseling and were actually committed to changing know that the truth can indeed set us free to be the persons God created us to be.

P R A Y E R:
*Loving Lord, give us the courage to seek the truth so that we may be healed of our self-destructive habits. Stay with us as we work on the changes we need to make. We desire healing and the freedom you promise. Amen.*
Suggested for Steps 4, 6 and 7

# JUNE 3

*"And it came to pass, that, as he was praying in a certain place,
when he ceased, one of his disciples said unto him, 'Lord,
teach us to pray, as John also taught his disciples.'"*
Luke 11:1

As we make a commitment to spend more time in prayer, it will help to consider the process of prayer. What are some prayer disciplines? First, we need to decide what we really need. We should be clear about our requests. Second, is our desire a Christian one? We cannot expect God to answer a prayer if what we want is not Christlike. Next, we should journal our needs and requests. If we write our prayers down on paper, waiting upon the Lord for answers will become more of a genuine commitment.

Next, we must quiet our minds and focus our attention on God. Then we need to talk *with*—not *to*—God about our prayer requests. We must listen to him before we speak and then listen again after we speak.

We also need to make a commitment to God about what we will do to make our prayer requests come true. Acknowledging our willingness to cooperate with him in helping to achieve answers to our prayers is also necessary. Prayer is action!

We need to ask ourselves if we expect answers to our requests and if we really believe that God will answer in our best interests. Finally, we have to thank God for answering prayer in his own way. God's delay may not be a refusal. Many times his "no" is not a denial of our prayers, either, but his assessment of our true needs.

P R A Y E R:

*Patient Lord, our feet stumble on the way to prayer. We are just learning to pray, and we need your help to center our full attention on you as we pray. Inspire us to pray according to your will. Discipline us to pray daily for our needs and those of others. Thank you for hearing us and for the fact that you do answer prayer. Amen.*

Suggested for Step 11

---

# JUNE 4

*"If any man thirst, let him come unto me and drink."*
John 7:37

If the Holy Spirit is going to be a genuine part of our lives, we must sincerely ask ourselves how seriously we want his presence and what we are willing to do to make that happen. We must recognize that we have a need. We must be willing to pray, "Lord, I thirst and desire to be filled." We need to be willing to admit our emptiness and express that need before the throne of God.

Are we at the point of being truly ready to have Christ transform our weaknesses into strengths? If we are holding onto old, destructive ways, what is getting in the way of our being willing to change? What is our payoff for staying the way we are? Do we fear change? Do we lack trust in Christ to see us through difficult times?

He has promised to fill us, but he requires that we come to him. We must acknowledge our need and humbly ask to be filled. Surely that is not too much to ask, considering the blessing we will receive.

P R A Y E R:

*Lord and Giver of life, thank you for your willingness to quench our thirst with living water. Help us to seek you humbly and to acknowledge this gift gratefully. Grant that we may share the blessing of your love with others who thirst. We ask that the Holy Spirit will become a genuine part of our lives, to fill and renew us. For all you do for us, we thank you. Amen.*

Suggested for Steps 2 and 6

---

# JUNE 5

*"What then?*
*Only that in every way, whether in pretense or in truth,*
*Christ is proclaimed; and in all that I rejoice."*
Philippians 1:18

Paul wrote these words in reference to those who preached but did not always have the right motives. I can relate to that. There have been times when I have felt phony because I have spoken about the love of God even though I did not feel his love. At times I was too discouraged, distraught or angry with God to feel good about him. My faith was not what I wanted it to be.

Unfortunately for me, I have survived so many tragedies in recent years that people have expected me to have unfaltering faith. Even when I bluntly told them I felt alienated from my faith, they wouldn't believe me. They looked to me for strength because they were convinced that I could encourage them to go on. I felt hypocritical when I proclaimed God's love although I did believe it existed myself.

Paul reminds us that even when we fake it, we are still proclaiming the name of Christ and that can have a positive influence on others. We need to take heart from this verse and stop criticizing ourselves for being imperfect. It is okay to doubt at times as long as we are willing to admit it and seek God's help in strengthening our faith. Sharing the gospel hesitantly is better than not sharing it at all. We may be more of a blessing to someone in our weaknesses than when we have it all together.

PRAYER:

*Loving God, thank you for your patience with us when we do not feel the firm conviction of your love. Help us to risk sharing our faith, as well as our lack of it, with others. Give us courage to show our humanness so that others will feel freer to share in return. Amen.*

Suggested for Step 2

# JUNE 6

*"It is good for me that I have been afflicted."*
Psalm 119:71

The powerlessness we experience in our lives is not always negative. We can receive genuine blessing from trials if we use them as times for reflection. We can develop a more meaningful relationship with our Lord if we turn to him for guidance. We can gain a new self-confidence in our own ability to deal with difficulties if we see them as opportunities for growth.

I would never have imagined it possible, but I gained many blessings in the past seven years. In some ways, they were the worst seven years of my life. A mugging resulted in a long hospitalization, an incurable disease and a permanent disability. My chronic health problem ended a 25-year career and a 27-year marriage. I lost four important people in my life through death, and two of them were suicides at relatively young ages. I was forced to change the priorities of my life and to focus upon God, who proved to be my true source of strength when all else failed.

PRAYER:

*Loving Healer, help us to be able to say with gratitude, "It is good for me that I have been afflicted." Thank you for the opportunities that our trials offer us. Give us strength to go through these times with our hands in yours. Grant us courage to share our experiences with others so that they, too, can know the hope that you give. Amen.*

Suggested for Step 11

# JUNE 7

*"Which hope we have as an anchor of the soul."*
Hebrews 6:19

This would be a distressing place to live if we did not have hope. Would we want to continue on day after day without hope that our lives can be better than they are now? For those with serious illness, what point would there be in continuing to suffer if they could not hope for a cure or at least some relief?

God's presence makes it possible for us to hope. He gives us reasons to hope in even the most hopeless of situations. He gives us strength to go on. When we are at our lowest point in life, he comes to us with the promise, "[I] shall supply all your needs according to [my] riches in glory through Christ Jesus."

Hebrews 6:19 promises that hope will be our anchor. God gives us hope as a premium for a life of faith. Hope is based on his power. Hope urges us to keep on keeping on even when everything seems to be going wrong.

PRAYER:

*Loving God, thank you for hope. Enable us to trust you so our spirits will calm. Change our attitudes of hopelessness and distrust into faith and hope and love. Help us to retain a simple, steadfast reliance on you and your will. Help us to share our hope with others. Amen.*

Suggested for Step 3

---

# JUNE 8

*"Anyone who is not for me is against me,*
*if he isn't helping me, he is hurting my cause."*
Luke 11:23, *The Living Bible*

This a powerful message for us to consider, especially in light of our Christian witness. People watch us as we go through life professing to be Christians. We are either helping or hurting the cause of Christ. If we can express his love and forgiveness, our lives will exemplify his love.

To be a Christian is a privilege, but with that privilege comes a serious responsibility. We cannot always do what we want to do when we want to do it. We cannot always have what we want to have when we want to have it. We need to pray for discernment so that we will know God's will. We need to ask ourselves, "Are my words and actions Christlike? Are my motives right, or is my behavior a result of lust, greed or selfishness?" If Christ would do what you are doing, it is the right thing to do. If what you are doing is contrary to his will or law, it is the wrong thing to do.

PRAYER:

*Heavenly Father, help us to remember that we are responsible for what we do and say. We know that we will suffer the consequences of our behavior. When we live destructive life styles, we hurt ourselves as well as others. Help us to remember the importance of our witness, and may our lives be pleasing to you. You have given us the example by which to live. Give us the wisdom to follow it. Amen.*

Suggested for Step 12

# JUNE 9

*"Blessed are they that mourn,*
*for they shall be comforted."*
Matthew 5:4

We all will experience a time of mourning. When this happens, it is important to know we can call upon our Lord and receive his comfort. Comfort in mourning is an experience of transformation. Through his transforming power, God helps us to look beyond our pain and loss and see hope. Yesterday's tears transform into today's courage and strength. Yesterday's despair transforms into today's hope and vision. Yesterday's sadness transforms into today's joy. Yesterday's anxiety transforms into today's serenity. Yesterday's doubts transform into today's understanding and assurance.

Transformation will take place in our lives when we recognize our powerlessness and turn our cares over to Christ. We know we need to work on letting go and accepting his will. If we hold onto our powerlessness, transformation will be impossible.

PRAYER:

*Thank you, Lord, for transformation. Help us to have willing hearts and minds to make transformation possible. Help us to fulfill our commitment to have you transform our weaknesses into strengths. Bless others in their powerlessness and help them to be open to your transformation. Amen.*

Suggested for Step 1

# JUNE 10

*"If any man hear my words, and believe not,*
*I judge him not; for I came not to judge the world, but to save the world."*
John 12:47

During Christ's ministry on earth, many "righteous" people criticized him for associating with sinners. Some critics were learned religious leaders who knew the letter of the law but did not practice the spirit of the law. Although Christ pointed out people's wrongs to them, he always gave them hope for redemption. He assured them of his love if they wanted it. He did not leave them in a state of condemnation, but let them know they could be healed.

Because of his unconditional love, Christ influenced many people. He loved them into choosing a life of faith in him. He did more than point out their sins, he offered forgiveness and the challenge to live constructive lives.

Unfortunately, too many of us who profess to be Christians unmercifully judge people according to our personal interpretations of God's word, for our own convenience and by our harsh standards. As a result, we project a poor image of Christianity. When we do this, we leave people without hope unless they are willing to become carbon copies of ourselves. That is not Christlike love, and it does more harm than good.

PRAYER:

*Loving Savior, help us to leave the judging of others to you. Teach us to love as you love. Help us to share the gospel of forgiveness and hope that will motivate others to desire transformation. Amen.*

Suggested for Steps 8 and 9

# JUNE 11

*"This is the victory that overcomes the world,*
*our faith."*
I John 5:4

In order to believe that Christ can transform our shortcomings, we need to make a personal commitment of faith. How wonderful it is to believe that with faith comes victory over the world, the whole world! "No enemy formed against us can prosper." We need not be defeated by losses or apparent failures. We can believe that even our failures are opportunities for us to grow and mature as Christians. We need not give way to fear and anxiety. We can feel confident that there is always another way, a new path, a new idea, that can head us in the right direction. God's love makes that possible.

The key to success is faith in the One who can make all things possible, all things new. We are blessed to be spiritual beings. We are filled with the Spirit of God, and his abiding presence makes it possible for us to accomplish many things.

When we believe with all our hearts, marvelous things can happen. Even at those times when our faith is a little less than the best, our Lord whispers to us, "If you have faith as the grain of a mustard seed, you can move mountains." We only need to be willing, and he will increase our faith.

PRAYER:

*Gentle Teacher, we acknowledge that we do not always have the faith we should have. We ask your forgiveness for our indifference. Teach us to trust you more completely and to share our faith with others. We want to learn to be the best that we can be—for you, for ourselves and for others. Thank you for your help. Amen.*

Suggested for Step 7

# JUNE 12

*"To comfort all that mourn."*
Isaiah 61:2

As Christian adults, most of us have had some experience of being comforted during a time of grief. Unfortunately, children are not that lucky and even in these modern times, children's grief is underestimated. Parents can easily overlook the grief of their children or misinterpret their behavior after a loss, especially when the parents themselves are going the grief process. Children grieve in a different way, and they express their grief differently. It is important for us to be sensitive to grieving children and to help them through the process with openness and love.

When I was ten years old, my 14-year-old brother died of cancer. He had been ill for more than a year before he died, and he spent most of that time in the hospital in the city, miles away from our farm. My parents spent most of their time with him at the hospital, and my older sister and brother were allowed to visit him regularly. I was thought too young to go to the hospital and see him.

So when he died, I had not seen him for almost a year. I didn't recognize him in the coffin. He weighed less than 50 pounds, and his hair was snow white. I could not believe that he was my brother. When I touched his thin fingers as I said "good-bye," something happened to me. I lost all memory of him, who he was, even the ten years we had laughing and playing together. After 40 years, I still cannot remember anything about him except that coffin experience. I have a rose from his lapel, but that is all that remains of my memory of him. My childhood grief was profound and long-lasting.

PRAYER:

*Lord, thank you for comforting us in our times of loss and grief. Help us to be aware of our children's needs and to help them through their grief process. Help us to teach them about your love and grace and how to turn to you when they sorrow. Help us to allow our children to express their feelings openly. Let us be willing to cry with our children so they will know that it is okay for them to cry, too. Amen.*

Suggested for Step 12

# JUNE 13

*"Come, let us walk in the light of the Lord."*
Isaiah 2:5

As we work at becoming entirely ready to have Christ transform our weaknesses into strengths, we need to remember this verse. When we are unsure of taking a new step, we need to pray for the light of his love. As we work on changes to be made, we ask God to guide and direct us. If we are struggling with a difficult decision, we must be willing to walk in his light. He will direct us if we are willing to be completely open to his will for us.

It is reassuring to know that we have a loving Lord to whom we can go for answers. Some times answers come quickly, and we feel confident that he is guiding us. Some times it seems that there is no answer to our problem, and we wonder why our prayers have not been answered in the way we expected or wanted. Then we need to remember that all of our prayers are answered in one way or another. Perhaps there is a special lesson for us to learn as we wait for his answer. Maybe we are not even ready to accept the answer for which we have prayed. We must continue to trust that he wants what is best for us. He is our light and our hope!

PRAYER:

*Lord, we thank you for your invitation to walk with you in the light. We thank you that because of your love, we need not struggle alone in the darkness. You make your presence known and felt when we invite you into our lives. Thank you for your love. Be with others who struggle in the darkness and bring them into your light. Amen.*

Suggested for Steps 6 and 11

# JUNE 14

*"Then he asked them, 'Where is your faith?'"*
Luke 8:25

Our Lord asked this question of many people when he ministered on this earth. Some had difficulty believing in him although they had heard or seen the many miracles he performed. Even his disciples, who knew him most intimately, had difficulty with their faith. Eventually they would become firm in their faith and willingly follow him even to death.

Christ questions us today, "Where is your faith?" We are reminded that it is much more blessed to believe without having seen proof. Some of us, even after we have seen some proof, still do not believe. One wonders what it will take for us to have the faith he wants us to have.

When we take an inventory of our lives, we need to ask ourselves what gets in the way of our having faith. Is our faith strong enough to sustain us during difficult times or barely strong enough to get us through good times? Do we believe our Lord's promise, "I will never leave you or forsake you"? If not, why not? Are we willing to take whatever steps are necessary for spiritual growth?

PRAYER:

*Lord, thank you for loving us even though we lose faith. Help us to be more committed to serving you with love. Give us a stronger faith that believes without having proof. Amen.*

Suggested for Steps 4 and 10

# JUNE 15

*"Choose this day whom you will serve . . .
but as for me and my house, we will serve the Lord."*
Joshua 24:15

Our Lord allows us to make our own choices. We do not always make the right choices, but we need to appreciate the fact that the decisions were ours. We can choose faith or fear. We can choose to be happy or unhappy. We can choose anger or forgiveness. We can choose to see the good in others, or we can see only their defects. We can choose the bondage of depression or the freedom that his healing love offers us. We can choose to trust him or to go our own way.

We can choose to walk with our Lord and experience his love, freedom and peace. We can choose to let go of the trials with which we struggle and let him lead us out of the wilderness. We can choose to be joyful rather than gloomy. We can choose to love him, ourselves and others. What will we choose this day?

PRAYER:

*Help us, Lord, with all these decisions and choices. Thank you for your strength and encouragement. Thank you for your constant love. Bless others as they struggle with choices and help them to make the right ones. Give them strength to continue on and give them courage to reach out for help when they need it.*

*This day, Lord, we choose you and your love. Amen.*

Suggested for Step 3

# JUNE 16

*"I will bless the Lord at all times;
his praise shall continually be in my mouth."*
Psalm 34:1

This should be the commitment with which we start every new day. "I will bless the Lord at *all* times." It is easy to be thankful to our Lord when things are going right, even though we may not take the time to thank him. But when we are healthy, we take it for granted. When we have enough food, clothing and shelter, we take it all for granted. When our children are doing well and our marriages are fine, we take the credit and take them for granted. Many times we do not fully appreciate all that we have until something threatens our security.

When things start to fall part, we pull out our emergency God and shout, "Help!" Or maybe we ask, "Why me, Lord?" We may not feel as loving toward our Lord during tough times as when all is well.

We need to discipline ourselves to bless the Lord *at all times*. Trials and crosses are often our greatest blessings in disguise. We need to thank him for the thorns in our lives, not just the roses. We come closer to our Savior through the path of pain. Our tears can even become beautiful rainbows that remind us of his presence.

PRAYER:

*Lord and loving Shepherd, we admit that we are not always thankful for the crosses in our lives. Teach us the glory of our crosses and give us the courage to face them willingly. Help us to share the beauty of our experiences with others who also see only the crosses, not the resurrection. Thank you for crosses! Amen.*

Suggested for Step 11

---

# JUNE 17

*"Then Jesus answered her,*
*'Woman, great is your faith! Be it done for you as you desire.'*
*And her daughter was healed instantly."*
Matthew 15:28

This story of one of Christ's miracles teaches the importance of trusting him. The woman represents a person of great faith and humility. She believed in his power to heal, and she was confident that he would grant her request for her daughter's healing. On the one hand, she came to him with a deep sense of unworthiness, willing to accept whatever crumbs might fall from the Master's table. Yet, she also came eagerly, trusting in the Master's love for his children.

As we become ready for Christ to heal our character defects, we need to see if we really believe he *can* heal them. Are we as committed as the woman in this story? Do we believe in him so completely that instead of living in fear, we step forward boldly as she did and cry out, "Have mercy on me, Lord. Help me"? Do we believe enough to dare ask him for any healing we need and then trust him enough to do what is best for us? Do we have enough faith in his love for us to pray *expectantly*? Let us journal about this important area of our lives.

PRAYER:

*Dear Lord, give us spiritual strength to have the kind of faith that trusts you completely. Help us to grow in devotion to the tasks that you have for us. Free us from the attitude of hopelessness and give us the never-failing trust of Christ our Lord. In all we do, may we have the faith that heals us in the name of Jesus Christ. Amen.*

Suggested for Steps 2 and 6

# JUNE 18

*"Behold, I will do a new thing;*
*now it shall spring forth; shall you not know it?*
*I will even make a way in the wilderness,*
*and rivers in the desert."*

Isaiah 43:19

There are times when we feel powerless and there does not seem to be any way out. It seems that no matter which way we turn, there is an obstacle too great to move. Many times, because we do not seek our Lord, we think we are struggling in the wilderness alone. We try to do it on our own, and it just does not work.

We have the promise that he will make a way for us in the wilderness. He does not promise that we will not have wilderness experiences, but he promises his presence if we ask! He will give us hope, strength, comfort, courage and guidance. He will see us safely through the wilderness if we believe!

We need to take a look at our wilderness experiences and the obstacles that seem to be in our way. Are we creating our own obstacles because we are doing our will and not his? Have we accepted limitations for ourselves with an attitude of hopelessness? We need to revise our awareness of the presence of our Lord and acknowledge him as the Giver of life. We need to hear once again that "with Christ, all things are possible" (Matthew 19:26). We need to be willing to give up our despair for the joy his love brings.

PRAYER:

*Loving Shepherd, thank you for making a way for us in the wilderness. We thank you for wilderness experiences and for the opportunities they provide to grow and mature in your love. Help us to be available to others in their wilderness experiences. Amen.*

Suggested for Step 1

# JUNE 19

*"Take therefore no thought for the morrow;*
*for the morrow shall take thought for things of itself.*
*Sufficient unto the day is the evil thereof."*
Matthew 6:34

In our 12 Steps for Christian Living program, we encourage taking just one day at a time. Our Lord gave us that wisdom when he walked this earth. He reminded us that there is beauty in living one day at a time. We are told that we need not worry. He is in charge. He showed us he not only cares for the birds of the air and the flowers of the field, but he cares much more for us. He assures us that he has created a natural order. Our heavenly Father greatly cares for every one of us.

He says to us that we are not to worry about yesterday and its griefs and mistakes. Yesterday is gone, and we can do nothing to change it. Forgive the past so that you can let go of the part of yesterday that is enclosing you. Also, forgive yourself for the mistakes you have made; that is the only way to let go of painful memories and recapture the beauty that surrounded past events.

He says to us, "Don't worry about tomorrow! Tomorrow has not yet been given to us, and we need all of our energy to live today!" He reminds us that this day has a sufficient amount of responsibilities to be handled one at a time. He assures us that he will be with us every step of the way. What more could we ask?

**PRAYER:**
*Loving Lord, thank you for this day. Help us to use it wisely. Help us to share your love with others and to be available to them in times of need. Teach us to let go of the past and not worry about the future. Touch others with your healing hand so they will no longer be burdened by the past. Free us all, Lord, so we can live one day at a time. Amen.*

Suggested for Steps 8 and 9

---

# JUNE 20

*"Rejoice always, pray constantly, give thanks in all circumstances;*
*for this is the will of God in Christ Jesus concerning you."*
I Thessalonians 5:16-18

Even when we feel tremendous fatigue in body, mind and spirit, we can rejoice and praise him. We can thank him during times of loss because he reminds us of his presence and strength. Even when our world is surrounded by darkness, he breaks the darkness with the light of his love.

We know that with his help, we can have the courage to go on. Because of his love, we have the capacity for renewal. We can believe that "this, too, shall pass away" and we will be revitalized. We just need to let go and let him lead.

The times we have the most energy and feel the best about ourselves are when we are in harmony with God, ourselves and others, therefore it is important to know which areas of our lives need to worked on in order to achieve that harmony. We must be open to the potential for healing, willing to release our self-doubts and wavering confidence. We know the Lord is with us every step of the way, and we thankfully claim that promise.

PRAYER:

*Thank you, dear Lord, for strengthening us this day. We are grateful that even though we doubt sometimes, we can always count on you. Bless others who need strength. Touch them. Help them in whatever way they need it most. Amen.*

Suggested for Step 2

---

# JUNE 21

*"The eternal God is your dwelling place,*
*and underneath are the everlasting arms,*
*and he thrust out the enemy before you."*
Deuteronomy 33:27

It is comforting to know that we can let go and know that his arms are always beneath us to hold us up. We can give him our burdens—the pain of loss, disappointments, frustrations, anger and even all the distressing memories of the past—and know that he will comfort us. He will enfold us with his love and peace. He will touch us with healing and joy. Even if we do not have total physical healing, he will heal us emotionally and spiritually.

Usually, before we can even begin to think about physical or emotional healing, we have to experience spiritual healing. In my experience with physical and emotional illness, I could not start the journey toward wholeness until I was willing to look at my spiritual illness. I was angry with God and gave up on him before my physical illness became serious. I'm sure that contributed to the worsening of the disease and severe depression. We can never become whole, or even come close to wholeness, until we become willing to seek healing in all three areas: the physical, the emotional and the spiritual.

PRAYER:
*Thank you, Lord, for the peace and healing you give us when we finally let go. Thank you for the assurance that you will take care of us. Thank you for your love. Forgive us for times when we refuse to let go and trust you fully. Be patient with us, Lord. We are slow learners sometimes.*

*Lord, there are so many who need to let go of the control of their lives. Touch them in a special way, and let them know it is all right. Let them know you have a better way if they will try it. Amen.*

Suggested for Step 3

# JUNE 22

*"I wait for the Lord, my soul does wait,
and in his word do I hope."*
Psalm 130:5

How many of us can say this verse and really mean it, especially during hard times? Waiting can be very difficult, whether we are waiting for something joyful to happen or for grief or pain to lessen. We need patience, and we need to be still and listen to the voice of God. We need to trust the process of life, and that is not always easy. We need to wait upon the Lord and allow him to fulfill his will for our lives.

Unfortunately, we often decide instead that our Lord has forgotten us and start trying to fix things on our own. At that point, we complicate the plan that Christ has for us and may even prevent the very healing we so desperately need.

If we are going to become entirely ready for Christ to transform our lives, we need to be open to his will. We need to pray for patience to wait for him to act rather than trying to find solutions ourselves. We may also need to accept the reality that we will have to endure some pain for a while longer. We have the assurance of his presence. He will give us the strength to wait.

PRAYER:
*Lord, thank you for your presence in our lives, which makes waiting more acceptable. We are grateful that your plan for us is the best plan. Help us to spend our time waiting wisely and not grudgingly. Help us to be patient with ourselves and others as we grow and change. Amen.*

Suggested for Step 6

## JUNE 23

*"I have fought a good fight, I have finished my course,*
*I have kept the faith."*
II Timothy 4:7

Perhaps the most effective way for us to witness to the message of Christ's love and forgiveness is by making these words our life style. This means that we do the very best we can. It does not require that we be perfect, for we will never be perfect until we are with our Lord in eternity. It does not mean that we do impossible things or even things that we are not gifted to do. It means that we do the very best we can at all times, praying for God's wisdom. It suggests that we be willing to risk new things and new relationships. It requires us to be about our Lord's business.

He does not expect us to stumble around blindly. He will direct our efforts. That involves risk taking, for some times we do not even recognize or acknowledge a gift we already have that he wants us to use. It requires openness, not only to his will for us, but to others who see a gift in us that we may not see ourselves. Using a new gift for the first time can be frightening, so we need to trust God to be with us. If he wants us to share the gift with others, he will give us the courage to use it.

PRAYER:

*Loving Father, thank you for the gifts you have given us. Thank you that although all of us have different gifts and different ways of using them, you combine our efforts in the body of Christ so that we effectively serve you together. To those who are too timid to share their gifts, give the courage to risk sharing them. Bless us to be a blessing through the gifts you give every one of us. Amen.*

Suggested for Step 12

---

## JUNE 24

*"I am the vine, you are the branches;*
*he that abides in me, and I in him,*
*the same brings forth much fruit;*
*for without me, you can do nothing."*
John 15:5

Those of us who have gone through a great deal of pain in our lives or struggled to change some difficult character trait know the truth of this verse. We may start out with the attitude that "I can do it myself," only to learn after much frustration that we cannot do it without Christ's help. We are unable to reap the rewards of a truly spiritual life style until we recognize our need for his guidance.

Quite often we take on more than we can handle, and then we are too proud to ask for help. Many people believe that the only way to get something done the right way is to do it themselves. Since we consider ourselves wise enough to care for our own lives, we often fail to solicit our Lord's help and try to carry the burden alone.

Burdens and responsibilities are much lighter when shared with others. Certainly we need to be willing to turn to our Lord for guidance. Independence is important for our self-worth, but interdependence and dependence on God are essential if we desire wholeness.

PRAYER:

*Lord, when we depend only on our own strength, you seem to be far away. As soon as we are able to acknowledge our need for you, you make your presence known. Help us to practice a healthy balance of independence, interdependence and dependence on you. Amen.*

Suggested for Steps 3, 6 and 7

---

# JUNE 25

*"I will greatly rejoice in the Lord,*
*my soul shall exult in my God;*
*for he has clothed me with the garments of salvation,*
*he has covered me with the robe of righteousness,*
*as a bridegroom decks himself with a garland,*
*and as a bride adorns herself with her jewels."*

Isaiah 61:10

We need to have a song in our hearts, to find joy in everyday life. We need to work at being enthusiastic about the things we do and to think positively even when times are difficult. We can choose to feel that life is good and see beauty around us, or we can feel that life is empty, barren and ugly. A lot depends on our attitude.

We need to make a commitment to change our attitude so that we will greet every new day with the expectation that good things will happen. We need to risk becoming involved with interesting people and interesting experiences so we feel challenged, vital and renewed. When that happens, we want to remember to give God the praise and the glory.

We need to look for the best in others and always have hope in them regardless of how destructive their life styles may be. Instead of being judgmental, we need to encourage them to align their wills with God's. If we cannot help, at least we can refrain from hurting them.

PRAYER:

*Thank you, gracious Lord, for those who touch our lives in special ways. Thank you especially for our families and friends. Bless us to be blessings to others. Amen.*

Suggested for Steps 11 and 12

## JUNE 26

*"Lead me in thy truth, and teach me,*
*for thou art the God of my salvation;*
*for thee I wait all the day long."*
Psalm 25:5

As we accept the fact that we must let go in order to have serenity, this verse gives us confidence to trust this promise. Our Lord assures us that if we will trust him, he will lead us. He wants the best for us. He has a perfect plan. As we become willing to let him fulfill that plan, we discover the joy and freedom he wants us to have.

Discovering his plan for us may take more time than we like. He may reveal it to us step by step, one day at a time, but we will experience a sense of achievement as his plan unfolds. Our own lives will become more blessed, and we will become more of a blessing to others.

We must be willing to participate actively in fulfilling God's plan. We must believe in him and trust his leading. Otherwise, we will sabotage his and our own efforts at change and miss the abundant life.

PRAYER:

*Heavenly Father, may we wait upon you and trust in your leadership. We know that every blessing comes to us from your hand. You share our hope. Help us to be worthy of the name Christian. Teach us how to share your love so others will come to know you, too. We acknowledge that we can do nothing without you. All power belongs to you. Thank you for being our guide. Amen.*

Suggested for Step 3

---

## JUNE 27

*"For I am the Lord. I change not."*
Malachi 3:6

God never changes! He is constant; his love is ever-abiding. In a world of unsure and changing relationships, he will never change. Our friends may abandon us, our parents may disown us, our spouses may decide that we are no longer wanted or needed. Neighbors move away, our jobs change, or we change and no longer relate to people as before.

With each loss or change in relationships, we go through a grief process. It is good to know that even in the midst of many changes, our Lord does not change! He is our lifetime Friend. He is committed to us even when we disappoint or ignore him. He is not angry with us when we fail him; instead, he forgives us. He stands by us.

PRAYER:
*Beloved and constant Friend, thank you for being the same for us, ever-present, never-changing. We praise you that unlike anyone else in our lives, you love us completely and unconditionally. Help us to see your example of real friendship and to practice that same kind of love with all our friends. Bless others in such a way that they come to know you as their Friend. Amen.*
Suggested for Steps 8 and 9

## JUNE 28

*"For in him we live, and move and have our being."*
Acts 17:28

Today we take time to appreciate how much God does for us. He is always available to help us, moment by moment, even though we may neither see nor hear him. Some times he helps us through a friend, a stranger, a spoken message or the printed word. In ways that we know and know not, we have his help.

He keeps us in his care. Some times it is through the trials that fret us or the walls that seem to close us in. He leads us along pathways easy and hard. Maybe he helps by a wide-open door or by a closed door. When joy is not forthcoming, he helps us to learn how to be thankful. He is with us during times of loss, and he helps us to grow toward Christian maturity.

He uses us according to his will—by way of a plan accomplished or by holding our hand and whispering, "Be still and know that I am God!" What we may see as a burden or even a failure may be one of our greatest opportunities to grow in his love.

PRAYER:
*Loving Friend, help us to keep open minds and hearts so that we may live according to your will. Let us work toward trusting you completely so we do not waste time in self-destructive activities. Let us always remember that we have your love and your help even when we don't sense your presence. Thank you for caring. Amen.*
Suggested for Step 2

## JUNE 29

*"Confess your faults one to another,*
*and pray one for another, that you may be healed.*
*The effectual fervent prayer of a righteous person avails much."*
James 5:16

Probably most Christians pray for one another, but to what degree do we really extend ourselves in praying for others? Do we pray not only for our loved ones, but for difficult people as well? Do we pray for those with whom we totally disagree regarding morals, beliefs and life styles? Do we earnestly pray for those who have deeply hurt us, or do we kind of forget their needs? We need to pray for one another, and that means for every one.

It can be distressing to pray day after day for persons we love and then watch them continue in their destructive life styles. Our prayers may not seem to be getting through to God. The harder we pray, sometimes, the more their lives deteriorate before our eyes.

We need to turn these loved ones over to the care of Christ. That does not mean we will cease to pray for them or even that we will cease to love them or try to help them when possible. It only means that we recognize our powerlessness to change anyone except ourselves. We need to continue to pray in a positive spirit, turning them over to Christ and expecting him to act on their behalf.

P R A Y E R :

*Lord, we pray for others this day—for loved ones, for strangers, for friends, for enemies, for all humankind. We lift our hearts to you in prayer for the needs of others. Thank you for all that you do for us. Amen.*

Suggested for Steps 11 and 12

## JUNE 30

*"If a city refuses you,*
*go out into the street, wipe the dust from your feet."*
Luke 10:10,11

As a people pleaser and caretaker, I need to think seriously about this verse. For most of my life, I expressed my love for people by doing whatever they wanted me to do. Many of these relationships were one-way. I did all of the work, all of the caretaking. They took what I had to give and gave nothing in return . . . except that many used or abused me. It was so important for me to feel loved and accepted that it didn't matter to me how they treated me. I was satisfied just to have them talk to me. At least while they were abusing me, I had their full attention. They were involved with me. I wanted to believe that meant they cared for me.

Gradually I realized that my behavior was too dependent and very self-destructive. It took me longer to realize that I deserve to be loved, not abused. I deserve to be accepted, not used. As a child of God, I deserve the abundant life that he wants for all of his children.

I found it difficult to detach these unhealthy relationships. It was hard to believe that it was okay for me to "wipe the dust from [my] feet." It took courage to risk new relationships with people who were willing to love me in return. The risk was worth the effort!

P R A Y E R:

*Lord, help us to take a close look at our relationships and detach from some of them if we need to. Help us to experience our self-worth so that we are willing to expect more for our lives than abuse. Help us to refrain from abusing others in any way. Amen.*

Suggested for Step 10

# JULY 1

*"Oh, return to me,*
*for I have paid the price to set you free."*
Isaiah 44:22

July is a month when we celebrate our freedom as a nation. Step 7 speaks of freedom, too. It reminds us that only God, through Christ, can transform our lives from slavery to sinful, destructive behavior, and transform us into freed men and women.

To be transformed means that we are called back to be with God—to be the persons that God created us to be. This verse reminds us that we will only find freedom in Christ. Christ paid the price of freedom by his suffering, death and resurrection. Being transformed means that we are loved into freedom by God.

Only Christ has the power to transform our lives. We cannot do it by ourselves. Only when we admit that we need him and allow him to work in us will we experience the freedom of the life in Christ's transformation.

May we know freedom not only as a nation, but freedom as individuals and children of God because we have been transformed.

P R A Y E R:

*God, you have created us for freedom. Thank you for paying the price for our freedom by sending us your Son, Jesus Christ, to set us free. Help us to have the good sense to want to return to you so that we might experience your transforming power in our lives.*

Suggested for Step 7                                   Vernon J. Bittner

# JULY 2

*"Know this, that when the way is rough
your patience has a chance to grow."*

James 1:3

Certainly when the way is rough we need a great deal of patience. But just when we need patience most, it is the most difficult to find. Some times we pray, "Give me patience, Lord, *right now!*" We want the rough times to be over with and our world to be fun and loving again. Perhaps we spend so much time bemoaning our predicaments that we fail to see opportunities in our pain.

We can grow during the difficult times if we are willing to be open to the healing power of God. Our faith can become stronger if we are willing to accept the challenge offered in suffering. True, suffering is hard to take, but it can produce a feeling of beauty and serenity that we have never known.

The secret is *to be willing to trust* in the process of God's love and will. We need *to believe* that if we surrender, he will take care of us. Believing that in the midst of pain is not easy because, to a certain extent, all of us are "doubting Thomases."

P R A Y E R:

*Help us, Lord, when times are tough to turn to you in complete trust for the patience we need. From each experience let us gain renewed faith in your ability to take care of us. Thank you for difficult times and for your presence to see us through them. Amen.*

Suggested for Steps 1, 2 and 3

# JULY 3

*"The Lord is my light and my salvation;
whom shall I fear?"*

Psalm 27:1

Remembering this verse and saying it every morning when we arise could bring us special blessings. We need not fear any person or any situation, for he is with us and within us. He gives us all that we need to meet every new challenge. We need to re-member to look for the good in all people and in all situations, remember-ing that he desires only good for our lives.

We release our problems into his hands, to do with them as he sees best. He will give us patience to accept the outcome of any situation and the courage to go on. Our problems can also be challenges to grow and mature in his love. Pray to be open to that possibility.

PRAYER:

*Thank you for your light, Lord. Thank you for the assurance that we need not fear, for you are with us. Thank you, especially, for your constant love. We pray that others will experience your light and your salvation and healing. Touch them with your warmth. Surround them with your love. Be with us, Lord! Amen.*

Suggested for Steps 6 and 10

# JULY 4

*"Blessed are the peacemakers;*
*for they shall be called the children of God."*
Matthew 5:9

The Fourth of July is a very important day in the United States. It is the day we set aside to celebrate the freedom that is so precious to us. It is a day we pause to remember that many people died to preserve the freedom we enjoy today. It is a day that we should give special thanks to God for the privilege of living in this country. We remember with gratitude all those who fought for religious freedom. Without their sacrifice, it would be more difficult for us to practice our faith today.

All four of my grandparents immigrated from other countries. They came to this land of opportunity so their children could be free to believe and to practice those beliefs openly. The freedoms offered here were important enough for them to leave their native lands, give up everything they had and move here.

They must have been very committed to the high ideals of freedom. They also must have had a strong faith in God to help them in their new homeland. They came with nothing and helped to build the foundation of what we enjoy today.

We can show our gratitude to those who have helped to preserve freedom for us by practicing peace. "Blessed are the peacemakers." We can be kind and loving toward one another. We can practice justice and mercy in all our affairs. We can refrain from setting one person against another and, instead, practice unconditional love.

PRAYER:

*Loving God, thank you for freedom. Help us to show our appreciation for all that we have by sharing it with others. Grant that we might share the peace and calm that your love brings us. Thank you for the blessing of living in this great nation. Amen.*

Suggested for Step 4

# JULY 5

*"Therefore all things whatsoever you would that men should do to you, do you even so to them; for this is the law and the prophets."*
Matthew 7:12

This verse is known as the Golden Rule, and if we truly practiced it, there would be a lot more love in this world. We spend so much time in anger and unforgiveness that we don't have time left to love as we should love. Our Lord has shown us how he responded to those who hurt him, yet we cannot seem to get beyond our pettiness and hurt to love as he would have us love.

My brother had a favorite saying, "Don't get mad, get even!" Too many people practice that slogan. He spent more time trying to get even with someone than he did looking for happiness in his own life. At times he was violent and did not hesitate to hurt someone who had "crossed" him.

He never learned the value of giving and receiving love, and when he died at the age of 49, he was a desperately lonely, tragic man. Many people had tried to love him, but when they got too close, he would turn against them. He could be so frightening in his efforts to get even that most people found it safer and easier to stay away from him. He was alone when he died, and he felt that no one loved him.

PRAYER:

*Loving Friend, help us to give and accept love, to be willing to treat others as we want them to treat us. Teach us to practice the forgiveness you taught by giving it to others and asking for it ourselves. Thank you for your love and forgiveness. Amen.*

Suggested for Steps 8 and 9

# JULY 6

*"Rejoice in the Lord always; again I say, rejoice."*
Philippians 4:4

We may not always feel this joyful even if we have a strong faith in God to see us through. When we are in the midst of pain and loss, we lose sight of the reasons we have to rejoice in the Lord. We can look back to a time when we came through a difficult trial and say, "Praise God," but not always in the midst of the trial. We are human, and we become discouraged.

When I was mugged, I was not able to say, "Praise God, I'm losing everything!" When I spent the first year in the hospital with so many surgeries, I did not feel like shouting, "Thank God for this disease and all this pain!" I was angry with God and everyone else. I felt lost and alone. I didn't feel faithful, and I certainly didn't feel thankful. In fact, I was too sick to care.

It was not until some time afterward that I could see what I had gained from my suffering. I did not forget what I had lost; God doesn't give us amnesia. I remembered much about the pain and loss, but God healed the pain of those memories. He permitted me to recognize a joy beneath all of my sadness. There is no hopelessness when we have faith! God's presence makes all the difference in the world.

P R A Y E R:

*Lord, who heals and restores, give us a deep faith that enables us to have joy in you through every circumstance in life. Teach us to rejoice even in the midst of our greatest trials. Help us to be available to others who suffer and are afraid. Help us to share our joy with them. Amen.*

Suggested for Step 2

---

# JULY 7

*"As for the man who is weak in faith, welcome him, but not to dispute over opinions."*

Romans 14:1

As we work on the seventh step, to "humbly ask Christ to transform our shortcomings," we need to think about how we treat others who appear to have less faith than we. We can be critical about others' commitment to the Lord. Maybe we don't think they pray enough because they don't like to pray out loud. Perhaps we criticize how much time they spend in church or how much money they give. Maybe they are not the kind of people to witness publicly about their Lord. We need to work at being more understanding and give the judging back to God.

This verse says we are to welcome the weak in faith, but not for the purpose of arguing with them about opinions. We will not convince others that they are wrong and we are right just by arguing with them. In fact, we might only succeed in turning them off or turning them away.

The most important way for us to show our faith is the way we live. Our actions will speak louder than any words. If we quote scripture but don't live it, we will be poor representatives of the Christian faith. We must not be judgmental of other people, nor can we criticize them behind their backs. That will turn them away and convince them that the Christian life is unloving. Let's journal about how we treat others who have less faith than we do.

PRAYER:

*Lord, when we ask you to heal our shortcomings, we need to pray especially for our tendency to judge others because we think they lack faith. Help us to pray for them instead and be willing to help them in any way we can to grow and mature as Christians. Strengthen us so that we may strengthen others. Amen.*

Suggested for Step 7

---

# JULY 8

*"But I have prayed for you, that your faith fail not; and when you are converted, strengthen your brother."*
Luke 22:32

This verse is from Christ's conversation with Peter in the upper room. Christ had told his disciples that one of them would betray him. Peter was upset and kept assuring his Lord that he would die for him. Christ told Peter that before the cock crowed three times, Peter would deny him three times. Peter was hurt and bewildered. He could not believe that he would ever do that.

Christ assured Peter of his love for him, saying in effect, "Peter, it's okay. Even though you deny me, I still love you and I know that you love me. I forgive you, Peter. Once you recover from the bad experience, you will be an even greater witness for me. Peter, I love you! Peter, I forgive you!"

Christ loves us so much that he forgives us for our wrongdoings if we are willing to admit them. Some times, like Peter, we know or have been warned that we will deny Christ, then go ahead and do it anyway. Still our Lord forgives us, but I believe he expects us to learn from our mistakes and do better the next time. Peter gained from his failure, and we can can from ours, too!

PRAYER:

*Loving, forgiving Lord, thank you for your unconditional love. We thank you that even when we knowingly fail you, you still love us. Help us to forgive ourselves so that we can gain from our failures. Help us to forgive others as you forgive us. Amen.*

Suggested for Steps 8 and 9

# JULY 9

*"So you have sorrow now,
but I will see you again and your hearts will rejoice,
and no one will take your joy from you."*
John 16:22

We need to concentrate on having more joy in our lives, regardless of the circumstances. We need to have a song of joy in our hearts to remember even when times are sad. A song of joy would be one that has positive words, one that gives credit to our Lord and for all things, joyful or sad. This song would be filled with love and life. This song would touch the child within every one of us. The child in us is that part of us with a free spirit to laugh, to giggle, to feel happy and free. Our song of joy would inspire us to keep going, not to give up.

God gives us a joyful song, but we do not always listen. We need to allow the joy of God that is within us to sing through us now. That God-given song can lift any emotional or spiritual burden we have been carrying.

God is the Composer, and he gives us a melody as well as lyrics so that we can express joy. With his help, we can sing our joy song even on the stormiest days. He will show us reasons to be joyful even when it seems there is no joy. But, we have an important part to play: we must be willing instruments, willing singers.

PRAYER:

*Thank you, great Composer, for a song of joy in our lives. Help us to seek that joy and to express it even on the darkest days. Let us be like the robin when spring first comes. It sings boldly because it senses that all its needs have been taken care of. It even sings when the branch beneath it gives way, rejoicing that it has wings. Let us, too, rejoice in you, O great Redeemer. Amen.*

Suggested for Step 6

# JULY 10

*"Jesus replied, 'I am the bread of life;
he who comes to me shall never hunger,
and he who believes in me shall never thirst.'"*
John 6:35

This verse is important to keep before us when we experience powerlessness in our lives. When we have reached the point where we realize we can no longer live with the unmanageability of our lives, we become willing to let go and let God. In order to do that, we have to trust that he will take care of us. We can let go of the steering wheel once we believe that a more capable person will take over.

What more could we ask than the promise in this verse? We shall never hunger. We shall never thirst. Our needs will be supplied by him, and we can feel secure in his love. We need to contemplate what we have to do to claim the promise in this verse.

First this verse says, "he who comes to me," and second it says, "he who believes in me." We must acknowledge our need. We must come to him and believe in him. This requires action *and* commitment. If we do not believe in him, we cannot benefit from his promise.

P R A Y E R:

*Lord, Savior, Bread of Life, thank you for providing all that we could possibly need. Help us to accept your gifts with joyful hearts and to repay you in part by sharing these gifts with others. Remind us that we need neither hunger nor thirst if we are willing to believe. Amen.*

Suggested for Steps 2 and 3

# JULY 11

*"If any man will come after me,*
*let him deny himself and take up his cross daily*
*and follow me."*
Luke 9:23

Jesus does not force anyone to follow him. He invites us to stop struggling with the pain of our powerlessness and follow him. He asks us to turn our wills and lives over to him. He desires that we live our lives more abundantly. With that invitation comes responsibility. First, we must deny ourselves. We must be willing to part with destructive character traits so that we can have a more spiritual life style.

Second, we need to be willing to take up our own crosses and follow him. A cross is not a pretty thing. We can reap the benefit of his cross, but only Christ could bear that cross. We cannot bear another's cross. We must bear our own crosses.

We may prefer to avoid the crosses in our lives. We would rather not lose the important people in our lives. If we avoid the crosses, we not only miss out on a lot of special opportunities to grow, but we live with denial. We need to see our pain as an opportunity to draw close to our Lord. If we are willing to rely on him, our crosses won't become too heavy. Through our experience of carrying our own crosses with his help, we will discover Christian maturity.

PRAYER:
*Lamb of God, thank you for the cross you bore for us. Help us to carry our crosses courageously and turn to you for support. Help us to benefit from our experiences so that we might encourage others as they struggle to bear their crosses. Amen.*
Suggested for Step 3

# JULY 12

*"Let your light so shine before men,
that they may see your good works,
and give glory to your Father who is in heaven."*
Matthew 5:16

Christ desires that we be the light of the world. We can be lights in many ways if we are willing to be used by him. We can shine with his love when we concentrate on the beauty in our lives. Certainly there is darkness, but when we allow him to fill our lives with his love, we become lights to light the way for others.

Many people represent only the sadness of life, the gloom and the darkness. Although many wonderful things may have happened in their lives, they only relate terrible events. They will not share the gains, for they are too busy counting the losses. They do not experience joy, for they feel and speak only sadness.

Others are lights that brighten the lives of everyone around them. Regardless of the trials that come into their lives, they find blessings in them and share those blessings with others. We are here to share the message of Christ's love and forgiveness with all those we meet. We can only do that if we feel good about our Lord, ourselves and others. If we are always gloomy, we drive people away. Have we experienced the light of Christ, or are we still living in darkness?

PRAYER:
*Precious Lord and Divine Light, we thank you that you are the Light of the world. We are grateful that you have asked us to help you share that light with others. Help us to willingly share the light of your love so others will be attracted to the source of that light. Amen.*
Suggested for Step 12

# JULY 13

*"And now, little children, <u>abide in him,</u>*
*that when he shall appear we may have confidence,*
*and not be ashamed before him at his coming."*
I John 2:28

A hymn writer by the name of Henry F. Lyte describes the meaning of this verse in his song, "Abide with Me":

*"Abide with me—fast falls the even tide;*
*The darkness deepens, Lord, with me abide;*
*When other helpers fail and comforts flee,*
*Help of the helpless, oh, abide with me!*

*"I fear no foe, with Thee at hand to bless;*
*Ills have no weight and tears no bitterness;*
*Where is death's sting? where, grave, thy victory?*
*I triumph still if Thou abide with me."*

Like so many others, he learned that the only true source of his comfort and aid was Jesus. His words "when other helpers fail and comforts flee" best describe how we feel when our lives are unmanageable and even other people seem unable to comfort us. Finally, in utter despair, we recognize that we must surrender our powerlessness to the one who can help us through because he loves us.

The writer continues by saying that he fears no foes, that ills have no weight and tears no bitterness. What a marvelous promise of what Christ can do for us when we put our trust in him! Our tears need not be tears of bitterness, and our burdens need not weigh us down. We do not carry our burdens alone, and with his help, even our tears can turn to joy. Even though we may not write famous hymns, we can have a song in our hearts.

P R A Y E R:

*Gracious heavenly Father, thank you that you abide in us and that we need fear nothing. We thank you for your comfort and strength. Help us to trust as little children and to have confidence in your ability to sustain us. Help us to share your love and abiding presence with others. Amen.*

Suggested for Steps 1 and 2

---

# JULY 14

*"He heals the brokenhearted, binding up their wounds."*
Psalm 147:3

Many of us carry a wounded child within us; hurts are so deep and painful that they still profoundly affect us. Some may have backgrounds of incest, violence, alcoholism, abuse and other acts that left us with damaged egos and low self-worth. The scars are deep. The pain is often unbearable. These unhealed scars keep us from wholeness today.

Our Lord has promised to heal the brokenhearted, to bind our wounds. But if we want to be healed, we need to be open to healing. We need to risk dealing with the painful past, to look at it honestly and boldly, to take a fearless moral inventory and to be willing to start changing. We will need to forgive those who committed evil against us in the past. We need to be willing to allow Christ to transform our weaknesses into strengths. We need to work to change our destructive character traits. With our Lord's help, we can restructure our lives so they will be pleasing to him and bring us pride and serenity.

P R A Y E R:
*Divine Healer, thank you that you heal the brokenhearted, that you bind our wounds. We thank you for the courage and patience it takes to look at the painful past and the strength to change so that we may be more whole. In a special way, bless those of us who are tormented by the past and help them turn to you in trust. We love you, Lord. Amen.*

Suggested for Step 4

---

# JULY 15

*"And Jesus said unto them, 'Because of your unbelief; for verily I say unto you, If ye have faith as a grain of mustard seed, you shall say unto this mountain, Remove hence to yonder place; and it shall remove; and nothing shall be impossible to you.'"*
Matthew 17:20

This verse is an important statement of faith. We do not have to have a great faith; it need only be the size of a tiny mustard seed. The act of believing will increase our faith until, with God's help, it will be adequate for any situation in life. We are also promised that if we have this faith, nothing will be impossible!

Do we believe it is possible to have this kind of faith? Is our faith strong enough to believe that we can be healed by God's grace? First, we have to believe that healing is possible. Second, we need to pray for healing, believing that God will answer our prayers. Next, we have to accept the healing that he offers and believe we are healed. We have to *act as if* we have been healed. In order to be healed, we need to believe that he *can* heal us; so, we are back to the essentials of faith.

We need to practice a lot of faith while we are working on the process of change. We need to have faith that with the power of God in us, we *can* change. We need to have faith in ourselves to believe that with

149

God's help, we *can* be healed of destructive character defects. We need to have faith in others and believe that they will be there for us and that they *can* help us in the change process. Perhaps we can journal about our faith today and how we can enhance it.

PRAYER:

*Loving Father, thank you for the privilege of faith and for your patience with us when our faith is not as it should be. Thank you for the promise that with you, nothing is impossible! Help us to believe in you and to trust you for healing. Then give us the courage to share that healing with others so they will want to know you better. Amen.*

Suggested for Step 2

## JULY 16

*"The effective prayer of a righteous man can accomplish much."*
James 5:16

We know that prayer changes things. We have experienced it many times when we have been truly willing to turn to our Lord with our needs. So, let us take time today to pray for the needs of other people.

We need to remember to pray for those who are lonely and whose loneliness becomes almost unbearable in the evening. We will pray that they will have a desire to reach out and touch lives around them and allow themselves to be touched in return. We will want to remember those who are far away from home and long for their families and friends. We need to pray for a special blessing for those who are ill and in pain, those for whom the night seems unending. We will pray that they will have periods of rest from pain so that they can renew body and mind. We will pray for their healing wherever in your will, it is possible and for courage for those when much-desired healing does not occur.

We will remember those who have hurt other people and those who have hurt us. We pray for those who make mistakes and because of them feel like failures. For those who have made mistakes, we will pray that they will forgive themselves for making the mistakes and find the courage to try again. We will ask for God's blessing on those who have been hurt by others. We will ask God to touch them with his healing love and let them know they are loved. We will pray that they will be able to forgive those who hurt them. We will remember as many others as we can in our prayers today.

PRAYER:

*Heavenly Father, thank you for the privilege of prayer and for the many answers to prayer that we receive. Help us when we pray to pray believing that we will receive answers that are best for us and others. Amen.*

Suggested for Step 11

# JULY 17

*"Only let your conversation be
as it becomes the gospel of Christ;
that whether I come and see you, or else be absent,
I may hear of your affairs, that ye stand fast in one spirit,
with one mind striving together for the faith of the gospel."*
Philippians 1:27

Our lives are to be worthy of the gospel of Christ. That is quite a challenge. Paul gave us a good example of how our words and our lives could be worthy even in the most dire of circumstances. While he was at Philippi, Paul had a prison for a pulpit. Even with the threat of death hanging over him, he continued to proclaim his love for Christ and the words of the gospel. He frequently said, "Rejoice." He must have been a powerful witness for his Lord.

We may not be as publicly visible to as many people as Paul was, but people are watching to see what kind of life we live. If we claim to be Christians, people will notice many things about us. Unless we are very careful about our words and actions, we could be poor witnesses for the cause of Christianity.

I found the truth in Philippians 1:27 when I was seriously ill for a long time. Most people respected the strength of my faith during some really trying times. There were days, however, when I admitted to people that I doubted the value of faith and God's love. Unfortunately, some people expected me to be perfect because I was a Christian. When I admitted that I was depressed, some well-meaning but judgmental people tried to shame me into believing that my love of God was inadequate. That didn't help me any! We need to love people where they are, even when they doubt. The best way to proclaim the gospel is with unconditional love.

PRAYER:
*Precious Lord, help us to proclaim your gospel by allowing yor love to shine through us. Keep us from being too critical and expecting perfection of others. Let us affirm one another as Christians and be willing to love those who are not yet Christians. Teach us to love as you love us. Amen.*
Suggested for Steps 10 and 12

# JULY 18

*"To everything there is a season,
and a time to every purpose under the heavens."*
Ecclesiastes 3:1

Healing takes time, but we do not always have the patience to wait. Working on the process of healing is difficult when we are overcome with pain and loss. It is even more difficult to believe that everything will work out fine and that we will experience joy again. Some times all we feel is a sense of loss so profound that we hardly feel anything else.

A year ago in January, my daughter lost her first baby. The little one was my first grandchild, too. We were so excited and filled with the joy of anticipation that we bought all kinds of baby things. We were even thinking how wonderful our Christmases would be with a child around. That baby was so loved and so wanted by everyone, and our hearts were so full of joy!

Unfortunately, that was not to be. The baby died, and a deep sense of grief followed. The death of a child seems to be such a senseless loss and it leaves a cruel emptiness. We wondered if we would ever experience joy again!

But, time does heal and change circumstances. One year later, my daughter had a beautiful, healthy baby girl. She is an absolute joy, and she has touched our lives in a special way. Although one child can never replace another child, a healthy, happy baby to hold and to love certainly helps with the healing process. God is so good!

P R A Y E R:

*Loving God, thank you for being with us when we experience loss. We thank you for the healing you give when we are receptive to it. Be with those who experience the loss of a child and touch them with your heaing comfort. Help them to reach out to others in their sorrow. Amen.*

Suggested for Steps 1 and 3

# JULY 19

### *"God is love."*
I John 4:8

This verse is both simple and profound. It can be used in all 12 steps because it encompasses every aspect of life as do the steps. In Step 1 we are reminded that we need not suffer with powerlessness because God loves us. Step 1 admits, "I can't, but God can." Step 2 recognizes that because of God's love for us, weaknesses can be transformed into strengths. Step 2 admits, "Christ can." Step 3 recognizes that because we love him and he loves us, we can turn our wills and lives over to his care. Step 3 admits, "I will let him."

Steps 4, 5, 6,7 and 10 talk about relationship to self. We know that God loves us unconditionally, but knowing that is not enough for us to achieve wholeness. We must love ourselves if we truly love God and if we are going to be capable of loving others. Love is important. To love God, ourselves and others is what it takes to find wholeness.

Steps 8, 9 and 12 have to do with relationships to others. Love is the necessary ingredient for maintaining a relationship. Some times our love is really tested when we are called to love those who are unlovable. Love is the most important quality we can have as we live our daily lives.

Are we instruments of love, joy and peace in the lives of others?

PRAYER:

*Loving God, thank you for your love, which is so complete and unconditional. Help us to love others as you have loved us. Help us to practice Step 11 by praying for the ability to love you, ourselves and others. Amen.*

Suggested for all 12 Steps

# JULY 20

*"Ho, every one that thirsteth, come to the waters."*
Isaiah 55:1

One song has become very important in my life. It came back to me after more than 30 years, at a time when my life was filled with pain and loss. The chorus goes like this:

*"Come to the water, stand by my side,*
*I know you are thirsty, you won't be denied.*
*I felt every teardrop when in darkness you cried*
*And I strove to remind you for those tears I died."*

The individual verses also had great meaning for me, and finding the song once again at that time of my life was a special gift from God. He spoke to me through this song in a most powerful way. Some times he speaks to me in ways that make it difficult to ignore. I am thankful that he is so persistent.

God invites us to come to him to be soothed, refreshed, cleansed and comforted. He tells us that when we are thirsty, if we will come to him, the Living Water, we will no longer thirst. He will meet us at the point of need even when we do not know what that is. Fortunately, he knows our needs before we ask.

PRAYER:

*Gentle, loving Comforter, thank you for quenching our thirst. We thank you for inviting us to come to the water and stand by your side. You know the reasons for our teardrops, and we are grateful for your love. Help us to be willing to receive the gift of life you offer so we can share it with others. Amen.*

Suggested for Step 1

# JULY 21

*"At their wits' end, then they cry unto the Lord in their trouble,*
*and he brings them out of their distress."*

Psalm 107:27,28

This is marvelous scripture on "letting go and letting God." Many times we have to be at our wits' end before we are willing to cry unto our Lord. We struggle too long to solve our problems our way, and we prolong our pain and anxiety. Some times life deals us cruel and shattering blows that bring our lives to a standstill. At those times we seem unable to keep our hearts full of hope. We experience despair at its greatest depth. We tend to see only gloom.

Fortunately for us, it is often when we seem to be at the lowest point, when we have really hit bottom, that we reach a place where our Lord can touch us and help us. He makes his presence known even though we do not always recognize him. He hears our pain even before we utter a sound. He knows our feelings of anxiety and hopelessness even before we cry out to him. We are reminded of his promise, "Lo, I am with you always." He invites us to trust him with our burdens.

PRAYER:

*Almighty and merciful God, thank you for your presence and grace, which sustain us during difficult times. Give us the courage to face trials in our lives with grace and beauty. Help us to remember that our hope is in you so that we are willing to let go. Let us be mindful of the needs of others who are also struggling through difficult and painful times. Grant that we may share with them your love, your hope, your promise, so that they, too, will believe. Thank you for your love. Amen.*

Suggested for Step 3

---

# JULY 22

*"For I the Lord do not change."*

Malachi 3:6

It is good to know that our Lord does not change. He is reliable. We need that assurance as we struggle with areas of our lives that are unpleasing to him. As we work on our shortcomings, we are comforted by his constancy. Change need not be fearful or harsh if we trust in God. We are aware that because we have the Spirit of God within us, we have the courage to change. We need to internalize his presence and power.

As we discipline ourselves to trust in the Spirit of God, we realize that we can grow through any change with grace and serenity. We need not be rigid in our thinking. We need not be judgmental of our own lives or others', for the Lord helps us to be flexible. We can adapt to any circumstance in our lives if we are willing to allow him to teach us acceptance. Our lives can be harmonious even amid change.

We have a responsibility, first, to be willing to change, and second, to put complete trust in him to help us through the change process. We need to begin today to listen to the voice of the Holy Spirit as it guides us.

PRAYER:

*Constant and loving Companion, we are thankful for the promise that you never change. We thank you that during our own difficult times of change, we have your promise as Lord and Friend that you are ever-present. Grant us the courage to look at our lives with microscopic lens and the determination to change what needs to be changed. Help us to be available to others who struggle to change the dark areas of their lives. Amen.*

Suggested for Steps 7 and 10

---

# JULY 23

*"Jesus said,*
*'They that are whole have no need of a physician, but they that are sick.*
*I came not to call the righteous, but sinners to repentance.'"*
Mark 2:17

I know some Christians who criticize people they feel are sinners, lost and condemned, because those people do not believe exactly as they do. Christ reminds us that he did not come to call the righteous; he came to call sinners to repentance. We are wrong to judge others by our own narrow standards. God is the Judge. His Son's life was shed in atonement for *every* sinner, and we are all sinners.

We cannot know what is in the heart of another person. We may not know the pain that causes him to seem to be more difficult. Instead of judging him, we need to turn to our Lord on his behalf and ask for his healing.

We need to remember that no one is lost to God. Everyone has an opportunity to turn to our Lord in repentance regardless of any wrong that has been done. It is not for us to decide who is good enough to be called a Christian. When we are judgmental, we become the sinners by condemning others. God loves all of us equally because he can see beyond the sin and he has brought hope for all.

PRAYER:

*Lord, forgive us for judging others and help us to spend our time more positively. Help us to serve you by loving others and being willing to see that they, too, have hope for their lives. Teach us patience. Remind us that we are the only ones we can change and help us to commit ourselves to changing our own lives. Allow us to see that the most significant witness is to tell others how Christ has transformed our lives. Amen.*

Suggested for Step 12

# JULY 24

*"I am the Good Shepherd;*
*I know my sheep and my sheep know me—*
*just as the Father knows me and I know the Father,*
*and I lay down my life for my sheep."*
John 10:14

We are blessed to have a loving Shepherd and know that he watches over us day and night. We are not always aware of his presence, and we do not always acknowledge his love. Yet, we know he is there and we need only turn to him. His love keeps us safe and sane in a sometimes hectic world.

It is so easy to get lost in the storms of life and forget whose children we are. We need to seek the forgiveness of our loving Father for those times of self-indulgence. We need to admit that we do not always "hear" the words of the 23rd Psalm and all the hope and promise it gives. We need to commit ourselves to staying close to our Good Shepherd.

We also need to accept that because of the Shepherd who loves us dearly, we can let go and put our lives into God's hands, trusting him to take care of us. We are his sheep, and we are assured that he will lead us in the right direction and take good care of us. He will protect us. He will lead us beside still waters.

P R A Y E R :

*Loving Shepherd, thank you for your guidance and protection. Help us to be willing to let go completely and trust you to lead us in the best way. Bless others who need your guidance. Touch them so they, too, will find the assurance that you are watching over them. Let them feel your presence and protection. Amen.*

Suggested for Steps 2 and 3

# JULY 25

*"And above all these put on love,*
*which binds everything together in perfect harmony."*
Colossians :14

According to this verse, love binds us together in perfect harmony. It is a reminder that the most important way to achieve peace and happiness is to be loving. Love is capable of healing hurt feelings. Love can make the difference between a life of loneliness and isolation and one of caring, committed relationships with others. Love is not only the most important aspect in a relationship, but it is often the most important ingredient in healing a physical or emotional illness. At times, it can even be more effective than a super drug or surgery.

Love is also the most important element in the process of forgiveness. Do we love enough to forgive unconditionally? If we say we have forgiven someone, yet are indifferent toward him or avoid him, we have not truly forgiven him. I am not saying that we need to put ourselves in a position to be "walked on," but we do need to be willing to love the unlovable and forgive even when the person doesn't ask for forgiveness.

Unconditional forgiveness means that we let go of hurt feelings and wounded pride. We allow ourselves to be open to the person who hurt us. We desire the best for that person and keep him in our prayers. Unconditional forgiveness is possible only when we love unconditionally because we have been loved unconditionally by God.

PRAYER:

*Lord, help us to forgive completely. Cleanse our hearts of hurt and anger. Renew our spirits so that we may practice your love, the love that will bind us together. We release our judgment and condemnation of others so that we can receive your love in our hearts. Thank you for teaching us about love by loving us. Amen.*

Suggested for Steps 8, 9 and 12

---

# JULY 26

*"When I am afraid, I will put my trust in you."*
Psalm 56:3

A couple of years ago a man broke into my home in an attempted rape, and I received several injuries. What happened was even more devastating because he had been hired by someone I loved. In fact, I had been warned 12 days earlier that he had hired this man to "rape [me] and break [my] bones." I had 12 long days to think about the violence before it happened.

My first reaction was fear. Most of all, I was afraid of being brutally murdered. My second reaction was anger mixed with genuine concern that this person I loved was about to commit a wrong against me that I could not forgive. Up to then I had always been able to forgive him and accept the fact that he was sick. My third reaction was, "What can I do to prevent the violence?" I knew that the answer was *nothing!* He was in control. He had the connections to have me seriously hurt or killed.

With the realization that I was powerless to do much to prevent it, I turned to God for strength and courage. I put my life in his hands and asked for his protection. Those 12 days were nerve-wracking, but the night the man broke in, carrying a knife, was terrifying. Although I had to have stitches in my face and received multiple injuries, he did not succeed in rape. I believe God helped me live through that experience and gave me serenity for the nightmares that followed.

P R A Y E R:

*Divine Protector, Comforter, thank you for helping us through really difficult times. Thank you for healing us of the bad memories that keep us tied to the past in a frightening, destructive way. Thank you for your presence and protection even though we don't always feel it or trust that you are near. Amen.*

Suggested for Step 10

# JULY 27

*"He shall not be afraid of evil tidings;*
*his heart is fixed, trusting in the Lord."*
Psalm 112:7

Another term for *evil tidings* is the all-too-familiar "bad news." For some of us, bad news comes more often than it does for others. We live in a stressful, often tragic world in which our lives can be adversely affected by total strangers. We are bombarded with news of war, poverty, hostages and a frightening increase in violent crimes. Some form of pain or loss touches every one of us at some time. How we deal with the bad news will depend upon our faith in Christ to sustain us.

When the psalmist wrote this verse, he must have known that the person whose faith rests upon the eternal God is on ground that does not shift or give way. It is wonderful to be able, in the midst of changes that are often drastic, to find something permanent. We can trust him to be with us. We hear the promise, "The eternal God is your refuge, and underneath are his everlasting arms." That is a wonderful comfort during difficult times.

P R A Y E R:

*Great God, Creator, thank you for the assurance that you are our resting place and that because our hearts are fixed on you, we need not fear evil tidings. We thank you, Lord, that you are the same yesterday, today and forever. You are our source of strength and security.*

Suggested for Step 1

# JULY 28

*"Contrawise you ought rather to forgive him, and comfort him,*
*lest perhaps such a one should be swallowed up with overmuch sorrow.*
*Wherefore I beseech you that you would confirm your love toward him."*
II Corinthians 2:7,8

In my 47 years of life, I had never seen this particular verse in the Bible. Then when I was struggling with the verbal threat that someone had been hired (by someone I loved) to rape me, this verse appeared out of nowhere. I wrote a letter of forgiveness to the one who had threatened me. I felt that if I put my forgiveness and love into a letter before anything happened, I would be honor-bound as a Christian to live up to it. That was a difficult letter to write and to mean.

Second Corinthians 2:7,8 reminded me that I must not only forgive, but that I must also comfort. I thought that was asking a bit much of me. I considered it noble just to be willing to work at forgiving him for initiating such a terrible action against me, but God knew I was capable of more.

In my letter I made the commitment to forgive him. I also agreed to work at loving him, and I offered to be there to help and comfort him if the time came when he was willing to get help to change his life style. I also shared my belief in God with him and the peace that relationship gave me in spite of what might happen.

My letter upset him. A letter of reciprocal hatred and threats would have been easier for him to accept. I believe he also realized that he had seriously hurt the one person who had always been there for him no matter what he had done. Six days after I was attacked, he committed suicide. His death was a great loss to me. I loved him unconditionally. He was my only brother and very special to me.

P R A Y E R:

*Loving, forgiving Father, thank you for helping us to forgive people who have hurt us. Remind us that no hurt is unforgivable if we are willing to seek your help. Be with us as we struggle through forgiveness. Help us to go beyond forgiveness and not only comfort them, but confirm our love to them.*

Suggested for Steps 8 and 9

# JULY 29

*"I take pleasure*
*in infirmities, in reproaches, in necessities,*
*in persecutions, in distresses for Christ's sake;*
*for when I am weak, then I am strong."*
II Corinthians 12:10

This verse is crucial to the process of letting go. Three times Paul asked God to remove the "thorn" from his flesh. The apostle must have realized after struggling in prayer that his weakness could indeed be his strength. He must have realized that much could be gained from weakness, mistreatment, distress and difficulties. In fact, often we are better able to reach others as a result of having been in a predicament similar to theirs. When they realize that we understand where they're coming from, it's easier for them to act on suggestions we make to help them help themselves.

Some might consider Paul a masochist, but most see him as a man of faith. His faith had been tried in painful ways, but he came out the victor because he was able to see the possibility of spiritual growth in suffering. To turn that possibility into reality took a tremendous amount of faith and persistence.

We can be like Paul. With God's help, our weaknesses can become our strengths. We can master our circumstances instead of giving in to them. The difference will depend upon whether or not we will be open to Christ's leading. We can rejoice in our infirmities, or we can spend our time complaining to God and have no energy left to help ourselves. We can experience the victory of the cross if we become willing to act on God's will for our lives.

PRAYER:

*Loving Teacher, thank you for all that you teach us through your own example and that of your followers. Help us to be open to the lessons that suffering can teach. Strengthen us in our need and grant us the courage to continue on. Bless others who suffer this day, and may they, too, benefit from Paul's wisdom. Amen.*

Suggested for Step 3

---

# JULY 30

*"And we all . . . are being changed into his likeness."*
II Corinthians 3:18

The process of change will be easier if we trust in this verse. My own life has changed so dramatically that it amazes me when I look back at what it was. My entire outlook is far better than it was because God's love is changing me into his image. I have survived a suicidal depression. I've physically improved, from lying flat in a hospital bed to taking care of myself quite well. I still have the disease and disability, and I still suffer from frequent pain, but acceptance and hope have changed how I look at my situation. The anger and unforgiveness I had toward God, myself and others has been healed, making it possible for me to be healed emotionally and, to a great extent, physically. My life is good now, and I am grateful for the experience of a life-threatening disease. I don't take either my life or my health for granted anymore.

I needed to go through the valley of the shadow of death in order to see the sunlight once again. I needed to think that I had lost everything before I could appreciate the fact that I actually had more than I ever needed. Some people don't have to hit rock bottom before they are willing to they change their lives, but I believe I was one of those who needed to lose everything before I was willing to turn to God.

PRAYER:

*Lord, thank you for healing. Thank you for giving us faith in your power to change our lives. Thank you that it is never too late to start anew. Thank you for faith and for prayer that can take us out of the dark shadows of self-pity and into the light of your truth. Thank you that our attitudes can change so that we believe in miracles even when it seems there is no hope. Amen.*

Suggested for Steps 4, 6, 7 and 10

# JULY 31

*"We are his workmanship created in Christ Jesus for good works."*
Ephesians 2:10

If we accept that we have been created in Christ Jesus for good works, we must concentrate on our strengths. As we take a fearless inventory of our lives, we must accept the good that Christ instills in us. We have something to offer, for we have special gifts to give. Our gifts can make this a better world. We may have been given the gifts of wisdom, understanding or patience to help us relate to people. If we experience limitations, we are reminded that God has given us all the gift of creativity to help us. In addition, we have gifts of gentleness, calmness and stability to offer those who are filled with anxiety and sorrow.

Our gifts can not only help us to become healthier physically, emotionally and spiritually, but they enable us to be a blessing to others who struggle for wholeness. Our responsibility is not only to recognize the gifts that we have, but to be willing to use them and share them with others. We need to spend less time concentrating on our weaknesses and more time building our strengths and gifts.

PRAYER:

*Heavenly Father, thank you for the courage to inventory our lives and for the patience to make necessary changes. As we look at our lives, we take the time to appreciate the gifts you have given us. We make a commitment now to share our gifts, especially the gift of love, with all those we contact today. Thank you that you created us for good and provided us with gifts to share that good. Amen.*

Suggested for Step 4

# AUGUST 1

*"He shall also make restitution*
*[amends] for what he has done amiss . . .*
*and he shall be forgiven."*
Leviticus 5:16

August is usually the month of the summer harvest. What was once a tiny seed in the ground has become a plant bearing a multitude of seeds. What a miracle! What a change has taken place in just a couple of months. God, our Creator, in his love for us has made it possible to harvest the fruits of the earth.

We, too, experience change. When we undergo the transforming love of Jesus, we feel constrained to apologize for the wrongs we have done. We "become willing," as Step 8 states, to make amends to all we have harmed. We are willing to let go of unforgiveness and be reconciled with the important people in our lives.

Unless we "become willing" to make amends, we will have difficulty experiencing forgiveness. God has forgiven all of us through the death of his Son, but it will be difficult for us to know that forgiveness if we haven't been reconciled with the important people in our lives.

Step 8 presupposes that we have had some changes, otherwise we will have difficulty making amends because the risk might be too great.

P R A Y E R:

*O God, you who are changeless, send your Spirit to empower us to change. Heal our hearts so that we "become willing" to make amends. Transform our lives so that we can make your forgiveness ours. Amen.*

Suggested for Step 8                                                      Vernon J. Bittner

---

# AUGUST 2

*"We must undergo many trials*
*if we are to enter into the kingdom of God."*
Acts 14:22

I do not believe that God purposely sends us trials just so that we can become better or stronger Christians. There has been much tragedy in my life and in my family of origin. In fact, by most standards, I would say that the sorrow has been excessive. If I believed that God caused tragedy solely to test or improve me, I would be forced to believe that he is a very unloving, punishing God. I would see him as cruel, and I would probably turn away from him rather than toward him.

As I look at myself and those I love, I can see where we cause a lot of our own problems. I can also see that our world has some very unloving and immature people in it who also cause us pain. Very simply, evil forces that do not originate with God affect our lives every day.

Whenever I have experienced trials, God has been with me to comfort and guide me. He has helped me through the trials and allowed me to see opportunity for growth, wisdom and maturity in everything that happened when I was willing to use the experience of pain to grow.

PRAYER:

*Heavenly Father, thank you that we are able to endure trials because of your love. Thank you for your presence when we feel overwhelmed. Thank you for your strength. Help us to be available to others in their trials. Amen.*

Suggested for Steps 1 and 3

---

# AUGUST 3

*"But the tongue can no man tame;*
*it is an unruly evil, full of deadly poison."*
James 3:8

This is a pretty strong condemnation of what we do with our tongues. The tongue is called "an unruly evil, full of deadly poison." James 3:8 also reminds us that we cannot tame the tongue on our own. We need the help of our Lord to change this destructive character trait. We not only hurt other people by the evil things we say, but if we call ourselves Christians we also put a stain on the image of Christianity.

We must not underestimate the damage we do as Christians. During World War II, the United States had a slogan, "Loose lips sink ships!" to stress the importance of not saying anything that our enemies could use against us. That would not only have cost many lives, but might have caused us to lose the war. We have to be careful what we say as Christians. The tongue is a powerful weapon that can work for good or for evil in our lives and in the lives of others.

As we work on Step 10 and do a daily inventory, we need to review this area of our behavior. Do our words reflect the condition of our inner spirits? Are we pure in heart, or do we reflect anger, pettiness and other negative traits that damage others and our image as Christians? Do we reflect Christ in our daily lives, or do we reflect bitterness? Let us journal about this important area.

PRAYER:

*Lamb of God, we do not always do the good that we want to do; instead, we do the evil we do not want to do. Help us to do the loving thing, to speak lovingly about you and others. Help us to reflect your presence in our lives by the way we treat others. Amen.*

Suggested for Steps 10 and 12

# AUGUST 4

*"Hitherto have you asked nothing in my name;*
*ask, and you shall receive, that your joy may be full."*
John 16:24

Many times we do not receive the special blessings that God intends for us because we do not ask. Perhaps we limit God by what we believe he can or will do for us. We may overlook the reality that God works through other people, and that expands the opportunity to bless us and touch us. Often we do not pray with the expectation that he will grant our desires in whatever ways are best for us.

We need to pray with trust and the assurance that he hears and answers our prayers. We need to pray believing that he knows our needs better than we know them ourselves. We need to pray in anticipation that we will receive answers that have been individualized to meet our specific situations.

We must pray in thanksgiving because we know that God is answering our prayers. We must prayerfully intercede for others because some times *prayer is action*, and we are motivated to reach out to others in their need. We must pray with others because prayer is a powerful vehicle to help us grow together in the Lord.

P R A Y E R:

*Precious Lord, thank you that you hear our prayers and know our needs even before we ask. Thank you for the surprise answers to prayer when we receive unexpected blessings. Keep us mindful of our need to communicate with you through meditation and prayer. Help us to grow spiritually so that we will know your will and have the courage to act on it. Amen.*

Suggested for Step 11

# AUGUST 5

*"To comfort all who mourn,*
*to give them beauty for ashes, the oil of joy for mourning,*
*the garment of praise for the spirit of heaviness."*
Isaiah 61:2,3

All of us take a turn with grief. Grief comes in vary degrees of intensity. Some times we are hit with more than one loss, reducing our ability to cope. Comfort and relief from grief come only when we experience God's love through others' concern. Significantly, we would not experience grief if we had not known love. Thank God for grief in that it assures us that we have been loved. Thank God for love because it heals us when we grieve.

Comforting love enables us to recover from grief and go on with our lives. This love helps us to rise above our sadness into light and joy. This love encourages us to risk loving again even though we may experience loss again. This love can transform the ashes of life into that which makes life beautiful.

Grief can be a growing experience if we allow God to lead us through it. We can gain greater insights and faith in God if we patiently allow the process of grief to run its course. We need to lay our sadness and loss at Jesus' feet. "Cast all your cares upon him, for he cares for you." We need to let go of our grief and allow Jesus' healing power to come into our lives.

P R A Y E R:

*Loving Counselor, Healer of all hurts, thank you that you understand our needs before we ask. Help us to trust you and others to be available to us when we experience grief. Touch us! Heal us! Be with all who mourn and help them to discover beauty amid the ashes of despair. Amen.*

Suggested for Step 1

# AUGUST 6

*"Follow peace with all men, and holiness,*
*without which no man shall see the Lord."*
Hebrews 12:14

To be at peace with everyone is not easy. When we have been hurt by someone, getting beyond that pain to even see the need for peace is difficult. We believe that if we forgive and risk placing our trust in their hands again, they will just hurt us again. That distrust is quite often built on conditioning beginning at infancy. We need to understand that if we are to have serenity, if we are to attain any degree of wholeness, we must actively seek this peace.

In order to experience this peace, we need to forgive those who have hurt us. We may even need to forgive God. Perhaps we have most difficulty forgiving ourselves. This requires a commitment of love, *unconditional* love! Love binds us together in Christian unity. Love directs us to see the good in others and forgive what we dislike about them. Love is the source of genuine peace.

We will be able to forgive others with Christ's help if we are willing to ask for his help. In some cases of deep hurt, I have had to turn to my Lord and say, "I am willing to forgive. Please help me to be able to forgive." He will help and let me feel his presence even while I am talking to him of my need. All things are possible through him, even forgiveness.

*PRAYER:*

*Lamb of God, you paid for our sins. You suffered at the hands of violent, cruel people and still prayed, "Father, forgive them for they know not what they do." Thank you for your example. Thank you that we can acquire peace if we are willing to live and forgive unconditionally. Bless those who struggle with this issue. Amen.*

Suggested for Steps 8 and 9

# AUGUST 7

*"It is vain for you to rise up early,*
*to sit up late, to eat the bread of sorrows:*
*for so he gives his beloved sleep."*

Psalm 127:2

When I was suffering with an active disease, I had great difficulty sleeping, partly because of physical pain and partly because of the side effects from the numerous drugs I was taking to treat the disease. I learned that the more I struggled to sleep, the more anxious I became and less able to relax and sleep. It seemed to be a vicious circle. Many nights I still have difficulty sleeping because of physical pain I can do nothing about.

I am not alone in the struggle to sleep. We all worry, some times over very little, or about things over which we have no control. We fear tomorrow or regret yesterday. We need to learn to give our worries to God so that we don't spend sleepless nights. We need to have a good night's rest in order to be renewed for the new day. If we sleep well, we send messages of relaxation to all parts of the body. Things always look better in the morning if we have had a restful sleep. Let us relax and put our lives into God's loving care, knowing that he is always with us. He can take better care of us than we can ourselves. If we are willing to turn our concerns over to him, we will sleep restfully and awaken refreshed.

*PRAYER:*

*O God, our Father, teach us to be calm and turn our cares over to you. When we struggle with needless anxieties, help us to remember to turn to you for comfort and guidance. We thank you for restful sleep that helps us to awaken refreshed and eager to meet the day's challenges and opportunities. Bless others who struggle to sleep because of disease or other anxieties. Amen.*

Suggested for Steps 1 and 3

# AUGUST 8

*"We give thanks to God always for you all,*
*constantly mentioning you in our prayers."*
I Thessalonians 1:2

These are the words of Paul. His desire was that the Christians at Thessalonica would not only know he was thankful to God for them, but that he prayed for them often. Praying for others is one of the most important things we can do, whether we are praying for family, friends, acquaintances or even enemies. The best way to love God is to love others, and we can show our love by remembering them before our heavenly Father in prayer.

We are often limited in what we can do for other people, especially those we care for deeply. If they are living self-destructive life styles, we cannot change them even though we want to change them. They must want to change themselves, and they must want it more than anything else; otherwise change will not occur. The best we can do for them is to let them know we care and that we pray for them daily.

We also need to ask our Lord for help in dealing with these people. It takes patience to watch someone we love destroy himself and not be able to help him. We need to ask the Lord to support our ministry of love so that we can be effective witnesses. If we lose patience and resort to ridicule or verbal abuse, the people we want to help will not see Christ in us.

P R A Y E R:
*Loving Friend, thank you for hearing our prayers and for the answers you give even when they come late or are unrecognizable. Help us to be willing to pray for others instead of trying to change them our way. Show us how we can best serve you by helping them to help themselves. Amen.*
Suggested for Step 11

# AUGUST 9

*"I will not leave you comfortless;*
*I will come to you."*
John 14:18

I'm sure all of us have felt comfortless at various times . . . when we've felt alone and believed that God deserted us . . . when we couldn't see any sign of his presence or help. Those are the times when we need to try even harder to take the time to talk with God. We need to be willing to cry out as Christ did from the cross, "My God, my God, why have you forsaken me?" We are thinking that then anyway, so we may as well be honest and admit it. If we are willing to risk that, we will be sure to find him. It is all right to be angry with God. He understands.

He has promised that he will never leave us comfortless, that he will come to us. Actually he has never left us although we may feel that he has. The Holy Spirit is always indwelling us; we need only acknowledge his presence. Once we acknowledge his presence, we will begin to feel his comfort and confidence that we are not alone. He is there to help, and we don't have to be alone in our pain. Too often we sit by ourselves in self-pity because we do not turn to him, but he promises, "I will not leave you comfortless; I will come to you."

P R A Y E R:

*Lord, thank you for your willingness to comfort us. Help us to be open to your will for our lives. Teach us to appreciate the influence of the Holy Spirit in our lives and tap into that power, so that you can transform our weaknesses into strengths. Amen.*

Suggested for Step 2

# AUGUST 10

*"There is one lawgiver, who is able to save and to destroy; who art thou that judgest another?"*
James 4:12

I loved my brother very much, but he was not loved by many people. Most saw him as a cruel, violent person. He was dependent on mood-altering drugs and for most of his life, on alcohol. His criminal involvement gave him the option to get even with people in ways most people never would. He hired people to hurt other people or their property when he wanted to get even. He took out a contract on them and made sure he had a foolproof alibi.

I was fortunate because I had known and loved my brother all my life. He had a special, positive influence on me. He saw the good in me. He saw my potential to become even better than he thought I was already. He was proud of me and what I had struggled to become, and he let everyone know how proud he was of his kid sister. Some times he bragged about me until I became embarrassed. He loved me even though at times, drugs and mental illness kept him from showing his love in constructive ways.

Many times he hurt me physically and emotionally, some times seriously. With Christ's help, I was always able to forgive him because I loved him so much. Beneath all the terror I saw a loving person who had given me much of my sense of self-worth. He ended his life three years ago. I'm glad I loved him while he was alive.

PRAYER:
*Lord, help us not to judge others, but to be able to see the good in them. There is good in everyone because you created us all. Help us to love unconditionally and to forgive unconditionally. Amen.*
Suggested for Steps 8, 9 and 12

# AUGUST 11

*"Any kingdom filled with civil war is doomed; so is a home filled with argument and strife."*
Luke 11:17, *The Living Bible*

This paraphrase is a little different from the *King James Version* of the Scriptures, but *The Living Bible* has an important interpretation for us. It speaks not only of the condition of many homes, but also addresses the kingdom within us as individuals. Our lives are unmanageable at times, and they do not reflect Christ's love. Homes break up, children are split between parents and important relationships terminate as people choose sides. All of us at some point are touched by the pain of failure and rejection.

Perhaps some of us do not take Luke 11:17 seriously. If we did, we would accept that the kingdom of God is within us. We are responsible for our actions because we have the potential to know and do God's will. We need to take more responsibility for our choices and to seek wisdom from our Lord so that we can be the very best we can be. Then we will be more open, more forgiving of others, and we will promote peace and harmony.

Still, relationships would end at times. If others refuse to change, there is nothing we can do. We cannot change the important others in our lives; but if we make sure that we are the very best that God intended us to be, at least we will be doing our part to bring about unity among ourselves and others.

PRAYER:
*Precious Lord, we seek your wisdom during difficult times. We are powerless without your help. Teach us to be gentle in our communications. Let us show your love by our actions. Help us to forgive the hurts and let go of those we cannot change by turning them over to you in prayer. Amen.*
Suggested for Steps 1 and 3

# AUGUST 12

*"Zaccheus stood, and said to the Lord,*
*'Behold, Lord, the half of my goods I give to the poor;*
*and if I have taken anything from any man by false accusation,*
*I restore him fourfold.'"*
Luke 19:8

Zaccheus was a despised tax collector. The people who heard Jesus say he was going to Zaccheus' house could not understand why he would go to a sinner's house. But Zaccheus was a repentant sinner. He was willing to make amends to everyone he had harmed. Although he was accustomed to enjoying his riches, he was willing to give half of his goods to the poor.

Zaccheus had discovered a new kind of wealth, the richness of Christ's love and forgiveness. Once he confessed his sins to Christ, he was transformed into a new creature. He was able to break with the past because he had hope of a new life with Christ.

It is important for us to reach the point in our lives that Zaccheus did. We need to acknowledge our wrongs to Christ, to ourselves and to another trusted person so that we can experience the grace of forgiveness and a sense of belonging to Christ. Christ must be more important to us than all of our material possessions. We need to set priorities just as Zaccheus did.

P R A Y E R:

*Lord, help us to be willing to admit our wrongs to you. Help us to be willing to break with the past and start over fresh with you in our hearts. Let us be willing to trust others enough to share all of who we are with them. Amen.*

Suggested for Steps 5, 6 and 7

---

# AUGUST 13

*"For we have not a high priest*
*which cannot be touched with the feeling of our infirmities,*
*but was in all points tempted like as we are, yet without sin."*
Hebrews 4:15

This verse is very important to us, for it reminds us that Christ is not far above us or too distant to feel our suffering. Many people have difficulty relating to priests or pastors because they have put them on a pedestal. They decide that clergy-persons are, for the most part, people who do no wrong. Shame prevents them from talking to the clergy about their own inadequacies because they do not believe they will be understood. That is unfortunate, for much is lost when we expect others to be perfect.

Fortunately, Christ is not like that. He can sympathize with us because he suffered in many of the ways we do. He is willing to share our suffering with us. He is willing to be our partner in sorrow. He understands and assures us that we need not experience it alone. As we see him so willing to share our suffering with us, we are reminded of how important it is for us to share in others' suffering. We need to reach out and touch other people at their points of need. We need to share their difficulties to enable them to experience Christ's love.

P R A Y E R:

*Lord, thank you for sympathizing with us in our weakness. We are grateful that you know how we feel and where we hurt and that you touch us with healing. Help us to trust that promise, for we know that we can turn our lives over to you because you know our needs better than anyone. Help us to be available to those who are suffering and grant that we might be instruments of your love. Amen.*

Suggested for Step 3

---

# AUGUST 14

*"A short-tempered man must bear his own penalty; you can't do much to help him. If you try once, you must try a dozen times!"*
Proverbs 19:19, *The Living Bible*

Anger destroys. Anger can make us physically, emotionally and spiritually ill. Anger can cripple us, taking so much of our energy that we cannot live our lives to the fullest. We cannot be good representatives of Christ's love when we allow anger to control us.

Anger may harm those on whom it is focused, but our anger is far more harmful to us. People can ignore us when we are angry and unloving, but we cannot walk away from ourselves and the devastating effects of anger on our bodies, minds and spirits. Besides, some times the people with whom we are most angry don't even know we are angry, and if they did, they could care less.

Scripture tells us to "let all bitterness, and wrath, and anger . . . be put away from [us]" (Ephesians 4:31). Christ does not take our anger lightly. It is a sin! We need to confess our sinful attitude to our Lord and ask for forgiveness. Once we confess, *we are forgiven*. As we yield to the power of the Holy Spirit, he will give us self-control. We do not need to be controlled by anger. God can free us if we will let him.

Finally, some think that God punishes us. I don't believe this. Holding onto destructive attitudes is our own fault, not God's. We are responsible for letting go of attitudes that destroy. The transforming power of Christ is our enabling power.

P R A Y E R:

*Lord, as we inventory our lives, we find that anger keeps us from being loving people. Forgive us for our anger and help us to let go of it. Help us to be loving examples of your love, joy and peace. Amen.*

Suggested for Steps 4, 8 and 9

# AUGUST 15

*"We know how dearly God loves us,*
*and we feel this warm love everywhere within us*
*because God has given us the Holy Spirit to fill our hearts with his love."*
Romans 5:5, *The Living Bible*

Some people are unsure of the first part of this verse. They don't know how dearly God loves them, and they never feel his warm love within them. Some whose lives are touched with pain have so much noise going on within them that all they can hear or feel is pain.

God's love is available to all who are willing to see it. We need to be quiet so that we can hear God's voice. We need to believe that the power who came in the person of Jesús Christ can transform our weaknesses into strengths.

Once we learn how to tap into the power of the presence of the Holy Spirit, we will become more confident of God's love. This kind of love will transform us into the persons God created us to be. This love will help us to see the good in others, even in those who seem to want the worst for us. When that happens, we will not only talk of his love, we will *be* it.

P R A Y E R:

*Spirit of the loving God, fall fresh on us. Fill us with your presence. Touch us with your love. Quiet our minds and hearts so that we may hear what you have to say to us. Teach us to be gentle in spirit and loving in communication. Thank you for your presence every day. Amen.*

Suggested for Step 2

# AUGUST 16

*"We should not trust in ourselves, but in God."*
II Corinthians 1:9

Second Corinthians 1:9 reminds me where I need to place my trust. As a survivor, I spent most of my life believing I was the only one I could trust. I shunned people who tried to show me that they loved me. My reaction, "Come close, but stay far away," turned most of them away. When I started to feel close to someone, I would find a reason why the person couldn't be trusted and end the relationship.

I hurt people by my actions and reactions, and I hurt myself even more. We cannot love God unless we are willing to love others and ourselves as well. I didn't love myself and most other people, but I convinced myself that I could still love God and all would be well in time.

Yet our Lord said so clearly, "Lovest thou me? Feed my sheep!" We can hardly obey his command when we avoid people. Others like myself who distrust people spend their entire lives avoiding relationships. They con themselves into believing that as long as they profess love for their Lord, they are good Christians and that is all he requires of them. How can we serve the Lord if we don't trust people? Perhaps it would be helpful to journal about why we some times find trusting people difficult.

PRAYER:
*Loving Shepherd, teach us to trust you because you have never failed us and you never will. Give us courage to reach out to others in love and trust. Help us let go of bad memories that keep us from taking risks today. Help us to be trustworthy to others so they, too, can learn to trust you. Amen.*

Suggested for Steps 2 and 12

# AUGUST 17

*"But seek ye first the kingdom of God, and his righteousness; and all these things shall be added unto you"*
Matthew 6:33

When we decide to turn our wills and lives over to the care of Christ, he reminds us that we must "seek first his kingdom and his righteousness." We must be willing to release ourselves to him and accept his will as our own. He is our only true source of being, and we need to acknowledge him.

Trusting God to supply all of our needs may be difficult for us in our materialistic world. We believe we have many more needs than we really do, and we are hesitant to do without some comforts. We need to ask ourselves if "things" keep us from loving God completely and if we are ready to make his kingdom our first priority.

Jesus said, "All these things shall be added unto you." What "things" is he talking about? He means peace of mind, security, freedom from fear, understanding, love, acceptance, forgiveness, strength, comfort, wisdom, as well as all of the other blessings that can be ours if we put God first. He will supply *all* of our needs. His blessings may not always fit our timetables, but we ought to take him at his word that we will experience the abundant life if we obey him.

P R A Y E R :

*Heavenly Father, we praise and thank you that you meet our every need even before we ask for help. Enable us to discipline ourselves to make your will our first priority and to claim your promise of the abundant life. Forgive us for being indifferent to you and for our greedy desire for more "things." Show us the true meaning of life.*

# AUGUST 18

*"Then shall your light break forth like the dawn and your healing shall spring up speedily."*
Isaiah 58:8

Today let us pray for healing in the lives of people who have specific needs, then be willing to help them in whatever ways we can. Pray for:

The hungry.
The blind and deaf.
Those oppressed by any injustice.
Those who are lonely.
Missionaries everywhere.
Unbelievers and those who doubt.
Those grieving over a loss.
Christian counselors.
Newborn babies and for the aging.

Those who are sick and in pain.
Those imprisoned for crimes
   or as prisoners of war.
The depressed or anxious.
Those fighting and dying
   for unpopular causes.
Committed Christians.
Our government and for those
   struggling for freedom.

P R A Y E R :

*Loving Healer, we pray for all these and for those we mention here by name* (individual petitions). *Give us hearts like the heart of Jesus Christ, more willing to minister than to be ministered unto, hearts moved by compassion toward the weak, the hurting, the angry. Help us to be willing to help others however we can. Bless all who are hurting today.*

Suggested for Step 11

# AUGUST 19

*"Jesus told them, 'A prophet is honored everywhere*
*except in his home town and among his relatives and by his own family.'"*
Mark 6:4, *The Living Bible*

Jesus warned his disciples that if they followed him, they might not be loved or accepted by the important people in their lives. He wanted them to realize that even their relatives might turn against them. They had to be aware that even though they were doing something good, they would be criticized. His love had to be enough for them in the event they lost the support of their friends and families.

The same thing can happen to us. The process of change is difficult, but it becomes even more difficult if we do not have the support of those who are important to us. We need to remember that God is with us so that we don't give up on our own commitment to change.

Those who come from dysfunctional families will get little credit for developing more sensitive behavior. In fact, the families quite often feel betrayed and may even turn against them. Then the risk of losing the primary relationship of the family causes complications. If we are risking a break with our families, we need to ask God for courage to continue on.

PRAYER:
*Precious Lord, thank you for the help you give us during change. It is hard to be committed to change when those we love turn against us. Help us to love them and forgive them. Give us courage to go on toward our goal of better lives. Help us to keep our faith and hope alive and active. Amen.*
Suggested for Step 6

# AUGUST 20

*"Choose this day whom you will serve."*
Joshua 24:15

I'm sure that all of us could admit that at one time or another, we chose the wrong service. We chose the world and the things of the world. We chose our own way rather than God's will for us. The result is always the same: confusion, unhappiness and frustration. We usually end up telling God that we're sorry and ask for his forgiveness, and then we are back in harmony with him and with our world.

Our Lord watches over us and protects us even though he allows us to make our own decisions and mistakes. He allows us to use our free will. Our choices are not always the best, but he loves us anyway and patiently stands by. He waits for us to see the error of our ways, then welcomes us back with open arms of love. He loves us unconditionally. He forgives us for ignoring him and doing our own thing. God is love.

175

PRAYER:

*Thank you, heavenly Father, for believing in our better qualities. Thank you for your patience and the lessons you teach us through trial and error. As we mature in the Christian life, we will make wiser decisions sooner, and we thank you for that wisdom. We choose to serve you and all that means. Help us to set our priorities straight. We are grateful for your presence and comfort when we experience powerlessness. Amen.*

Suggested for Steps 1 and 10

# AUGUST 21

*"Above all hold unfailing your love for one another, since love covers a multitude of sins."*

I Peter 4:8

When we love as God has commanded, we are different people. When we love unconditionally, we are willing to forgive unconditionally. Love frees from anger, resentment and pettiness. When love is in our hearts, even though we may remember past hurts, the pain from those memories is gone and we can see Christ's reflection in other people. When we are loved and loving, we are open to see their hurt and willing to try to understand why they act as they do.

Forgiveness is Christlike love, Christlike living. Love allows us to trust again, to risk involvement though we have been hurt before. Love gives us freedom and confidence. When love is truly in our hearts, we feel love, we radiate love; and in doing so, we invite love and trust in return. When we love, we are at peace and feel happy and blessed. Love gives us patience to love others who can often be unlovable.

PRAYER:

*Help us to be loving, Lord, and let that love shine to others. Let our love be sincere and steadfast so others feel they can trust us to love them unconditionally. Grant those who feel unloved and unaccepted your special healing. Amen.*

Suggested for Steps 8 and 9

# AUGUST 22

*"Jesus said unto them, 'Come after me, and I will make you fishers of men.'"*

Mark 1:17

Christ expects us to decide if we will be his followers. His bold statement in Mark 1:17 demanded an immediate response. He said, "Come with me *now*." Some of those he addressed were fishermen. Others were social outcasts. Some had even abused other Christians. Significantly, they were all *broken*. Jesus didn't say, "Think it over, and let me know in three weeks." He said, "Come with me." They followed!

How do we respond to Christ's call to be "fishers of men"? He does not require the same sacrifice that he asked of his disciples. If he did ask us to give up whatever we were doing and follow him, we might have many objections.

Many of us are concerned about our financial security. We would worry about our pension plans or profit sharing. We would wonder if we would have enough money to pay for our cars, boats, houses, even our essentials. How many of us would be willing to disrupt our comfortable lives to follow this Man who had so many public enemies? How many of us would be willing to die as martyrs for his sake? We probably cannot answer that question honestly, but we need to think about it.

PRAYER:

*Lord, we are so comfortable that we lack the motivation to serve you. We even become comfortable with the destructive parts of our lives and are unwilling to let go and let you take over. Help us to be more willing. Take our lives and let them be consecrated, Lord, to you. Amen.*

Suggested for Steps 3 and 12

# AUGUST 23

*"As the Father hath loved me, so have I loved you: continue in my love."*
John 15:9

We are reminded that love comes from God and challenged to live his way of life, his way of love. We are asked to love as we have been loved. If we love as God loves us, we will love with tolerance, we will love unconditionally. We will separate the behavior from the person. We may not like what people do to us, but we can still love them.

Unconditional love is not easy. Loving in this way means that we look beyond a person's behavior to see the person God loves. We let go of our hurt and anger and try to love him as we have been loved. We may need to ask God to help us love someone who is particularly difficult to love. Then we will have to trust that God knows how to handle the relationship.

PRAYER:

*Loving God, thank you for your love. No matter how much we ignore your will for us, you continue to love and forgive us. Help us to love others the way you love us. Amen.*

Suggested for Step 12

# AUGUST 24

*"He is not afraid of bad news;*
*his heart is firm, trusting in the Lord."*
Psalm 112:7

Some times we suffer from heart trouble, but not the physical kind. Our hearts are not always as pure or as filled with Christ's love as they should be. They are not always filled with God's love, and that keeps us from being whole. Materialism can get in our way. Grieving over a loss can hinder our spiritual receptivity so we fail to let God fill our hearts with his love. Hurt and anger toward another person can close the heart's door so we do not hear God urging us to forgive. Unrealistic fears keep us from trusting him completely, and our days are filled with anxiety.

God will help us to become pure in heart. If we seek to be witnesses of his love and forgiveness, we will need to be loving in our relationships. We will need to turn to him for patience to deal with people who are difficult to relate to. Some times we are so preoccupied with the pain in our lives that we forget to turn to God and relinquish our powerlessness to him. We do not need to struggle on our own. God is always with us to guide us. We need to turn to him in every situation.

PRAYER:

*Giver of life, help us to turn to you when we become distracted by our fears and buried in hopelessness. Let us be willing much sooner to turn to you so that our hearts can be filled with your loving counsel. Make our motives pure and help us relate to others lovingly. We pray for those whose lives are so filled with despair that their hearts cannot respond to your love. Thank you for your unconditional love. Amen.*

Suggested for Step 1

---

# AUGUST 25

*"Be perfect, be of good comfort, be of one mind, live in peace;*
*and the God of love and peace shall be with you."*
II Corinthians 13:11

It is not always easy to live in peace and harmony. Even when this is our choice, we are affected by others who choose not to live that way. We cannot do anything about them and the way they choose to live. We need to work at finding peace and harmony ourselves in this world so often filled with hatred and disharmony. Achieving this can be difficult.

First, we need to feel peace and harmony within ourselves. We will never find peace with others if we are filled with inner turmoil. We have to tame the unrest within before we can tame the unrest without. We have to recognize our self-worth, be loving and allow ourselves to be loved.

Second, we must seek and find peace with God. We will not be able to find peace until we have found serenity with God. Jesus said, "You shall love the Lord your God with all your heart, and with all your soul and with all your might. And you shall love your neighbor as yourself." Peace and harmony are only possible when we love ourselves, God and others.

PRAYER:

*God of love and peace, thank you for the harmony we can experience when we love as you love. Help us to be honest with ourselves as we look at our lives in the light of peace and harmony. Let us desire peace for others just as we desire it for ourselves. Amen.*

Suggested for Step 10

---

# AUGUST 26

*"In God I have put my trust:*
*I will not be afraid what man can do unto me."*
Psalm 56:11

This is a penetrating statement of trust. If we trust God, we can release all of our fears and put our lives into his hands. Surrender requires a firm commitment of faith. As we look at our lives, we will see that people, both past and present, have controlled and manipulated us. Unresolved events may cause us to fear being close to people. Hurts of the present can result in this fear, too. Fear of being hurt can even affect our self-worth because isolation results in feelings of inadequacy. God created us for relationships, and without them we feel unloved and worthless.

We need to change that destructive area of our lives. We must turn to our Lord in trust, believing that we need no longer be afraid. We will take responsibility for ourselves and not allow others to abuse us. We will ask our Lord for confidence and begin to live the abundant life that he desires for us. We will be as kind as possible in detaching those who manipulate us, but we will no longer be conned. We have a new chance because Christ will give us the courage. As we change, we will acquire more of the self-esteem we have needed for so long.

PRAYER:

*Thank you, Lord, that we need no longer fear what anyone will do to us. Too often we have been powerless because we gave our power to others who used us. Help us to let go of that destructive part of our lives and trust you. Amen.*

Suggested for Step 3

179

# AUGUST 27

*"I do not do the good I want,*
*but the evil I do not want is what I do."*
Romans 7:19

This could be the theme song of struggling Christians. We often contend with the tendency to be contrary to God's will, whether we are trying to keep our faith, to fight depression, to overcome alcohol and other addictive behaviors or to heal some other self-destructive attitude. The more we struggle to do what is right, the more we do what is wrong. This is frustrating for all of us at times.

When we reach the point of frustration that Paul did in Romans 7:19, we need to turn to our Lord and admit our powerlessness. We must humbly ask him to transform our shortcomings into strengths. We need to be patient and keep on working on our lives. We need to pray for guidance and then be open to God's will.

Perhaps we are struggling too much on our own. We cannot succeed alone. We need the help of our Lord, and we may need the help of a professional counselor as well. We also need to find a trusted friend so that we will have someone in whom we can confidently confide. Above all, we need to "be still and know that [God is] God." Let him be God!

P R A Y E R:
*Lord, we confess that we are sinful, that we have gone against your will in thought, word and deed. We ask your help with our frustration. Help us to seek to do good and be committed to that which is good. Remind us that we can't do it alone. Trying to control our lives by will power alone only leads to more frustration, Lord. Help others who struggle in this area, that they, too, may realize that it is through your power that our lives are transformed. Amen.*

Suggested for Step 7

---

# AUGUST 28

*"Father, if you are willing, remove this cup from me;*
*nevertheless, not my will, but thine be done."*
Luke 22:42

Our Lord experienced anxiety just as we do. He experienced the same kind of humanness that we do. We want to avoid painful, difficult experiences. We want more joy and fewer trials. We want the easy road. We want our lives to be made up of weddings, baptisms, birthday parties and other happy times, not sickness and funerals.

Yet, we know that the times we have gained the most have been when we seemed to be losing the most. God blessed us by turning our trials into opportunities to learn more of his love. He stayed with us and gave us strength and courage. We thank him for that!

We need to look at the example Christ gave us in Luke 22:42 and be willing to admit when we feel powerless. It is okay to cry out, "Remove this cup from me!" when we experience fear and pain. We can let God know how we feel. He will give us strength to get through any trial.

P R A Y E R:

*Father, we want to give you the same commitment you gave so willingly and sacrificially, "Nevertheless, not my will, but thine be done." Whatever your will is for us, we leave our lives in your hands. We are willing, Lord. Help us to do your will. We especially thank you for your example to us. Amen.*

Suggested for Step 3

---

# AUGUST 29

*"Be still, and know that I am God;*
*I will be exalted among the heathen,*
*I will be exalted in the earth."*
Psalm 46:10

How rewarding it is when we are finally willing to be still and listen to God! When we do, tension and stress disappear, anxieties and fears become unimportant. God is always in our midst, a mighty, healing, renewing power. As we become aware of his life-giving presence, we feel his healing.

Whatever our need, he is with us. Whether we desire reassurance, comfort, strength or healing, he is present. He soothes, strengthens and heals in a loving, beautiful and perfect way. He helps us to make the best decisions for our lives, ones in accord with his will.

We will not be able to hear God speaking to us unless we believe Psalm 46:10 and take time to be still. We need to quiet the noise outside of ourselves as well as within us. If we are feeling anger, grief, anxiety or any other of life's draining forces, we will have a difficult time hearing God speak to us of his will for our lives.

P R A Y E R:

*Thank you, Father, for your presence in our lives and for supplying all of our needs so abundantly. We thank you for quiet times alone with you. We pray for others who are struggling. Teach us the importance of taking time to be still and experience your presence. Help us to trust you enough to let go of anything that blocks us from you.*

Suggested for Steps 2 and 11

# AUGUST 30

*"'No weapon that is formed against you shall prosper,*
*and every tongue that shall rise against you in judgment*
*you shall condemn. This is the heritage of the servants of the Lord,*
*and their righteousness is of me,' says the Lord."*
Isaiah 54:17

Isaiah 54:17 is very important to me. This verse came to me one day when I really needed it and has been a strength to me every since. No matter if the weapon is physical or emotional illness, alcoholism, family abuse, doubt or fear, this verse says, *"no weapon formed against you shall prosper."* Those are strong words and a firm promise that our Lord backs up with action.

But to claim the promise of this verse, we must believe it. No matter what evil comes into our lives, it will not and cannot win if Christ is with us. We need to trust him completely in order to know how to deal with the particular weapon used against us. Claiming this promise works, but we need to remember that God writes the timetable.

Seven years ago I was mugged and as a result, suffered many losses and presently have a disease. Only within the past year have I been able to see the blessings in the tragedy. I can now say, "Thank God for the day I was mugged." Through that trial I experienced a miracle.

P R A Y E R:

*Lord, Defender, thank you for your promise in Isaiah 54:17. We do not need to fear anything, for if you are in our lives, we will be all right. Help us to share the joy of this knowledge with others. Amen.*

Suggested for Step 6

---

# AUGUST 31

*"Be imitators of God, as beloved children."*
Ephesians 5:1

Paul challenges us to imitate God. In order to do that, we must become aware of what God is like. He is wise, so we must learn wisdom. He is a God of discernment, so we need to practice making good choices. He is a God of love, so we, too, must be loving. He is also a God of forgiveness, so we must forgive as he has forgiven us.

Fortunately, we can learn and practice these qualities once we realize that his Spirit dwells within us and guides us. God's qualities are available to us if we are open to receive them.

We do not need to spend our lives in frustration and confusion. The Spirit of God will lead and inspire us. Our Lord promises, "I am the way, the truth and the life" (John 14:6). We will experience new creative potential when we allow the Spirit of God to direct us. We will discover the wisdom to make right choices when we seek him. He will continually supply us with the qualities we need if we only ask him for them.

P R A Y E R:

*Spirit of God, fall fresh on us. Fill us with your presence today and help us to trust you completely. Help to mirror your love to a world that desperately needs love.*

# SEPTEMBER 1

*"Be gentle and ready to forgive; never hold grudges.*
*Remember, the Lord forgave you so you must forgive others."*
Colossians 3:13

September is the beginning of the school year and our getting back into the swing of the fall routine. It reminds us that the life that came alive in the spring and summer is rapidly coming to an end.

Step 9 speaks of the importance of being reconciled with the important people in our lives. It is important that we do this now and not wait until it is too late. This step indicates that there are times when it is necessary to make direct amends to the people from whom we are alienated. Some times in order for us to restore a significant relationship, we have to make a direct apology or tell someone personally that we forgive him.

This is difficult to do some times. We have to swallow our false pride. We need to risk not only possible rejection, but also the reality that the person with whom we want reconciliation may not desire the same. This will be painful for us, but at least we will have the satisfaction of having done all that we can do to bridge the gap between us. What is important is that we will have done our part, been "gentle" with that person and "ready to forgive."

P R A Y E R:

*Thank you, Lord, for giving us the courage to reach out and make direct amends in a gentle and forgiving way. May we always be willing to do our part in the process of reconciliation so that we will continue to experience your forgiveness and the serenity that comes from doing our part. Amen.*

Suggested for Step 9                                    Vernon J. Bittner

# SEPTEMBER 2

*"The fruit of the Spirit is love, joy, peace,*
*longsuffering, gentleness, goodness, faith."*
Galatians 5:22

We would like to have our lives produce
all of these fruits, but we are well aware that we do not always have these
characteristics. Some times we withhold our love because we are hurt or
afraid. Some times we are sad instead of joyful because we think too much
about losses and not enough about gains. Some times we miss out on
peace by not fully trusting Christ to help us with a difficulty. We are not always patient, and we know the only way we can become patient is to rely
on him for wisdom.

Certainly we are not as faithful to him, to our beliefs or to others as
we need to be. When we are frustrated, we are not as gentle as we should
be and not always in control of ourselves. All of these things require a special commitment and awareness of what is going on within us as well as
others. We do not always possess that commitment or awareness, and we
know that the only way we can is to rely on Christ.

PRAYER:

*Thank you, Lord, for these beautiful gifts and your part in helping us*
*live them. We know that as these things become more obvious in our lives,*
*others will notice and respond accordingly. We ask your blessing for others*
*who struggle. Help them to succeed in their endeavors to love more com-*
*pletely, to love unconditionally. Then the fruits of the Spirit will become a*
*regular part of all our lives and how wonderful we will feel! Amen.*
Suggested for Step 4

# SEPTEMBER 3

*"There are friends who pretend to be friends,*
*but there is a friend who sticks closer than a brother."*
Proverbs 18:24

We need to thank our Lord for
friendship, that friends can love one another enough to promote their
mutual good and happiness. A friend makes joyful events more joyful. A
friend lifts the burden of sorrow by sharing a shoulder with a friend in
need. Friends remind us of the love sent by the Father to make our lives
fuller. We are especially thankful for those friends who share our love for
him and are willing to witness to others. We are thankful for prayer friends,
comrades who will pray with and for us, as we do for them.

We also need to consider what kind of friend we are to others. Do we
support them in every way we can? When someone criticizes a friend or

spreads gossip, we must do more than just stand idly by. We need to confront the critic about his unloving behavior. Above all, we must not contribute to his destructive action by participating in the gossip. We need to look for the best in people, and if we can't say something good about someone, it is best for us not to say anything at all. We need to be friends as Christ is a Friend to us and love unconditionally.

PRAYER:

*We remember all of our friends today, Lord, and ask you to bless them in whatever way they need to be blessed. Reassure those who are afraid. Comfort and strengthen those who are in pain. Help those who are angry or dealing with a lack of forgiveness. Grant our friends your peace, serenity and love. We pray for those who have no friends, who isolate themselves from the comfort of others. Give them courage to risk becoming involved with others even though they are afraid of being hurt again. Heal them. Amen.*

Suggested for Step 12

# SEPTEMBER 4

*"He who is in you is greater than he who is in the world."*
I John 4:4

Some times the world's pull on us is stronger than our desire to do God's will. We can sympathize with Paul when he says, "For I do not do the good I want, but the evil I do not want is what I do" (Romans 7:19). The desire to go against God's Word and will is strong.

Yet, that is no excuse to disobey him. The Spirit of Christ within us sets us free from the belief that we are victims of our circumstances; that misconception does not need to limit our lives. Past mistakes or present feelings of inadequacy needn't bind us because Christ is within us to guide and help us.

When the Spirit of Christ is within us, he gives us faith and courage, the love and wisdom, the understanding and patience, for every situation in life. We can be filled with peace and joy, the abundant life he wants for us, if we will allow his Spirit to dwell within us.

PRAYER:

*Holy Spirit, fill us with your presence and guide us every day. Help us not to accept a mundane existence as our burden, but that we may expect and receive serenity and joy. Thank you for your mighty power that sustains us and grants us your commendation, "Well done, thou good and faithful servant." Amen.*

Suggested for Steps 2 and 3

# SEPTEMBER 5

*"Why are you cast down, O my soul? and why are you disquieted in me?*
*hope in God: for I shall yet praise him for the help of his countenance."*
Psalm 42:5

The psalmist's question and answer are simple enough, but life is not that simple. When we become committed Christians, we start off with such zeal that we cannot imagine ever feeling cast down or without hope. Then when grief and hurt do overwhelm us, we become even more discouraged because we feel cast down.

As we mature spiritually, we discover that just the fact that we are Christians is no guarantee that we will not suffer. Certainly Christ was more committed to his Father than any of us will ever be, yet he suffered. We will not always walk in green pastures beside still waters. The sun will not shine every day of our lives. We will experience desert and wilderness, too. We will feel cast down and disquieted. We will feel hopeless.

As we experience powerlessness, we need to be gentle with ourselves. We can grow in these difficult times, our weaknesses can transform into strengths. It is okay to lose our faith and feel depressed; those experiences will help us turn to God. It is okay to fail; we can learn from our failures. Christ does not expect perfection from us. We want perfection, but we will never achieve it on this earth. Christ asks only that we do our best and turn to him for guidance.

P R A Y E R :

*Lord, help us to turn to you when we feel powerless. We thank you for your presence during difficult times even though we don't always acknowledge you. Help us to be available to others who struggle with unmanageable lives. Teach us patience and help us be willing to share our faith with them. Amen.*

Suggested for Step 3

# SEPTEMBER 6

*"You are my friends, if you do what I command you."*
John 15:14

Do we usually think of Christ as our Friend, or do we only look at him in sterner ways? Do we see him as a task master, a disciplinarian, a punisher, a judge, a master who rules with an iron hand? When we do, we fail to see the tenderness, the gentleness, the caring, the fairness of our Lord. A friend is someone who wants the best for us. A friend is someone who loves us even when we do things that are unlovable. A friend forgives us when we make a mistake and invites us with open arms to continue to be friends. A friend shares both joy and sorrow. A friend accepts us with both our strengths and our weaknesses. Jesus will be that kind of friend to us if we let him.

Let us take the time to do some journaling today about how we see this important person in our lives, the Lord Jesus. If we fear him, why do we fear him? If we are reluctant to trust him, why do we feel that way? If he does not fill the role of a friend, why do we think so?

PRAYER:

*Loving Friend, help us this day to make a commitment of friendship to you. Help us trust you with all that is important to us. When you are truly our Friend, perhaps we can be friends to others as you would have us be. We must love you and ourselves before we are fully able to love others. Amen.*

Suggested for Step 11

# SEPTEMBER 7

*"A little child shall lead them."*
Isaiah 11:6

My first child was born one week before Christmas. Her birth brought about a very important commitment in my life. She was a beautiful baby with a lot of dark, naturally curly hair. When the nurse laid her in my arms for the first time, I was proud like never before. I also felt an overwhelming sense of responsibility for this tiny life that had been placed in my care. Suddenly, motherhood required a great deal more than I thought I had to give.

I wanted my child to feel loved and to hear "I love you" every day of her life. I wanted her to know her feelings and be able to share them without being ashamed. I wanted her to know that it is okay to cry, to feel down, to be imperfect. I wanted her to have a strong faith that would not only help her to be a better person, but would give her strength during difficult times.

I wanted her to know she was loved unconditionally and always would be. I wanted her to be loving and accepting of other people and to practice unconditional love herself. I wanted to teach her to love herself and appreciate her gifts. I wanted all that, but I didn't know how to achieve it. I had help from a lot of people and a lot of help from God.

PRAYER:

*Heavenly Father, thank you for the blessing of children. They are a big responsibility, Lord, and we need your guidance. Help us to seek your wisdom and that of others so that we do our very best for our children. We must teach them love and forgiveness by our own example, not just with words. Help us to love them unconditionally as you love us. Amen.*

Suggested for Steps 10 and 12

# SEPTEMBER 8

*"Jesus said unto him,*
*'Thomas, because you have seen me, you have believed:*
*blessed are they that have not seen and yet have believed.'"*
John 20:29

Christ could say much the same thing to many of us, I'm sure. Several times I have doubted not only his love, but his very existence. On one such occasion I was depressed because I was physically, emotionally and spiritually exhausted. I went for a walk on a rainy, overcast day. I'd taken my camera with me because I wanted to take a picture of how I felt: gloomy, depressed, dark and hopeless.

As I walked along, I talked to God about my anger. "Lord, if you are anywhere around, give me a sign. You will have to hit me over the head with a very large board. I can't see you! I can't hear you! I can't feel you! I wonder if you even exist and if you do, whether you even care."

Then I photographed the dark sky and forgot the whole incident. As usual, I didn't really expect an answer to prayer. Two weeks later when I picked up the print and negative at the camera shop, I was stunned. Shining through the dark clouds was a very bright light in the perfect shape of a cross with a brilliant circle of light in the center. All around the cross were the same dark clouds I remembered. The photo gave me goose bumps, and it has had a similar effect on others who've seen it.

I had demanded proof, and God gave it to me. I had not expected any answer, but he gave me a sign I could not deny. That God would actually answer my frustrated demand both frightened me and made me feel ashamed. At that moment, I knew the meaning of the words, "Blessed are they that have not seen and yet have believed." I have seen a miracle, and I will never forget it. When you pray, ask believing, and you will receive God's answer.

P R A Y E R:

*Thank you, Lord, for answers to prayer. Forgive us for not believing that you will answer any prayer in the way best for us. Amen.*

Suggested for Steps 2 and 11

---

# SEPTEMBER 9

*"God meant it for good."*
Genesis 50:20

God wants us to see and enjoy the beauty of the world he created. As we do Step 10 and continue to take a daily inventory, we need to look at our attitude about life. Do we look for good in everything? In every situation, no matter how tragic, there is something good. Many times we cannot see the good because of loss or hurt, but the good is there. God will help us see it if our hearts and minds are open.

Do we see only what is wrong, or do we see right and good as well? Do we focus only on injustice, or do we trust God to be just and believe that justice will somehow prevail? Do we look only at our limitations, or do we appreciate the abilities God has given us? Do we experience only want and need, or do we see the abundance God provides for us? Do we experience only loss and pain, or can we see the glory in our cross?

God's will for us is always good although we doubt that many times. He does not want us to hurt one another. He wants us to have life, joy, peace and the abundant life. We need to believe that and look for the good in every day.

P R A Y E R:

*Heavenly Father, thank you for surrounding us with so many good things and so many good people. Help us to find peace and beauty in this world, not war and ugliness. Help us to look for the best in one another rather than for what might be wrong. Help us to share the good we see with others so they will see it too. Thank you that every trial carries the seed of your love and the possibility of more of your abundant life. Amen.*

Suggested for Step 10

---

# SEPTEMBER 10

*"There is no fear in love;*
*but perfect love casts out fear; because fear hath torment."*
I John 4:18

We fear many things. Some times we fear things that are real to us, but other times we fear things that are intangible. Some times our fear is realistic, and some times it is irrational. We waste far too much time being afraid. The things we spend so much times worrying about usually never come to pass, so we worry for nothing. We need to let go of our fears and remember that where there is faith, fear cannot exist. We need to turn to our Lord when we are afraid and rely on him to get us through the times of fear and doubt.

We can conquer our fears through faith in God. He will give us the confidence we need no matter how real our fears may be. We have many promises of his ability to still our fears. Jesus said to his disciples, "Fear not, little flock." He says to us, "Fear not. I am always with you. Fear not, for I am the resurrection and the life." Fear is worst when we are alone, so we need to remember that he is with us even then.

PRAYER:

*Thank you, loving Friend, for faith, hope and courage to deal with fear. Thank you for your presence that assures us we are never alone. Help us to remember that because of your love, we need not fear anything. Thank you for that assurance. We pray for others who are afraid. Touch them and let them know your healing power. Give them the assurance that your "perfect love casts out fear" and help them to experience that love by believing and turning their cares over to you. Amen.*

Suggested for Step 4

---

# SEPTEMBER 11

*"You will walk on your way securely, and your foot will not stumble."*
Proverbs 3:23

Have you ever climbed down a very rough, steep hillside, with unsure footing and the fear you might slip and slide down into a ravine? For those of us who have disabilities of the hips or legs, the climb is even more frightening because we are afraid of more injury. We are tense until we are again sure of our footing.

We are just as tense and unsteady when we doubt God's faithfulness to his word. Some times when we are angry, grieving or hurting in some other way, our faith seems unsure and the path is rocky. We may even feel that we are falling headlong down the hill, with nothing and no one to stop us.

But, our Lord promises us that we will walk securely and not stumble. We are assured of that when we are willing to walk hand-in-hand with our Lord. He levels the path and directs our feet. We need not fear. He will not let us slip if we trust him completely. Even if we are trying to find our own way and slip, he will redirect us and put us back on safe ground.

PRAYER:

*Thank you, Lord, for your promise in Proverbs 3:23 and for all the times you walk with us and keep us safe. Be with others on their journeys and keep them safe, too. You are our Guide, and we thank you for that. Amen.*

Suggested for Steps 1 and 6

# SEPTEMBER 12

*"O Lord, thou hast searched me and known me."*
Psalm 139:1

We know that our Lord sees our every deed, knows our every thought. He sees us when we are loving and when we are not. He sees us when we live the kind of lives he would have us live as his disciples. He sees us when we dishonor the Christianity we profess. He knows our needs before we ask. He knows our fear even before we tremble. As he searches us, he sees in us the ideal person he wants us to become. He wants the very best for us, but he leaves final choices to us. If we could not make choices, we would be slaves, know it and resent him for it.

Many times when God searches us, he is happy because we are living lives of love. Other times when he searches us, he becomes sad because we have turned away from him and his will. We do not always live Christlike lives.

PRAYER:

*Help us, precious Lord, to be worthy of your love and your trust. Fill us with your Spirit so we may become the way you want us to be. Help us to witness to others of your love so they, too, may have hope. Let us love as we are loved. Thank you for your constant vigil. Amen.*

Suggested for Step 7

---

# SEPTEMBER 13

*"We glory in tribulations also, knowing that tribulation works patience; and patience, experience; and experience, hope."*
Romans 5:3,4

We usually struggle to avoid tribulations because we dislike pain and anxiety. We become all upset and try to figure out how we can go over, around or under circumstances that cause suffering. Of course we are never successful, and sooner or later we realize that we must experience tribulation and turn to God for help.

It takes us a while to relinquish control of our lives to Christ. Yet, we know that "tribulation works patience; and patience, experience; and experience, hope." We always grow from our trials after we accept them and let the Lord guide us. We usually learn from tribulations if we are patient and trust God, in his love, to change them into blessings.

PRAYER:

*Thank you, Father, for tribulations. Thank you for the patience we learn from them, for the hope you give us. Help us to be worthy of your love by enduring trials in a way that will speak to others of our faith in you. Let others*

see the beauty and assurance of your love in our witness. Bless others during their times of touble. Give them the courage to endure. Give them your peace and assurance, and help us to help them whenever we can. Amen.*
Suggested for Step 1

---

# SEPTEMBER 14

*"By this all men shall know that you are my disciples,
if you have love one for another."*
John 13:35

Do we really want to be Christ's disciples? If we do, we must love one another. By his own example, our Lord showed us how to love, and the Apostle Paul carefully describes the characteristics of a loving attitude in I Corinthians 13:4-7.

Paul says, "Love is patient and kind; love is not jealous or boastful; it is not arrogant or rude. Love does not insist on its own way; it is not irritable or resentful; it does not rejoice at wrong, but rejoices in the right. Love bears all things, believes all things, hopes all things, endures all things."

The verse challenges us to love more perfectly. We are called upon to live I Corinthians 13 lives, not just to memorize the scripture. There is no acceptable excuse for side-stepping this verse. If we are to be true followers of our Lord, we must receive God's word and put it into action. He will help us to love as we are loved.

PRAYER:
*Loving Lord, we want to be your disciples. Help us to be loving. Teach us to be sensitive to others' needs. We are grateful for your love, and we want to exemplify it to others. Amen.*
Suggested for Steps 8 and 9

---

# SEPTEMBER 15

*"You are all the children of God by faith in Christ Jesus."*
Galatians 3:26

A child's faith is a marvelous phenomenon. Children believe simply and trustingly. They do not intellectualize and look for reasons not to believe. They do not ask for proof that someone exists or even that they are loved by special people. They believe in Santa Claus, the tooth fairy and the Easter bunny even when older children laugh at them because common sense says they're wrong.

The young ones continue to love and hope, even for parents or caregivers who abuse them. When they have been hurt, children forgive and believe that bad will become better. They have a free spirit that most of us lost long ago. Children have much to teach us about faith and love.

Could we practice childlike faith? We need to believe in the existence and love of our Lord without demanding proof. We need to believe that he loved us enough to die for us, without demanding that we see his nail-scarred hands. We need to accept his presence in our lives even though we do not have visible proof.

PRAYER:

*O great Creator, Redeemer, help us to have simple, childlike faith so that we will believe in you without demanding proof. Help us to be open to your presence and the work of the Holy Spirit on the basis of your word alone. Amen.*

Suggested for Step 1

---

# SEPTEMBER 16

*"Set the believers an example*
*in speech and conduct, in love, in faith, in purity."*
I Timothy 4:12

We do not always set good examples. Our speech does not always reflect godly discipline. Our conduct is some times less than desirable. Although love is important to us, we isolate ourselves or allow pettiness to get in the way of our relationships. When we appear anxious or afraid, we share a testimony of fear, not faith. We need to concentrate more on discipleship qualities of purity in motive, faith and witness.

When I first met my mother-in-law, she told me the rule of the house: "If you can't say anything good about a person, don't say anything at all." That is a good rule, and she lived it. She found good to say about everyone. She never spoke of Christian principles, only of genuine human compassion. Yet, I saw more Christian values in her than I have found in some Christians. I have always appreciated her example of love in action.

PRAYER:

*Forgive us, Lord, for times when we set poor examples. Help us to be conscious of how we represent you and your kingdom. Help us to practice Christlike living. Help us not to be slovenly in speech or conduct. Help us to love unconditionally, to exemplify pure and honest faith. Let us show others that your love makes life worth living. Amen.*

Suggested for Step 12

# SEPTEMBER 17

*"God is not the author of confusion, but of peace."*
I Corinthians 14:33

Noise and confusion in our lives make clear thinking hard. Confusion can even bombard our Christian beliefs. We say to ourselves, "If God really loves me, if God can really perform miracles, if God knows my needs before I ask, if he hears my prayers before I pray, why am I confused? Why do I hurt? Why all the losses? Why do I feel so lonely? Why do I have so many doubts? Why can't I feel God's presence? Does he really care about me?"

The questions are needless, and we may never know the answers. We have to have faith. We have to believe even in difficult times. God is always with us, even when we do not "feel" his presence. God is with us *wherever we are*—even when we do not want him there!

PRAYER:

*Thank you that you are the God of peace, not a god of confusion. Lord, help us to realize that we cause much of our confusion and dismay. Help us to spend our time seeking and experiencing your peace instead of concentrating on the confusion within and around us. Bless others who feel confused, frustrated or fearful. Amen.*

Suggested for Step 3

# SEPTEMBER 18

*"My presence shall go with you, and I will give you rest."*
Exodus 33:14

Exodus 33:14 has always comforted me. No matter what happens, God will come with me. Regardless of the storms raging in my life, he will never leave me. The only time I get into real trouble is when I leave my Lord and strike out on my own against his will.

This verse was especially important to me when I was in the hospital. Twice I nearly died. It was important to me as I struggled to accept and learn to live with an incurable disease and ugly disability. It was important to me when I learned that my husband of 27 years could not accept my physical condition and divorced me. It was important when two people whom I loved dearly committed suicide while I was struggling with failing health and a failing marriage.

We need to plant this verse very deeply in our hearts and minds. We need to get it into our unconscious thinking so that when we face trials, that assurance will always be there. We need not be afraid. We need to remember that no matter what happens, God will come with us.

PRAYER:
*Precious Lord, we are grateful that you will come with us wherever we go. Help us to be aware of your presence and willing to experience it with a positive, thankful attitude. Thank you that we need never be alone. Help us to be available to one another, too. Amen.*
Suggested for Step 2

# SEPTEMBER 19

*"Every branch in me that bears not fruit he takes away;*
*and every branch that brings forth fruit, he purges*
*so that it may bring forth more fruit."*
John 15:2

Our Lord reminds us in John 15:2 that if we are to be productive for him, we will be challenged. The lessons we learn, whether in sorrow or joy, prepare us to serve him effectively. When we humbly ask Christ to transform our shortcomings, we acknowledge our willingness to cooperate with him. That is the only way for change to take place.

Some people believe God singles them out for punishment. They continually ask, "Why me?" They do not see *opportunities* in suffering.

Our greatest growth comes when we are willing to put ourselves in God's hands and trust him completely. That is not always easy; it takes a firm commitment of faith. We need to be willing to go through the desert, without expecting lush, green valleys. Most of all, we need to truly want our lives transformed.

PRAYER:
*Lord, thank you for staying with us as we struggle to change. Thank you for your patience and for the courage you give us to keep on. Help us to be available to others who struggle to change. Amen.*
Suggested for Step 7

# SEPTEMBER 20

*"Because you are sons and daughters,*
*God has sent forth the Spirit of his Son into your hearts,*
*crying, 'Abba, Father.'"*
Galatians 4:6

Those who were abused as children can hardly think of themselves as sons and daughters of a loving Father, much less call him the endearing term of "Abba" (Daddy). The anger, hurt and

195

even hatred of the past complicate their free expression of love to God their Father.

How can we tell them about the loving Father and his gift of the Holy Spirit? First we need to help them through the process of forgiveness. We need to help them understand that although they were not loved by their earthly fathers, their heavenly Father loves them very much. We need to encourage them to trust him even though others in their lives have not been trustworthy. Most of all, we need to be gentle with them until they can work through the process of learning a new life style.

P R A Y E R :

*Precious Lord, help us tell others about our Father's love. Help them to work through the process of forgiveness so they can let go of the hurt. Help them to risk loving you as you love them. Amen.*

Suggested for Step 2

---

# SEPTEMBER 21

*"In returning and rest you shall be saved,*
*in quietness and trust shall be your strength."*

Isaiah 30:15

For workaholics, this advice is nearly impossible to follow. I was a workaholic until a serious illness put a stop to it. I remember believing that the only way I could be worthwhile was to work hard. Between my home, husband, children, numerous foster children, job, hobbies and volunteer work, I seldom had time to think, let alone pray and meditate. Rest was an excuse for lazy people. There would always be time for God, maybe tomorrow!

To be forced by illness to rest and take time for God was not the most admirable way for me to approach him. Unfortunately, for me that was the way it had to be. How much better it would be if we set time aside without being forced to do it. Hopefully, God will have first place in our lives from now on.

We continually need to assess our priorities. Are we spending all of our time striving for personal and professional success and excluding God to achieve our goals? That may work for a while, but my personal experience proved to me that there is no true or lasting success without God. Unless we commit ourselves to spend time with him every day, we cannot know his will for our lives, nor can we excuse our way of living.

P R A Y E R :

*Lord, help us to commit ourselves to daily prayer and meditation with you. Fill us with your presence. Guide us with your wisdom. Touch us with your healing. Slow us down so that we rest in you. Help us to evaluate our lives every day. Thank you for your love. Amen.*

Suggested for Step 10

# SEPTEMBER 22

*"My mouth shall speak wisdom*
*and the meditation of my heart shall be understanding."*
Psalm 49:3

As we work on Step 7 and humbly ask Christ to transform our shortcomings, we need to think seriously about this verse. Do our mouths speak wisdom? Is the meditation of our hearts understanding? Some of us struggle to overcome being judgmental, gossipy, even hateful. We criticize other people unmercifully, even in the name of Christian concern. We decide that what other people do is morally and spiritually wrong, and we want to make sure that everyone else knows how terrible they are! We crucify them without a hearing.

When we meditate, does our meditation reflect understanding, or are we condemning others before our Lord? To speak and to pray out of sincere love and Christian concern is noble, but to speak and meditate in order to condemn is as wrong as anything a friend might do that we condemn. When and where have we been judgmental? Journaling about this might help us to change attitudes that prevent us from being understanding and compassionate.

P R A Y E R :

*Precious Father, help us to speak wisely and to meditate on you so that we nurture understanding hearts. Forgive us for judging others. Transform our lives so that we, too, can possess the gifts of patience and acceptance. Amen.*

Suggested for Step 7

# SEPTEMBER 23

*"Henceforth I call you not servants;*
*for the servant knows not what his Lord does;*
*but I have called you friends;*
*for all things I have heard of my Father*
*I have made known unto you."*
John 15:15

There is no question that Christ represented an authority figure when he ministered on earth. He was called Master, Lord, Messiah, Counselor, Leader, King and many more titles of authority. When he spoke, he spoke authoritatively from knowledge and experience. He told the people how they could serve him and his Father.

Christ assures us in John 15:15 that he does not just consider us servants. He calls us friends! This is an important concept because it has implications for our ministry to others. Christ not only ministered, but allowed others to minister to him. He asked John the Baptist to baptize him.

He allowed a woman to wash his feet. He served others and was served by them. Serving with an attitude of love and allowing another to reciprocate is the foundation of friendship. Christ wants us to know that he desires close, intimate friendship with us. He is not solely our Master.

Are we entirely ready to have Christ come into our lives on an intimate basis? Can we trust him as our Friend, or do we see him only as judgmental and punitive? Does our fear/mistrust of authority figures, reminiscent of the past, stand in the way of our friendship with Christ? Perhaps we could benefit from journaling about this.

PRAYER:

*Loving Friend, help us to get to know you as our Friend. Help us to love you as a friend and accept your love as a friend who truly cares about us. Grant that we may share with others the friendship we have with you. Amen.*

Suggested for Steps 2 and 12

---

# SEPTEMBER 24

*"I am the good shepherd; I know my own and my own know me,*
*as the Father knows me and I know the Father;*
*and I lay down my life for the sheep."*
John 10:14,15

We are blessed to have a loving Shepherd and to know that he watches over us day and night. We are not always aware of his presence, nor do we always acknowledge his love. Yet, we know he is there and we need only turn to him. His love keeps us safe and sane in a hectic world.

We can get lost in the storms of life and forget whose children we are. We need to ask forgiveness for those times of self-indulgence. We do not always "hear" the words of the 23rd Psalm and all the hope and promise it gives. We need to stay close to our Good Shepherd and believe that he can lead us better than we can lead ourselves. He will not forsake us even if we wander off by ourselves and do our own thing. He lovingly waits for us to return and is happy to have us back. He knows all of his sheep and loves each one in a special way.

PRAYER:

*Precious Lord, thank you for all of the promises in John 10:14,15. Thank you for being our Good Shepherd and for leading us in the way we should go. Forgive us when we stray and ignore your will. Bless others in this area of their lives. Help them to know and trust you as their Shepherd. Touch us with your healing and then send us out to serve others. Amen.*

Suggested for Steps 1, 2 and 3

# SEPTEMBER 25

*Will all your worries add a single moment to your life?"*
Matthew 6:27, *The Living Bible*

We worry about so many things, and yet this verse tells us that our worry cannot add "a single moment" to the length of our lives. You may be interested in a simple exercise. Try listing the things that you worry about and then date the list. From time to time, read through your list and see how many of the things you worried about actually happened. Ask yourself if you could have done anything to prevent them from taking place. Did worry help?

After a few years, go back to the list again. You will discover that your list represents a lot of time and energy wasted on worry. Then ask yourself which items on the list should have been turned over to your Lord for care and keeping. You will be surprised to learn that the Lord was willing to help you with many of the things you worried about. You did not need to fret about them at all.

Worry keeps us from having a more spiritual life style. We need to commit ourselves to turning our needless worries over to the care of Christ. He can share our burdens and make all things new.

PRAYER:

*Gracious Father, thank you for your presence in our lives. We thank you for lifting our worries and for the serenity we receive when we trust you. Grant that we may discipline ourselves so that we will turn to you when we feel worry coming on. We want to be a comfort to others.*

Suggested for Step 6

# SEPTEMBER 26

*"Let your speech be always with grace, seasoned with salt, that you may know how you ought to answer everyone."*
Colossians 4:6

Colossians 4:6 represents quite a challenge, one which we probably do not live up to very well. As witnessing Christians, we need to be graceful in speech. What we say should reflect our Christian values. Our words should show that we are slow to anger, ready to forgive and interested in the persons to whom we speak. We should not take our Lord's name in vain, nor should we resort to name-calling others.

If we are truly loving Christians, we should be sensitive to the needs, hurts and disappointments of other people. Even when we find it necessary to be firm with someone, we should be careful what we say so that no unkind word slips from our lips and no harsh tone is heard in our voices. When we are hurt or angry, we find it hard to be careful, but then we need to remember that the Holy Spirit dwells within us. If we allow him to have control, his love will show in what we say and how we say it. Our speech can be either a blessing or an offense. The choice is up to us.

P R A Y E R:

*We pray, precious Lord, that your Spirit will be within us so that our speech will reflect your love. Help us to show your gentleness and caring by what we say and how we say it. Amen.*

Suggested for Step 12

# SEPTEMBER 27

*"We also thank God for this,*
*that when you received the word of God which you heard from us,*
*you accepted it not as the word of men but as what it really is,*
*the word of God, which is at work in you believers."*

I Thessalonians 2:13

Are we grateful for the privilege of being believers? God's word teaches us to believe in God, in ourselves and in others. We believe that God is a God of love, that he is good and that he has a special place for every one of us in his creation. We believe that we are one with God and he with us. We believe that God works in many wonderful and mysterious ways in and through our hearts and minds to makes our lives the best they can be *with his help.* We believe that God turns every circumstance of our lives into our benefit, whether through pain or joy, loss or gain, if only we trust him.

We believe that he is always with us, even when we feel lost and alone. We can believe that anything is possible in his will and know that the limitations most difficult to overcome are the ones we've set ourselves. We know we work at our best and live up to our highest potential when we make God our partner. We are a team, and we work much more creatively together than apart.

Finally, we believe in God, and he helps us to believe in ourselves and others. In order to benefit from his counsel, we need to put our wills and lives into his hands.

P R A Y E R:

*Dear God, we love you and thank you for the privileges of belief and serving you. We pray that others will come to believe in you as the one who can make the difference in their lives, transforming them from simply being to fully living. Amen.*

Suggested for Step 2

# SEPTEMBER 28

*"If you love those who love you,*
*what reward have you?"*
Matthew 5:46

When it comes to loving others, we need our Lord's help. We need a large dose of compassion and the ability to let go of our ill feelings. When someone we care for hurts us, we have a hard time being around him and treating him in a loving way. The deeper the hurt and the more important the person is to us, the more difficult it is to reconcile the relationship. We become afraid to trust again for fear of another hurt or rejection.

Our Lord was often disappointed with the behavior of his friends while he was here on earth. He must have been deeply hurt on many occasions, and then he was crucified. Christ taught us the ultimate example of forgiveness when he died on our behalf. He reminds us that we must not only love those who are easy to love. Life would be simple for us if we were only required to love the lovable, but he asks us to do more than that. Our Lord wants us to love as he loves us. We need to ask him to help us love and forgive as we should.

PRAYER:

*Help us, precious Lord, to love as you love and to forgive as you forgive. Mark Twain said, "Forgiveness is the fragrance the violet shed on the heel that has crushed it." Regardless of how much someone may have hurt us, holding a grudge is neither Christlike love nor living. Remind us of that when we need your help. Amen.*

Suggested for Steps 8 and 9

---

# SEPTEMBER 29

*"God shall supply all your needs*
*according to his riches in glory by Christ Jesus."*
Philippians 4:19

It is good to know that God will supply all our needs. We only have to ask. Every morning we should ask him to help us be patient with the things we do and the people to whom we relate. When a task becomes difficult, we need to ask him for perseverance. When a problem is hard to solve, we need to ask him for the wisdom to find the solution. We need his help to keep trying even when failure seems most probable.

We need to ask God to help us to love difficult people in difficult situations. We need to take time to listen to anyone who needs to talk through their fears or concerns. We need to love as Christ loves us. We need to be willing to work in his will just as he worked in his Father's will when he was ministering in Judea and Galilee and Samaria. He always projected love and compassion.

We have to discipline ourselves to be about our Father's work. We are so easily sidetracked, yet God graciously, lovingly cares for us in spite of our erratic responses to his direction.

P R A Y E R:

*God of love, thank you for supplying all of our needs even before we ask you for help. Thank you for guiding us. Please forgive us when we resist your will.*

*Bless those who seek you but have difficulty in committing their lives to you wholly. Teach them that they can trust you to supply their needs, and help us to be available to them and encourage them. Amen.*

Suggested for Step 6

# SEPTEMBER 30

*"You have taken away my gods which I have made . . .*
*and what have I more?"*

Judges 18:24

In this Bible story, Micah is devastated by the robbery of his household idols. He cries, "What is left for me?" The figurines must have meant more to him than anything else, but they could not answer him, return to him or help him. A more familiar Old Testament figure, Job too experienced losses, among them his health. He cried, "God, why didn't you let me die?" God talked to Job, showed him his power, restored Job's health and blessed him far beyond anything he had known.

Unfortunately, like Micah we some times worship our own handpicked gods instead of the one true God who created all that is good in life. We need to spend time with him. Our false gods are no use to us in the midst of suffering, when we need a friend, when we face eternity . . . so why are they important to us? Journaling could be a way to discover why we look to false gods for what we *want* instead of going to God for what we *need*.

P R A Y E R:

*Loving God, you are the same yesterday, today and forever. You promise us everlasting life. Help us to be willing to give up our false gods and worship you in spirit and truth. Touch our hearts with the desire to see ourselves as you see us so that we will turn to you to find your abundant life. Amen.*

Suggested for Step 4

# OCTOBER 1

*"I don't mean to say I am perfect.*
*I haven't learned all I should even yet,*
*but I keep working toward that day when I will finally be*
*all that Christ saved me for and wants me to be."*
Philippians 3:12

October is one of the most beautiful months of the year in Minnesota. Looking over the countryside, one can see a multiplicity of colors. We are reminded of how wonderful a Creator our God is.

Step 10 calls us to take a daily inventory of our lives. This process helps us to focus on our positive and negative behavior during the day. To walk through our day with the Lord reminds us of how great he is to guide us, forgive us and also empower us to change and grow toward being what "Christ saved [us] for and wants [us] to be." Working the tenth step calls to mind how gracious and wonderful God is.

Having the Lord walk through our day with us can be a joyful experience even though we fail at times. Continuing to experience forgiveness, being thankful for how he has guided us in positive behavior, and knowing the excitement of being transformed by his power is experiencing the abundant life.

Traveling with our Lord daily, evaluating our lives with him on a daily basis, is also necessary for spiritual growth. Unless we look at our behavior every day, we will not only slip back into old destructive behavior, but we will not be "working toward that day when [we] will finally be all that Christ saved [us] for and wants [us] to be."

Becoming what Christ saved us for requires that we work at it "one day at a time."

PRAYER:

*Lord, thank you for keeping us through the day and preparing us for a new day . . . of your guidance, forgiveness and transforming power. Amen.*

Suggested for Step 10 Vernon J. Bittner

# OCTOBER 2

*"He has shown you, O man,*
*what is good; and what does the Lord require of you,*
*but to do justly, and to love mercy, and to walk humbly with your God?"*
Micah 6:8

God has shown us what is good. We must follow his example and be willing to love God and our neighbors as ourselves. Part of doing good is to see the good in others. This old world needs love! Love is the only language that everyone can understand. It is better to be deceived occasionally than to think that everyone is bad and untrustworthy. We miss out on a lot of loving when we are too afraid to risk trusting others.

We are also asked to be fair in our relationships. We're not to steal, lie, gossip, judge or do anything else that would be harmful to others. To wrong only dishonors ourselves and shows disrespect for others. We are also to love mercy and practice forgiveness. We need to be benevolent toward those who hurt us—not an easy thing to do, but possible with God's help. Because we have been forgiven, we can forgive the unlovable.

Finally, we are "to walk humbly with [our] God." We need to acknowledge him as the sovereign power in our lives. We need to look to Jesus as the author and finisher of our faith. We need to be in daily communion with him and glorify him by living as he has taught us to live. We all have difficulties of one kind or another; but when we try to do justly, when we love mercy and when we walk humbly with God, we will not fall beneath our cares even though we falter from time to time.

PRAYER:

*Gracious heavenly Father, draw us nearer to you in fellowship so that we may walk humbly with you. Give us faith and strength to live so that we will be pleasing to you and helpful to others. Amen.*

Suggested for Step 12

# OCTOBER 3

*"Who can understand his errors?*
*Cleanse me from my secret faults."*

Psalm 19:12

As we attempt to do Step 5 honestly, we need to think about the implications of Psalm 19:12. To do the "searching and fearless moral inventory" required in Step 4, then admit our wrongs in Step 5, we need to be willing to understand ourselves, to discern our strengths and our weaknesses. We are not always willing to look at our errors with honest eyes. We do not always see our faults because as the psalmist says, they are secrets even to us.

Even when we can see our faults clearly, we cannot easily change them. We are so comfortable with our old ways that the inconvenience and unfamiliarity of new ways make us reluctant to make necessary changes. We have to discipline ourselves just to examine our faults.

We need to be willing to look at our lives honestly and then admit our mistakes. We may need to ask our friends for help in learning about ourselves. If we encourage their honesty and support in this learning process, we may get valuable insights into how others perceive us. When we allow them to share their feelings with us, we need to be open enough to hear what they have to say and honestly take it for its worth.

PRAYER:

*Precious Lord, thank you for encouraging us to try to understand our errors. Thank you for loving us in spite of our faults. Give us courage to look at the changes we need to make in our lives. Cleanse us from our secret faults. Amen.*

Suggested for Step 5

---

# OCTOBER 4

*"Be still and know that I am God."*
Psalm 46:10

I am sorry to say I usually have to be forced to practice Psalm 46:10. I don't always turn to God when I should, and because of that I suffer more and longer than I should. When I become really careless, God sends me a vivid reminder of his love.

On one such occasion, my mother had nearly died from a combination of drugs. Her heart had stopped, and she had to be flown by helicopter to a hospital. When she got there, she was unconscious. The medical staff worked for hours to save her. I was worrying.

In the middle of the night I awakened with these lyrics running through my mind: "Turn your eyes upon Jesus, look full in his wonderful face; and the things of earth will grow strangely dim in the light of his glory and grace." I went back to sleep, only to wake up once more with the same lyrics impressed on my mind. I leafed through an old hymnal and found these verses to the song:

*"O soul, are you weary and troubled?*
*No light in the darkness you see.*
*There's light for a look at the Savior*
*And life more abundant and free.*

*"His word shall not fail you—he promised,*
*Believe him and all will be well;*
*Then go to a world that is dying,*
*His perfect salvation to tell."*

God reached out to me when I was too tired and torn apart to pray. He did it gently, yet in a way that would capture my attention. When sorrow overwhelms us, we need to admit our powerlessness and turn to our Comforter. He knows our needs. We need to do whatever we can and then put ourselves and others in God's hands.

PRAYER:

*Heavenly Father, thank you for helping us when we are too distraught to pray. Thank you for drawing our attention to you so that we will receive your comfort and courage. Amen.*

Suggested for Step 3

# OCTOBER 5

*"Whoever does not bear his cross and come after me
cannot be my disciple."*
Luke 14:27

Jesus does not mince words when he tells us what he expects of us. He does not say, "Come along for the good times! Come and share the joy of the Christian life with me. Come and share the resurrection. I have prepared a beautiful, happy place for you." All of this can be ours, but he asks far more of us. He does not merely ask us to weep at the foot of *his* cross. He says, "Take up *your* cross and follow me."

He warns us that we will be like lambs for slaughter. He tells us that not everyone will welcome us when we witness for him. He expects us to love him more than anyone else, more than anything else. He must be first.

Discipleship is costly. We need to ask ourselves if we are Christians because of what we can get out of him or because of our love for him. We must not deceive ourselves. He doesn't want lukewarm followers. He asks no more of us than he is willing to do for us. Are we willing to follow him if it means we must bear our own crosses? We need to be willing to follow him wherever he leads us.

P R A Y E R:

*Lamb of God, who takes away the sin of the world, have mercy on us. Help us to be worthy of your sacrifice. Give us courage to take up our crosses willingly and follow you. Teach us patience and perseverance for difficult days. Help us to be willing to follow you not only because we can't find the abundant life any other way, but because we love you. Amen.*

Suggested for Step 1

---

# OCTOBER 6

*"The Lord said to her,
'Martha, dear friend, you are so upset over all these details!
There is really only one thing worth being concerned about.
Mary has discovered it.'"*
Luke 10:41,42, *The Living Bible*

We need to set priorities. Jesus cared enough about Martha to show her that there was some thing more important than preparing the meal and serving her guests. She was fussing over the details of having Christ in her home, while Mary was more concerned about keeping Jesus in her heart by listening to his words. Martha was not wrong to be concerned about practical matters, but she had her priorities mixed up. We need to learn the lesson that she learned.

We need to do whatever is necessary for daily living; that's only practical. But if time is short, we may have to *make time* for prayer and meditation with our Lord. If we are to know his will for us, we need to spend time with him. We have to be quiet long enough to hear him speak to us. We need to be expectant and receptive.

PRAYER:

*Loving Lord, thank you for listening to us during those quiet moments when we are alone with you. Help us to discipline ourselves to set aside time for prayer and meditation every day. Help us to be willing to accept your will for us so that we will serve you effectively. Help us to share our prayer life with others by praying with and for them. Thank you, too, for answering our prayers. Amen.*

Suggested for Step 11

# OCTOBER 7

*"Love your enemies, do good to those who hate you,*
*bless those who curse you, pray for those who abuse you.*
*To him who strikes you on the cheek, offer the other also;*
*and from him who takes away your cloak do not*
*withhold your coat as well."*

Luke 6:27,28

These can be hard words to hear, but we have to reach the point in our Christian lives when we treat our enemies with a loving attitude. We have to turn to God often for strength and determination because loving our enemies means to do good for them, to pray for their happiness, to ask God to bless them.

Some people in my life have hurt me in many ways, some resulting in serious physical injuries, even a permanent disability. I could not forgive on my own. I had to pray, "Lord, if you want me to more than forgive, to actually convey my love to them, you will have to help me." He gave me the gift of understanding, which enabled me to forgive them for even the greatest of hurts. Understanding is often the key to loving the unlovely and forgiving those who do not seek forgiveness.

PRAYER:

*Gracious Lord, thank you that even when we are buried in hurt, you penetrate our pain and help us to forgive. Thank you for teaching us how to forgive and love the unlovable. You forgave Peter when he denied you, Thomas when he doubted you, the criminal who was crucified beside you. You taught us that our hurt is not as important as our love and forgiveness. Help us to love as you love, unconditionally. Amen.*

Suggested for Steps 8 and 9

# OCTOBER 8

*"For freedom Christ has set us free;*
*stand fast therefore, and do not submit again to a yoke of slavery."*
Galatians 5:1

This day is devoted to adult children of alcoholics and to others who grew up in homes with little if any nurturing. Far too often those from this kind of environment live unrewarding lives as adults. They have low self-worth and believe they don't deserve to be loved. They feel guilty for anger toward their parents and blame themselves for negative circumstances.

Those who are tied to the pain of the past cannot experience serenity and joy unless they look at what happened, understand how it affected them, let go of the past and begin to rebuild their lives. They need to forgive those who did not love them, realize that their self-worth is not dependent on those inadequate relationships and believe they deserve to be loved because they have become children of the loving heavenly Father.

Unless we break the ties that bind us to the past, we will continue to falter under the yoke of slavery. Low self-worth is one of the most painful forms of slavery. We need to believe that our Lord can set us free! We need to trust him to heal our brokenness so that we don't put ourselves into other relationships that would enslave us.

PRAYER:

*Loving Father, thank you for the freedom you offer us. Give us courage to look at our lives and to work on the painful areas that need healing. Heal our brokenness and then send us out as wounded healers. Help us to risk being vulnerable to others, but not being enslaved by others. Amen.*

Suggested for Steps 7 and 10

# OCTOBER 9

*"Blessed are all who hear the word of God*
*and put it into practice."*
Luke 11:28

Hearing the word of God is one thing, but putting it into practice is quite another. We often hear only what we want to hear and shut out the rest. We interpret scripture for our own convenience because we don't like what it says and would rather not make the required commitments.

As we work on Step 11, we need to study our prayer life. Do we take enough time to meditate on God's word? Do we spend enough time reflecting on what the scriptures mean for our lives? Do we journal about the meaning of each of the 12 Steps and their impact on us?

Do we intercede in prayer for others? Do we pray with the important people in our lives? Do we offer to share the 12 Steps with other people to help them structure their spiritual growth? Are we willing to risk allowing others to come close to us so they, too, can experience the fellowship of the Christian community? If the answer is "no" to any of these questions, hopefully we will feel motivated to make appropriate changes so that we become wholly committed to our Lord and to others.

PRAYER:

*Loving and patient Lord, thank you for your promise in Luke 11:28. Help us to be more open to sharing our life stories so that our witness for Christ will be more authentic and credible to others. Bless those who struggle toward wholeness and help them to risk sharing themselves so they can put God's word into practice and grow spiritually. Amen.*

Suggested for Step 11

# OCTOBER 10

*"We walk by faith and not by sight."*
II Corinthians 5:7

The Apostle Paul's statement in II Corinthians 5:7 reflects the mature Christian life. Unfortunately, we do not always live up to that standard even though we know that the degree to which we experience the abundant life in Christ is closely linked to the degree of our faith in him. It would be nice if we did not need proofs of his love and presence, especially when trials beset us and losses pile up. We are quick to believe he doesn't care about us then.

Faith provides many of the qualities necessary to a meaningful Christian life. Faith helps us overcome limitations, whether they are self-imposed or imposed by others. Faith reminds us that God is greater than our circumstances, greater than any condition or difficulty that life has to offer.

Faith helps us to fear less, risk more and expect the freedom God's love gives us. Faith reminds us that as long as God is our source of strength, as long as he is beside us and within us, we can accomplish his will for our lives. We will experience trials, but we will overcome them. Faith helps us to be steady, calm and trusting during turbulent storms. When we trust God, we live joyfully and victoriously.

PRAYER:

*Almighty God, author and finisher of our faith, thank you for challenging us to walk by faith and not by sight. Thank you for the gifts that you give us when we trust you. Give us courage to share our faith with others so they will learn to know and trust you, too. Amen.*

Suggested for Step 2

# OCTOBER 11

*"A merry heart makes a cheerful countenance;*
*but by sorrow of the heart the spirit is broken."*
Proverbs 15:13

When I was young, I read that frowning exercises more muscles than smiling, so I thought lazy people would naturally prefer to smile. Since then I have learned far more important reasons to have a merry heart and cheerful countenance. As I struggled through a serious disease that nearly ended my life, I learned the healing power of laughter. I learned that it is healthy to feel good about myself and my life.

In fact, a serious and long-lasting depression was draining me of life faster than the physical disease raging through my body. With God's help and good Christian counseling, I started my life over again. I found reasons to love myself, reasons to laugh. Laughter has been healing. In fact, I have taken up clowning not only to assist my process of healing, but because I know how important laughter is in the healing of others.

Research has proved that laughter has a therapeutic, healing effect on body, mind and spirit, whereas depression has a deteriorating, occasionally fatal effect. I know that is true because within the past six years, I lost two important people to suicide. Because their lives lacked meaning, they were dead long before they killed themselves. We need merry hearts for very important reasons. As we inventory our lives, we need to ask, "Do I have a merry heart? If not, why not? What am I willing to do about it?"

P R A Y E R:
*Lord, we know we should feel happy because we have your love and that should be enough. We allow life's circumstances to depress us. Help us to turn to you. Give us merry hearts and cheerful countenances, and grant us opportunities to share our joy with others. Amen.*
Suggested for Steps 4 and 12

---

# OCTOBER 12

*"Be of good courage and he will strengthen your heart,*
*all you that hope in the Lord."*
Psalm 31:24

Courage is so necessary to win through in life, yet so difficult to attain. Perhaps that is because we must find it within ourselves. Courage is a spiritual quality that requires the practice of three disciplines. The first of these is *self-control*. We must practice self-control before we can find courage. If we discipline ourselves to achieve a life style that we value, the accomplishment will develop our self-respect and give us resolution to take on new challenges.

The second discipline is *understanding*. We must have a genuine comprehension of life's values, purpose and meaning. We need to be willing to understand people and their values if we are bravely going to stand up for them. We need to understand, or at least be willing to learn, God's will for our lives; and in order to do that, we must realize the significance of turning our wills and lives over to Christ.

The third discipline is *trust*. Many factors cannot be changed, many things are beyond our power to do anything about. We must be willing to trust God to see us through difficult times. When we are anxious or afraid, we must trust him and believe he is with us.

So the three ingredients of courage are *self-control, understanding* and *trust.* With God's help, we can attain them and discover that the gift of courage is ours.

P R A Y E R:

*Loving God, grant us courage to live boldly. Strengthen, guide and keep us in your care. Give us ability to share with others whose burdens may be greater than our own. Help us to find our strength in you and to practice the disciplines of self-control, understanding and trust so that we will experience your gift of courage. Amen.*

Suggested for Steps 1 and 3

---

# OCTOBER 13

*"The righteous will answer him,
'Lord, when did we see thee hungry and feed thee,
or thirsty and give thee drink?'"*
Matthew 25:37

"When the Son of man shall come in his glory, and all the holy angels with him, then shall he sit upon the throne of his glory: and before him shall be gathered all nations . . ." (Matthew 25:31,32). At that point in future history, Christ, the Son of God and Son of man, will reward all the believers of the ages for their faithfulness to give him something to eat when he was hungry, something to drink when he was thirsty, a place to rest when he was a stranger, clothing when he had none; for visiting him when he was sick, for ministering to him when he was in prison.

God's children will ask him, "Lord, when did we see thee hungry and feed thee, or thirsty and give thee drink?" Though we may consider ourselves insightful and think we see clearly, the Bible says that on that day we will still ask him *how* we could have served him because if we did see

211

him, we didn't recognize him. We too often wear blinders so that we cannot see our Lord's reflection in people's eyes. We do not see how much they need his love, nor do we realize that he considers our helping them to be helping him. We make our own judgments about others, too often deciding whether or not they are worthy to be helped or if we are willing to make the effort to help. We forget that they, too, belong to him. They, too, are redeemable regardless of the way we see them.

Matthew 25:37 speaks not only to physical needs, but to spiritual and emotional needs as well. Someone may be in a prison of depression, needing our assistance to find the key to the lock. Someone may be hungry for the spiritual fruits of love, joy and peace. We can nurture that one in Christlike living. Whatever the hunger or thirst—physical, spiritual or emotional—we can encourage the one in need to look beyond himself. Christ will be there to help him, and we are to be there, too. Christ wants us to look for him in other people, to build on their strengths and help them to become healed.

PRAYER:

*Loving Shepherd, we do not always seek out people with whom to share your love and forgiveness. Help us to be more willing to be available to people wherever they are at in their lives. Forgive us for our indifference toward one another and you! Amen.*

Suggested for Step 12

# OCTOBER 14

*"You have not received the spirit of bondage again to fear; but you have received the spirit of adoption, whereby we cry, Abba Father."*

Romans 8:15

Abba Father is a loving term that carries with it gentleness, caring and trust. It reminds us that we have a loving Father in heaven who will hold us securely in his arms. When we are afraid or discouraged, we need to imagine climbing up onto his lap and crying, "Abba, Abba Father!" He will comfort us. All we need to do is ask and he will respond in love. To know God's comfort and love is to experience peace beyond all understanding.

Unfortunately, many people have difficulty believing in a loving heavenly Father. For those who had non-nurturing or abusive fathers, trusting God is hard. Unconsciously they relate God the heavenly Father to their earthly fathers. Yet, they can only experience God's love when they release the pain of the past, and they can only release the pain of the past with God's help. Loving God and being reconciled with the past go together.

Some who learned early in life that nothing they did would ever be considered good enough by their parents, whose mistakes seemed to be written in indelible ink, whose successes went unnoticed, mistakenly think that God keeps the same kind of records. If this was our experience, we need to learn to believe in the heavenly Father who truly cares for his children. We need to approach him in childlike faith, climb onto his lap and cry, "Abba, Abba Father." Then we will experience his unconditional acceptance and love.

P R A Y E R:

*Heavenly Father, thank you for responding in love when we cry, "Abba, Abba Father." If our earthly parents were lacking, help us to forgive them for not caring enough. As we take a daily inventory, let us be willing to give up our distrust and trust you to be the loving Father you are. Amen.*

Suggested for Step 10

# OCTOBER 15

*"A time to rend, and a time to sew;*
*a time to keep silence, and a time to speak."*
Ecclesiastes 3:7

Ecclesiastes 3:7 is an important reminder to us as practicing Christians. It is not easy to keep silent, especially if someone is insulting us. We want to defend ourselves. We want to get even. We play the game of "one-up-manship," and we want the last word. We want to hurt others the way we have been hurt, but is that the best solution? At times we need to pray for strength to keep silent.

Our Lord gave us the finest example of dignified silence. When he was brought before Pilate under false charges, he did not speak one word in his own defense even though there was much he could have said. Keeping silent is often more noble and Christlike than defensively retorting with our own point of view or to put someone else down.

Some times we find ourselves arguing with people we care about. We know that what they are saying or doing is wrong. They may be acting immaturely because of alcoholism, emotional illness, repressed anger or grief, or any one of many other reasons. Arguing will not change them. We need to pray for them and put them in the Lord's care.

P R A Y E R:

*Loving Savior, help us to refrain from fretting to get in the last word. Teach us patience, acceptance and love. Remind us that there is a time to be silent.*

Suggested for Steps 8 and 9

# OCTOBER 16

*"Every one of us shall give account of himself to God."*
Romans 14:12

We need to remember Romans 14:12 not only while we are taking a personal inventory of our lives, but also when we confess our sins to Christ. Are we ready to admit the "exact nature of our sins," or do we still try to water them down? Do we make excuses or offer justification for our destructive character traits, or are we willing to admit everything? Not until we are ready to be totally honest with our Lord will we receive healing. Only then will we experience his peace and be on the road toward wholeness in body, mind and spirit.

This is a good day to start admitting our wrongs and to do something to change them. Today is the day to be willing to be open to the Holy Spirit so we can be filled with comfort and assurance. Are we ready today to give a full account of ourselves to God, or are we still making excuses? It will be helpful to journal about this area of our lives.

PRAYER:

*Loving Lord, thank you for listening to our confessions. Thank you for forgiving us and that "our sins are remembered no more." Help us to be honest with you when we go to you in prayer. Help us to approach you with contrite hearts, ready to be healed. Fill us with your Spirit and stay with us as we go through the process of change in our lives. Help us to be willing to be available to others as you have been available to us. Amen.*

Suggested for Step 5

# OCTOBER 17

*"Turn you to your God:*
*keep mercy and judgment, and wait on your God continually."*
Hosea 12:6

We do not always turn to God at the appropriate time even though that is exactly what we need to do for comfort and strength. In my life, things have gotten really bad before I've turned to God. On one occasion, shortly after my 41-year-old sister-in-law committed suicide, I suffered traumatic amnesia. My disease was at a critical point and I was dependent on drugs to stay alive. I had gone deep into the woods to my cabin to grieve her loss. The cabin had no phone or other modern conveniences. Upon my arrival, I immediately lost my car keys and my memory. I was helpless because my legs were so badly infected that I could not walk far enough to get help. Anyway, I couldn't even remember who I was.

I stayed like that for six terrifying days. My medication was gone, and my fever was climbing. On the sixth day, as I was strolling in the woods near the cabin, I said to myself, "God wouldn't leave me in a mess like this!" As soon as I acknowledged my need for God, my memory started to return and I found my car keys. I quickly returned home for help. I'd been angry with God for not preventing my sister-in-law's death and blocked him out of my mind and heart when I needed him most. Yet he was there to help me as soon as I acknowledged him and admitted that only he could transform my life.

PRAYER:

*Dear Lord and Father, help us to turn to you sooner so that we do not suffer needlessly. Give us courage to get through difficult times. Help us to allow others to be available to us in our pain. Thank you for your healing and the grace you have given us to wait on you. Amen.*

Suggested for Steps 2 and 3

# OCTOBER 18

*"We grope for the wall like the blind;*
*and we grope as if we had no eyes;*
*we stumble in noon day as in the night;*
*we are in desolate places as dead men."*
Isaiah 59:10

Isaiah 59:10 is very familiar to those of us who have struggled to change character defects. We may earnestly, honestly inventory our lives and set out to work on what needs to be changed, only to stumble around blindly. Old habits are apt to be more comfortable than struggling to change them, so we lose our bearings in frustration.

We need to stop and think. Are we living destructively? Are we trying to do everything ourselves? Do we need the help of our Lord or of some of our friends? Do we need to talk to someone who can more objectively point out areas of our lives that we need to work on? Perhaps a professional counselor. We are not our own best physicians even if we do try. Physicians are not their own best physicians.

PRAYER:

*Kind Father, help us to be honest enough with ourselves to admit when we need help. Help us not to waste time stumbling around in the dark. Help us to turn to you sooner. Give us courage to find professional help if we need it. Once we seek that guidance, help us to be open about our feelings and problems and allow someone to help us. Amen.*

Suggested for Step 4

# OCTOBER 19

*"If the world hates you,*
*know that it has hated me before it hated you."*
John 15:18

We would rather be loved than hated. Most of us like to be liked. Hate makes us feel insecure, worthless and frightened. Most of us, at one time or another, have felt the intensity of someone's hatred for us. Even though continuing to hate is wrong, they have tried to convince themselves and others that we deserve their wrath. When this happens to us, we feel mistreated and find it difficult to love them in return.

All of us need acceptance and respect from the people who are important to us. We want to feel that we are morally right, and we feel put down when others attack our beliefs or actions. But Christ tells us that if we truly love him and are willing to serve him in a spirit of true commitment, we probably will be hated by some. Those who do not believe in Christ will be disturbed by our love for the Lord. They may verbally or physically abuse us for our beliefs. For some of us, being Christians means living with genuine fear. Choosing to serve the Lord means that the people important to us might cut us off from their fellowship.

P R A Y E R :

*Lord, thank you for being our strength and comfort. Thank you for your presence in our lives that gives us the courage to serve you. Teach us to love those who hate us. Help us to see that one way to love them is to be willing to pray for them. Amen.*

Suggested for Step 7

# OCTOBER 20

*"He will give his angels charge of you*
*to guard you in all your ways."*
Psalm 91:11

The most important lesson I learned from serious illness is that I do not have total control of my life. At a point of desperation, I was forced to "let go and let God." In a hospital isolation room, unable to care for myself, I was aware that the doctors were unable to do little for me, either, other than to try to keep me comfortable. They told me they could not cure the disease and might not be able to save my life. That was hard for me to accept.

By the grace of God, I survived 16 unsuccessful surgeries, every one of them leaving me physically weaker and more spiritually and emotionally depleted. When I had the least going for me, I realized that God had been taking care of me all along. His angels were in charge over me.

As ill as I was, I never felt the fear that many people do when seriously ill. What the Lord wanted from me was my cooperation in the healing process and my willingness to share that healing with others. Once I made that commitment, my health began to improve.

PRAYER:

*Loving God, how wonderful it is to know you are with us! We need not struggle on our own. Help us to be strong in faith, to believe in your power and to trust your promises. Thank you for healing us wherever you see our greatest need. Amen.*

Suggested for Step 3

---

# OCTOBER 21

*"Bless the Lord, O my soul, and forget not all his benefits: who forgiveth all thine iniquities; who healeth all thy diseases; who redeemeth thy life from destruction; who crowneth thee with lovingkindness and tender mercies."*

Psalm 103:2-4

I must confess that all too often I forget all that the Lord has done for me. I was born in a Minneapolis slum in the Depression years. I knew what it was like not to have the basic requirements of food, clothing and adequate shelter. Our family struggled to exist. As I think about those days, I realize that trying to raise four children close together was no small accomplishment. Both parents were young, and much of the time my father was unemployed. That was before the days of welfare and other programs to help struggling families.

I have come a long way since then and received blessings too numerous to count, but like so many others, I still take blessings for granted and fail to appreciate that my life today is a miracle of God's love. Two weeks ago, when the sewer backed up in the house, I was reminded of how far I'd come since the Depression. Having to limit the amount of water used until the problem could be cleared up reminded me of when we didn't have running water either inside or outside of the house. A slop bucket had to be carried out in the morning and an outhouse emptied three times a year. That was a terrible job! And, heating the house in those days was not as simple as setting a thermostat the way I do now. Wood had to be cut, split and stacked, and Mother got up before dawn to build a fire to warm the house. I'm grateful for those times because they remind me of how fortunate I am today.

PRAYER:

*Loving Lord, help us to be thankful for all that you do for us and for all that we have. Remind us now and then of how blessed we are. Let us be willing to share our blessings with others. Don't let our self-pity block us. Amen.*

Suggested for Steps 5 and 10

# OCTOBER 22

*"He said unto him the third time, 'Simon, son of Jonas, lovest thou me?'*
*Peter was grieved because he said unto him the third time, 'Lovest thou me?'*
*And he said unto him, 'Lord, thou knowest all things; thou knowest*
*that I love thee.' Jesus said unto him, 'Feed my sheep.'"*
John 21:17

Peter was saddened by Jesus' repeated question. Peter loved Jesus, and he was also sure that Jesus knew that he loved him; but the Lord was not looking so much for reassurance of Peter's love as he was looking for a life commitment. Peter's love had to be strong and resilient because it would be tested. Eventually Peter had to give up his life for his Lord.

This dialogue in John 21:17 reminds us that words without action to back them up can be very empty. "I love you" are important words, but we must demonstrate their value in a more tangible way. Those words may require a sacrifice of time, effort, money, personal comfort, perhaps the exclusion of some thing we would prefer to do.

Christ also says to us, "Lovest thou me? Feed my sheep. Take care of my lambs!" He asks us to get to work. We may have to love an unlovable person in order to demonstrate Christ's love to that one. Are we fully committed to loving and serving our Lord? Only we can answer that question. It might be helpful to journal about how we show our love for other people and for our Lord.

PRAYER:
*Lord and loving Master, thank you for asking us difficult questions that motivate us to do your will. Thank you for challenging us to love you in ways that are more concrete. Give us courage to love you by loving our neighbors as we love ourselves. Amen.*

Suggested for Steps 2 and 4

# OCTOBER 23

*"Who shall separate us from the love of Christ?*
*Shall tribulation, or distress, or persecution,*
*or famine, or nakedness, or peril, or sword?"*
Romans 8:35

As we work on becoming entirely ready to have Christ heal the defects that prevent us from have a more spiritual life style, we need to trust the promise implicit in Romans 8:35. Some of the trials listed may make us shaky, but Christ will love us through all of them. Although tribulations should turn us to him, we often turn away instead. We especially need his help in times of trouble; but if we become depressed or angry, we may forget our source of help.

Broken relationships with other people can also distract us. When we are hurt or angry because we feel separated from the important people in our lives, we are usually out of touch with God, too. People who are afraid of being hurt maintain superficial relationships with many people but are never really close to anyone. They avoid intimacy and keep so busy that they manage to avoid a close relationship with God as well. Angry people avoid intimacy in another way. Both the hurt and the angry separate themselves from the love of Christ because they are not willing to be involved with him or anyone else.

P R A Y E R:

*Precious Lord, thank you that when we are willing to commit ourselves to you, you welcome us with open arms. You have promised us that "in all things we are more than conquerors through him that loved us" (Romans 8:37). Help us to become entirely ready by committing all of who we are, including our strengths and weaknesses, to you. Amen.*

Suggested for Step 6

# OCTOBER 24

*"This day is a day of good news."*
II Kings 7:9

If we really try, we should be able to see the truth in II Kings 7:9 every day. When our lives are filled with trials, we may have to concentrate to find good in the pain. A commitment of faith in our Lord helps us to believe that good will always prevail because of his love for us.

When I was desperately ill and struggling to survive, I could see very little that was good about serious illness and the loss of important people in my life. Some times I couldn't see *any* good and just wanted to die.

The truth is that there's good all around us. God loves us. Some of us have the love of spouse and children, and most of us have friends and Christian fellowship. Even trials are blessings if we patiently look for the good in them.

P R A Y E R:

*Loving Father, thank you that there is good in every day of our lives, even in the midst of pain. Help us to remember to turn to you n prayer, not only for guidance and strength, but for thanksgiving. Bless others who struggle, and let them see the good in each day. Bless us to be blessings whenever, wherever possible. Amen.*

Suggested for Step 2

# OCTOBER 25

*"Though we have never yet seen God,*
*when we love each other, God lives in us*
*and his love within us grows stronger."*
I John 4:12

Several years ago I bought a painting that fascinated everyone who saw it. Other paintings at the art show paled next to it. The piece was of two men, one white and one black. The heads were so close together that they shared an eye in the middle, giving the illusion of one face, half black and half white. Behind them was a figure of Christ, with a hand on each shoulder as if holding the men together. Then behind the figure of Christ were swirling brushstrokes resembling the turbulence of a storm.

I asked the artist what he was feeling or thinking as he painted that piece. He said he wanted to depict the thought that some day we will "see eye to eye." He explained that eventually, with Christ's help, the turbulence of prejudice and hatred will be stilled and we will all see with the eye of love.

That painting hung in the living room all the years that my children were growing up. Many people who visited us were affected by that picture, and it was a special influence in my life.

P R A Y E R:

*Precious Lord, help us to love one another and to be willing to see through one common eye of love. Let us show the light of your love by the way we treat other people. Help us to let go of the ignorance of prejudice and hatred and trust you to teach us unconditional love. Thank you for our differences and for the ways in which we are alike. Amen.*

Suggested for Steps 8, 9 and 12

---

# OCTOBER 26

*"And, behold, a woman of Canaan came out, and cried unto him, saying,*
*'Have mercy on me, O Lord.'"*
Matthew 15:22

This woman of Canaan knew where to turn when she experienced utter despair. She was not too proud to turn to the Lord and ask him to help her. She must have realized that he was her only true source of help. We need to do what she did.

When life seems most desperate, when the future seems hopeless, God is with us. Our extremity is his opportunity to bless us in a very special way. He adds purpose to our misfortunes and meaning to our lives even in the darkest hours. He fills us with courage and hope.

But, we must be willing to admit our powerlessness to him. We must humbly ask him to help us, and we must ask in faith, believing that he will help us in the way we most need his help. We must be willing to let go and let God control our lives. When we yield, we will realize the power of his love to transform our lives

PRAYER:

*Lord, help us to become aware of our own inability to change some of the circumstances of our lives. Help us to recognize our powerlessness and be willing to cry to you, "Have mercy on me, O Lord." Teach us to love one another so that we can comfort one another. Amen.*

Suggested for Steps 1 and 3

# OCTOBER 27

*"God saw everything that he had made and behold, it was very good."*
Genesis 1:31

What do you see when you look in a mirror? Do you see a beautiful, worthwhile person made in God's image? Do you see yourself as a child of God who is loved, accepted and valued? Do you see a healthy, happy, free person with a feeling of wholeness? Do you recognize and acknowledge your inner beauty, or do you see only the exterior part of yourself that you consider less than perfect?

Unfortunately, many of us fail to see ourselves as God sees us. We may spend so much time remembering and reliving our past mistakes (as we see them) that we never get around to seeing the good. We need to remember that what God makes has his stamp of approval on it.

God loves us. He sees our good. We need to concentrate on our strengths, not just on our weaknesses, and remember that if God sees us as worthy, we must be worthy. One reason we need to believe in our own goodness is that we tend to project ourselves to others the way we see ourselves. Making the effort to see ourselves as God sees us is an important way to develop a healthy self-image. Another way is to share all of who we are with others and experience God's love through them.

PRAYER:

*Loving God, thank you for loving us and seeing good in us. Help us to accept your evaluation, that we are worthwhile individuals with potential to grow in your love. Every morning when we look into the mirror, we should practice saying, "I am a beautiful, worthwhile person because God loves me." Give us the confidence to believe that and the courage to risk sharing our real selves with others so that we will experience your love for us more fully. Amen.*

Suggested for Step 5

# OCTOBER 28

*"Heal me, O Lord, and I shall be healed;*
*save me, and I shall be saved; for you are my praise."*
Jeremiah 17:14

Our Lord heals us physically, emotionally and spiritually. We need to trust his healing power at work within us. We must trust on no other power for this healing. We can relax as we allow the soothing, restoring, healing power of God to take over our lives. We are grateful for this wondrous transforming power and the peace it gives us.

Many people have been told that their physical condition is incurable or that their disability is permanent. For others, chronic pain is a way of life. Yet, we know that healing is possible outside of the medical world. We need to believe it, to expect it, to claim it! We need to trust God for whatever form of healing is best for us.

We must also remember that if we continue to have a physical disorder, we can be healthy in other ways. Physical health is important, yet we are all going to die. Physical healing does not last. Ultimately, physical health is unimportant, perhaps even a luxury. What matters is our willingness to be healed emotionally and spiritually.

P R A Y E R:

*Thank you, Lord, for the physical healings we have received; but most of all, thank you for heaing us emotionally and spiritually. Thank you for comfort and strength in difficult times. Touch those who need your healing. Let them feel your presence and have the assurance of healing. For those in pain—whether physical, emotional or spiritual—grant a time of rest so that they will have strength for a new day. Amen.*

Suggested for Step 3

# OCTOBER 29

*"God has caused me to be fruitful in the land of my affliction."*
Genesis 41:52

Genesis reminds us again that our suffering need not be in vain. We can be fruitful in spite of our afflictions. Sharing our experience of suffering and grief often becomes a way for us to understand ourselves. We can become wounded healers just as our Lord is our wounded Healer. We can empathize with suffering more easily if we have suffered ourselves. When those to whom we attempt to minister know this, we become more credible to them and they stop using the words, "You don't understand."

We must give our misfortunes, losses and failures to Christ and allow him to transform them for us. Life's painful experiences can become opportunities to grow, mature and serve our Lord more fully. Peter was transformed from a person who denied Christ to the rock upon which Christ founded the Christian church. Jesus took Peter, in Peter's weakness, and loved him into being the founder of the Christian church. From the ugliness of the crucifixion of our Lord came the glory and hope of the resurrection. There are so many examples of how suffering has brought out the best qualities in people. Therefore, we can learn from our afflictions if we are open to that possibility.

P R A Y E R:

*Blessed Savior, thank you for the opportunities that our afflictions give us. Even though we may not always see good in suffering, help us to turn to you for guidance. Let us draw our strength from you. Give us courage to share our spiritual journeys, our strengths and weaknesses, even our failures, with others so that we can benefit from the difficult experiences of life. Amen.*

Suggested for Steps 1 and 6

# OCTOBER 30

*"I waited patiently for the Lord, and he heard me."*
Psalm 40:1

These are King David's words. From experience we know it is not always easy to wait patiently for the Lord. Some times we do not even hear him when he answers our prayers because his answer is not the one we expected, perhaps not one we wanted. When that happens, we decide that he did not hear us.

Or we don't wait for an answer. In his wisdom, God some times lets us wait a little while for his answer because we are not actually ready for it. If we believe that he loves us, we have to wait patiently, confident that he will answer when the time is right.

We need to believe and to wait. We need to expect God's answer to be the best answer, and we need to be patient.

P R A Y E R:

*O God, teach us to be patient in prayer. Help us trust you to answer our prayers in ways best for us. Teach us to expect an answer and to trust the promise that you do hear us. Amen.*

Suggested for Step 11

# OCTOBER 31

*"Neglect not the gift that is in you."*
I Timothy 4:14

If most people are like me, they underestimate their gifts. I know many people who refuse to believe they have any gifts at all. When you ask them to facilitate a 12 Step group, teach Sunday school, whatever, they will reply, "I can't do that. I'm not gifted that way." Because they refuse to try to do new things, they cannot develop new gifts. They miss out on a tremendous blessing when they refuse to develop and use God-given gifts.

When I was first advised to serve as an emergency chaplain in a local hospital, I hit the panic button. The position was a requirement of some training I was taking, but I really became anxious. How could I do the work normally performed by an ordained minister? How could I possibly represent God's love in such difficult surroundings?

I agreed to take it on because I knew I had no choice if I wanted to continue my training. The challenge turned out to be one of the greatest blessings of my life. I discovered that I was very good at dealing with people and sharing the love of Christ with them in crisis situations. I received a lot of affirmation about my work, and that improved my self-worth and self-confidence. I discovered a new gift of helping that I would never have found if I had not been forced into sharing myself. I'm thankful that someone who believed I could do it pushed me into developing a new gift.

PRAYER:

*Kindly Lord, you give us gifts so that we can share them with others. We don't always share them because we are afraid and insecure. We need courage to risk sharing ourselves with others. Help us to risk being vulnerable so that we may discover new ways to share your love. Amen.*

Suggested for Step 4

---

# NOVEMBER 1

*"Grow in spiritual strength and become better <u>acquainted</u> with our Lord God and Savior, Jesus Christ."*
II Peter 3:18

November is the month that reminds us of our need to be thankful. Thankfulness is not only an important part of our spiritual life, but also for our personal relationship with Christ.

Step 11 calls us to get our wills in tune with God's will through prayer and meditation. An important part of our prayer life is thanking and praising God for what He continues to be for us. Unless we approach him with this attitude, we will not be open to hear what he has to say to us. We will also not be open enough to know what his will is for us, nor find the strength in him to carry it out.

Peter has some good advice. Not only does he call us to get to know Jesus better, but to "grow in spiritual strength" so that we have the power to act on God's will for our lives. Being thankful is a necessary part of making that happen.

Many of us have difficulty being thankful some of the time. Oh, it is comparatively easy to be thankful for the good things in life such as food, clothing and shelter. But it is hard to be thankful for the less pleasant experiences in life.

Having a thankful attitude is hard when life is stressful and unpleasant. Yet, it is often these experiences that help us to "grow in spiritual strength" and realize our need for Christ.

May God help us all to seek through prayer and meditation to know his will for our lives. May we also approach him with grateful hearts so that we are open to his will and find the "spiritual strength" to act on it.

P R A Y E R:

*Lord, help us to be thankful for the crumbs of life because we know that you are even able to use them to fill the world with bread. Let us be thankful, trusting that you make all things work together for good when we love you and desire your will for our lives. Amen.*

Suggested for Step 11                                                    Vernon J. Bittner

---

# NOVEMBER 2

*"See how very much our heavenly Father loves us,*
*for he allows us to be called his children—think of it—*
*and we really are!" But since most people don't know God,*
*naturally they don't understand that we are his children."*
I John 3:1, *The Living Bible*

To be called the children of God is a privilege beyond our comprehension. We are his children, and he is our loving Father. He loves us in a way that no one else does. He provides for our every need before we ask. We need to think about what it means to be a child of God.

Do we know what it means to be a child? Children trust more easily than adults. We need to learn to trust with childlike faith. Children do not hang on to pettiness and anger like many adults do. They can quarrel and be friends again the same day. Parents can abuse their children, and the children still love and forgive them. Children will hope and believe in their parents' ability to change. We need to learn to be as forgiving as children.

If children grow up in healthy environments, their spirits are free and their minds are creative. We need to tap into the child within each one of us. We need to experience the joy, laughter, play and freedom of a childlike spirit. As we take a daily inventory of our lives, we need to look for the childlike spirit inside of us; if we can release it, we will be happier, healthier people. Can you find the child within you? Let it out to play. You might find journaling about this helpful. Why is childlikeness some times difficult to express and experience?

PRAYER:

*Heavenly Father, thank you for the privilege of being your children. Help us to be willing to find the child inside each of us and let it out to play. Release our inhibitions and touch us with a free spirit. Help us to be supportive of others who are seeking to express the childlikeness within them. Amen.*

Suggested for Step 10

# NOVEMBER 3

*"He will keep in perfect peace all those who trust in him, whose thoughts turn often to the Lord."*

Isaiah 26:3

Turmoil can make us forget to turn to our Lord for his perfect peace. Often the pain speaks so loudly within us that we cannot hear him speak words of encouragement. We are too busy asking, "Why, Lord? Why me? Why now?" We cannot calm down and allow his Spirit to fill us, so we go on in our insanity. We continue to hurt, and we fail to get the help we need.

*Trust* is the key word in Isaiah 26:3. If we would trust God to manage our lives, to provide our needs, we would experience the "peace that passes understanding." We must also remember the second phrase of this verse and often turn our thoughts to the Lord. We will not experience his peace unless we are willing to welcome him into our minds and hearts.

PRAYER:

*Dear Father, today in our prayers we remember others who struggle to find peace. Help them to trust in you, Lord. Help them to turn to others for solace. Remind us that we need to spend time with you in prayer and meditation in order to keep our thoughts turned to you. Amen.*

Suggested for Step 2

# NOVEMBER 4

*"He spoke this parable unto certain which trusted in themselves*
*that they were righteous and despised others."*
Luke 18:9-14 (Read the entire passage.)

Another version translates this verse "Certain persons who were sure of their own goodness and look down upon everybody else. . . ." I'm sure we all know people who are sure of their own goodness and consider themselves just a bit above the rest of God's children. We may have felt that way about ourselves at one time. It is so much easier to see the faults of others than our own. We can be very self-righteous.

We may be judgmental about people who are unemployed and must rely on public support. We may be critical of people who maintain different moral values or religious beliefs. We may condemn people who are in prison, or people with different sexual practices. We can be so legalistic in interpreting the Bible that almost everyone comes under our condemnation. We see them as doomed.

But our Lord warns, "Judge not lest you too be judged." It is no less a sin to set ourselves up as judges than what anyone else is doing that we condemn. Sin is sin, and *anything* that separates us from God is sin. We need to leave judgment up to God and pay attention to our own lives. Our priority should be to become the very best persons we can be and let God deal with all of the others.

PRAYER:

*Help us, Lord, to be aware of our failures and to be less critical of one another. Help us to realize our own shortcomings. Grant us pardon for judging others. Help us to be willing to pardon others. Help us to show our love for you by loving others unconditionally. Amen.*

Suggested for Steps 8, 9 and 12

# NOVEMBER 5

*"Jesus beholding him loved him, and said unto him,*
*'One thing you lack; go your way, sell whatever you have*
*and give to the poor and you shall have treasure in heaven.'"*
Mark 10:21

Jesus tells the rich young ruler to sell all that he owns and give the money to the poor. If he does that, he will receive eternal riches in heaven. Evidently the young man prized his possessions and considered them his security against the future. At least for the moment, giving up his earthly security was more than he could handle. The price of following Jesus was more than he wanted to pay. He did not realize that he would find lasting security if he trusted the Lord.

We need to ask ourselves what our response would be if Jesus gave us the same instructions. Would we be willing to give up everything we have if Jesus asked us to? Could we give up our earthly security, our comfortable life style, if that was what he wanted?

Are we "entirely ready" to have Christ transform our lives, or are there things we need to hold onto? Would we sacrifice our earthly riches or our creature comforts? Would we change some of our character defects that we find quite comfortable? Would we give up everything, take up our crosses and follow him?

PRAYER:

*Lord, we say we want to follow you, yet some times it seems like you ask more than we want to give. Help us to be willing to follow you no matter what the cost may be. Let us place our wills and our lives in your hands, knowing this is the only way to experience serenity and the joy of serving you. Amen.*

Suggested for Step 6

# NOVEMBER 6

*"Even if a mother should abandon the child of her womb,*
*I will never leave you or forsake you."*

Isaiah 49:15

For many people, fear of abandonment is the greatest fear of life. The fear may have begun early when parents or other important people abandoned them. Some were physically abandoned, others emotionally abandoned. Unless what happened in the past is courageously addressed and resolved, the hurt and distrust will continue.

Some people believe they were abandoned or unloved because they were not worthwhile. They take the responsibility for their rejection instead of putting it on those who rejected them. They often expect rejection because they feel unlovable, and their suspicion does turn people away from them.

Our Lord tells us that no matter who may have abandoned us, he will never leave us. He also wants us to know that we are lovable and worthwhile to him. He does not concentrate on our faults, but on our positive characteristics and potential as we grow in the image of his Son. We need to learn to love ourselves as much as he loves us.

PRAYER:

*Gracious Lord, thank you for your promise that you will never abandon us. Help us to trust others to be there for us when we feel abandoned. Help us to know that we deserve to be loved and cared for; when we are not, remind us that it is not because we are unlovable. Help us to forgive those who don't love us so that we can trust your unconditional love for us. Amen.*

Suggested for Steps 4 and 10

# NOVEMBER 7

*"With him they crucify two thieves;*
*the one on his right hand, and the other on his left."*
Mark 15:27

Mark 15:27 reminds us that it takes all kinds of people to make up this world. We need to be tolerant of people, those who are very beautiful and those who are very sick. I feel that my life has been blessed by having a wide range of personalities among my family and friends. Several members of my family have been incarcerated for one reason or another, and that has provided a learning experience in love and forgiveness.

My brother was in a Wisconsin prison for 18 months, a 700-mile round trip from my home. I took his wife and children to visit him on weekends. It was difficult to see my brother in that place, progressively difficult as the months went by, and I longed for his freedom.

In another part of this devotional I mentioned my nephew who was sentenced to 20 years in prison for one count of murder and two counts of attempted murder. He had already spent 20 of his 31 years in prison somewhere. I first learned of the incident on the nightly news, and I was shocked. It was hard for me to think of him as a murderer. I had watched him grow from the day he was born. He often stayed with me as a child He was my brother's only son and a very special person to many of us.

Those circumstances changed my whole attitude toward people who commit murder and other crimes. They are humans just like you and I, but with some special problems that get them into trouble.

P R A Y E R:

*Lord, when you ministered here on earth, you taught us to love and forgive others. Teach us tolerance. Remind us that regardless of the labels we put on people, they are special to someone. When they fail miserably, heartache touches many lives. Bless those who have loved ones in prison or enslaved in any way. Amen.*

Suggested for Step 12

---

# NOVEMBER 8

*"No temptation has overtaken you that is not common to man.*
*God is faithful, and he will not let you be tempted beyond your strength,*
*but with the temptation will also provide the way of escape,*
*that you may be able to endure it."*
I Corinthians 10:13

The Apostle Paul's promise in this scripture can encourage us in difficult times. Often we feel so overwhelmed that we cannot see any way to carry on, even losing sight of our Lord and isolating ourselves from family and friends. This isolation is very destructive and in some cases results in such severe depression that people become suicidal. We are not only acutely aware of our powerlessness (Step 1), but we interpret our situation as hopeless and our despair is overwhelming. The result may be fatal.

Our Lord understands when we experience this desert land. He compassionately promises that even in this especially difficult time, he will provide a way for us to bear it. We have a wonderful Lord, and we need to turn to him in trust and expectation.

PRAYER:

*Divine Comforter, thank you that even when our lives are out of control, you comfort us and provide a way for us. Thank you for your love that surrounds us, warms us, assures us and comforts us. Help others as they struggle with powerlessness. Encourage them to turn to you in complete trust. Amen.*

Suggested for Step 1

---

# NOVEMBER 9

*"We are ambassadors for Christ."*
II Corinthians 5:20

The role of an ambassador of a country is to fulfill the solemn responsibility of reconciliation and promotion. The polished diplomat in this honored position not only represents the values of his government, but attempts to encourage and maintain peaceful relations between his own country and the country hosting his nation's consulate. He must interpret official statements and act as a mediator in volatile situations. His life is often in danger from reactionary militant groups, at times the official government itself. Above all, he needs to be loyal and committed to his own country.

As II Corinthians 5:20 indicates, we are ambassadors of Christ and his kingdom. Our own ethical and moral standards must be very high, and our commitment must be sincere. As ambassadors, we are images of our Lord to the world. In order to be as clear reflections as possible, we need to be enthusiastic and willing to be involved with people.

What kind of ambassadors for Christ are we? If we were going to go to a city where no one had heard the gospel, how would we introduce people to our Lord? What could we say that would make them eager to learn about him? Would our love of Christ show that it is possible to love other people in a special way? Would people be encouraged to hear more about him because of our life style? Or, would they *hear* us speak of a love and life style that we did not actually *live* ourselves every day of our lives?

P R A Y E R:
*Loving Father, thank you for appointing us your ambassadors to the world. Help us to serve you in a way that will encourage others to seek you and serve you. Let us remember that we are always on center stage, that others are watching to see how we represent you. Amen.*
Suggested for Step 12

# NOVEMBER 10

*"Always give thanks for everything to our God and Father in the name of our Lord Jesus Christ."*
Ephesians 5:20

We have many things for which to be thankful, and we set this day aside to give thanks. We are thankful for our faith, which helps us to accept the things we do not understand. We are thankful for the loyalty of friends who bless our lives every day. We are especially thankful for love—the love of one another and the love of our God.

We are thankful for our health. Those of us who have disabilities give thanks for the abilities we have. We thank the Lord for the sickness and trials that help us to appreciate health and good times. We are thankful for the ministry of the Holy Spirit who touches us so deeply and intimately. We remember all the gifts that we receive from God, our Father. We are thankful for friends and their love. We will always remember to give thanks. Let's journal about all of the things for which we can be thankful today.

P R A Y E R:
*Lord, thank you for all of your marvelous gifts. Help us to share them with others so they can experience your love through us. Give us strength to obey you and fill our hearts with your love so that we will willingly serve others. Forgive us if we have failed to use the gifts you have given us for service to you and your kingdom. Help us to make amends. Amen.*
Suggested for Step 11

# NOVEMBER 11

*"When you are praying, first forgive anyone you are holding a grudge against, so that your Father in heaven will forgive you."*
Mark 11:25

If we approach our Lord with unforgiving hearts, we cannot expect to receive forgiveness from him. But if we ask him, he will enable us to forgive so that we can be forgiven. We cannot show his love to others if we do not forgive and love the people we've resented. We cannot find peace ourselves unless our relationships with others are right. We cannot be faithful ambassadors of our Lord and his kingdom unless we represent him as the loving, forgiving God.

We need to think seriously about our relationships. We can work on the eighth and ninth steps and list everyone we have harmed so that we can begin to make amends to them. We also need to list those who have harmed us so we can be sure that we have worked through the process of forgiving them. Let's journal about our relationships and be honest about those we have harmed.

PRAYER:

*Help us, precious Lord, to be ambassadors of your love by making amends wherever necessary. Help us to let go of our false pride and to admit when we are wrong. Help us to accept the humanness of others and readily, willingly forgive them when they wrong us. We pray for those who are struggling with anger, resentment and guilt because of their inability to forgive. Thank you for forgiving us. Amen.*

Suggested for Steps 8 and 9

# NOVEMBER 12

*"He said unto another, 'Follow me.'*
*But he said, 'Lord, suffer me first to go and bury my father.'"*
Luke 9:59

In Luke 9 we read of the man who thought he wanted to follow Jesus, but had other business to attend to first. We may have felt just as he did that other priorities are paramount, and they get in the way of our total commitment to Christ. They seem like legitimate reasons to delay serving him. Our intentions seem good, but we are just not quite ready.

If we are going to follow Christ, we will have to be willing to follow his directions implicitly, whenever and however he leads. We will have to be willing to love and forgive as he did. We can no longer retain unforgiving thoughts about anyone. We must love ourselves and others. We will leave past hurts where they belong, in the past.

If we follow him, we will be filled with love. We will let go of our pettiness, criticism, impatience, fault-finding and other negative attitudes that keep us from loving and being loved. We will reach out to others and be blessed by our willingness to bless them. We will be compassionate because our Lord is compassionate to us. As we follow Christ, his love will transform us. To grow in his love and his likeness, we will work at sincerely seeking and obeying his will.

PRAYER:
*Precious Lord, thank you for asking us to follow you. Help us to be willing to set our excuses aside and to follow you wherever you lead us. We want to follow you in love. Teach us your way. Amen.*
Suggested for Step 10

# NOVEMBER 13

*"I will lift my eyes unto the hills
from whence cometh my help."*
Psalm 121

For today's devotional I would like to share a poem based on Psalm 121. I wrote it when I felt powerless to deal with disease, divorce and other losses in my life. This is the first of 140 poems I wrote during those difficult times.

*I will lift my eyes unto the hills
To seek your solace, Lord;
I will lift up my eyes believing
You will quiet my discord.*

*I will lift my eyes unto the hills
And seek your gentle touch;
I will lift my eyes believing
You love me, oh, so much.*

*I will lift my eyes unto the hills
And seek your tender care;
I will lift my eyes believing
My burdens you will share.*

*I will lift my eyes unto the hills
To seek your loving face;
I will lift my eyes believing
I will receive your grace.*

*I will lift my eyes unto the hills
And seek release from pain;
I will lift my eyes believing
My strength you will sustain.*

*I will lift my eyes unto the hills
In times of doubt and fear;
I will lift my eyes believing
You will always be there.*

*Amen.*

Journaling, whether in poetry or prose, has been very important in my healing process and spiritual growth. Before the simultaneous crash of trials in my life, I had never journaled. I encourage you to keep a daily journal; it can become a vital part of your life.

Suggested for Steps 1 and 11

# NOVEMBER 14

*"Now the God of hope fill you*
*with all joy and peace in believing,*
*that you may abound in hope,*
*through the power of the Holy Ghost."*

Romans 15:13

Hope, joy and peace are not easy to claim as our own, especially during the difficult times of our lives. Too often we grieve over what we have lost, what we don't have, what we might've had *if only*, that we forget our blessings. If we reflect on the positive aspects of our lives, we might find energy to transform the destructive aspects. If we concentrate more on blessings than on disappointments, our whole attitude toward life will change. Emphasis on the positive will allow us to hope in God and experience the joy and peace only he can give.

Hope comes from God. We can hope in him because of Christ's ministry on earth, his death and his resurrection, his intercession on our behalf at the throne of God the Father. Instead of wishing we were somewhere else or someone else, we need to pray for hope so that we can accept who we are and where we are in life. When we acknowledge the God of hope, we will know the power of hope, the joy and peace of trusting God. We will also know the serenity of being okay with our station in life because we have allowed the Holy Spirit to transform our discontent into hope.

PRAYER:

*God of hope, thank you for all that you do for us. Thank you for giving us hope when our lives seem hopeless. We are grateful for the joy and peace we receive when we believe and trust in you. Thank you for breaking in upon us with your Spirit of hope so that we are able to know the joy and peace of believing. Amen.*

Suggested for Steps 2, 4 and 6

# NOVEMBER 15

*"Pray constantly,*
*give thanks in all circumstances."*
I Thessalonians 5:17,18

Few of us pray constantly, and we certainly do not give thanks in all circumstances. Prayer must become an integral part of our daily experience if we desire spiritual growth and rich, fulfilling lives. Through prayer we remain receptive to God's will as well as his comfort, encouragement and power to accomplish his purposes.

Prayer keeps the line of communication open. We can talk to God about our personal needs and the needs of friends and loved ones. We can know the power of his presence. Prayer can calm our anxieties. Going to God in prayer helps us to find the serenity we need to face life. Prayer helps us to experience the assurance that nothing is impossible as long as we trust him.

How is our prayer life? Can we do anything to improve it? Perhaps we need to spend more time in prayer. Reading God's word or a devotional can be a catalyst for quieting and centering our minds on him. We need to find a quiet place and make time for prayer and meditation with our Lord so we can enjoy his companionship and counsel.

P R A Y E R:

*Lord, thank you for hearing and answering our prayers. Help us to wait and listen. Help us to trust that you know what is best for us. Help us, Lord, not only to hear you, but to incorporate what you have to say to us so that we will truly love and serve you. Amen.*

Suggested for Step 11

# NOVEMBER 16

*"On the day I called you answered me,*
*my strength of soul you increased."*
Psalm 138:3

The truth of Psalm 138:3 is undeniable. I know from personal experience that when I call, God will answer and strengthen me. As I've mentioned elsewhere, God helped me the time I went through traumatic amnesia following my sister-in-law's suicide. Though my memory was gone, he enabled me to call out to him in despair, and he responded. The time a man broke into my home to rape me, God was there to protect me and to heal the nightmares that followed. When I doubted God's existence and took a picture of dark, stormy rainclouds, God gave me a sign by putting the outline of a cross right in the middle of the snapshot.

God has proved his love for me many times. In the midst of suffering, even when I've thought that he deserted me, God was near to strengthen and comfort me. Some times I asked him for help. Other times, even when I did not ask, he let me know he was with me.

Psalm 138:3 reminds us to ask God for help. We must be willing to acknowledge our need to God. It is important for us to be willing to work out the first step, to admit that we are powerless and that, at times, our lives are unmanageable. God cannot help us until we are ready to give up the control of our lives and place ourselves in his hands. Do we really believe he will be there for us? Do we trust him? Let's journal about our faith today. Where are we spiritually? Are we filled with belief, unbelief or a mixture of both?

PRAYER:

*Loving Father, thank you for being with us even when we do not acknowledge your presence. Give us courage to admit that we are out of control in some area of our lives and need your help. Help us to let go and let you take charge of our lives so we can experience your healing. Help us to be open to your healing and available to others who need healing. Amen.*

Suggested for Steps 2 and 3

# NOVEMBER 17

*"Those who decide to please Christ Jesus by living godly lives will suffer at the hands of those who hate him."*
II Timothy 3:12, *The Living Bible*

We may strive to live godly lives, only to discover that people will persecute us for our beliefs. Others will either make fun of us or ignore us. They will question our reasoning, and they may give us a hard time about how we feel about Jesus. Our Lord has warned us that we might be persecuted because we love him. We may not be crucified as Christians were at the time of Christ and the early church, but we will experience discomfort. If and when we are ridiculed, we will find it difficult to keep a dignified silence like Christ or to be so receptive to God's Spirit that he can witness through us.

We will need an extra portion of patience to deal with people who persecute us for our beliefs. We cannot "repay evil with evil." We must continue to project the love of Christ that is within us, sustaining and supporting our faith. With our Lord's help, we can endure insults. We need to remember his promise, "No weapon formed against you shall prosper." Love will overcome.

P R A Y E R:

*Thank you, Lord, for helping us to endure when others abuse us. Help us to maintain our Christian beliefs in the face of adversity. Keep us kind, loving and forgiving so that the disparagement we receive from others will not shake our love for you. Amen.*

Suggested for Steps 8 and 9

---

# NOVEMBER 18

*"Fear not, for I am with you,
be not dismayed, for I am your God;
I will strengthen you. I will help you.
I will uphold you with my victorious right hand."*

Isaiah 41:20

Have you ever felt too tired to move or breathe? We all feel that weary at times, and some times that feeling completely overwhelms us. Perhaps other times we are worn out by losses and feel that our situation can never be any different. We may grieve and fall into severe depression.

God promises to strengthen us, and we need to believe that he will be true to his word. Whether or not trust is difficult for us, we must do our best to place our faith and lives in his hands. We may trust him completely but expect him to stop the pain and the losses, and when that does not happen, decide that he is not trustworthy.

It is important to understand the reason for our fatigue. If there is no physical reason, we should explore other possibilities. Anger or depression can cause great fatigue, and until we resolve the reason for our emotional overload, we will continue to be tired.

P R A Y E R:

*Forgive us, Father, for not trusting you completely. Help us to risk trusting you and others and to understand that there is no pain-free life on this earth. There will always be losses. Let us trust you to handle them with us. Bless all who are struggling with losses and give them strength and courage. Bless those who live with the pain of sick or dying children; may they find comfort in you, the nurturing Father of us all.*

Suggested for Steps 1 and 3

---

# NOVEMBER 19

*"I sought the Lord and he heard me,
and delivered me from all my fears."*

Psalm 34:4

We spend a lot of time in unecessary fear. Many of us fear what *might* happen to us. The "might happens" seldom happen, and some that do can't be prevented anyway, so we waste time and energy worrying. Franklin D. Roosevelt said, "The greatest thing we have to fear is fear itself." The Bible teaches that fear cannot exist where faith abides. Faith is the solution to our fears.

Psalm 34:4's key words are *sought* and *he heard*: "I *sought* the Lord and *he heard* me." First, we must actively seek God. He is not hard to find. He knows our fears. He hears us before we pray. Second, we must believe that he will hear and answer us. Then, we must go one step further; we need to believe that he will not only hear, but he will *take action* on our behalf. He will deliver us from our fears! To benefit from this promise, we need faith, trust and action. Can we make that commitment?

PRAYER:

*Loving Savior, thank you that when we seek you, you hear us and deliver us from our fears. We are grateful for your steadfast love. Help us to be available to people who are afraid. Teach us patience and acceptance of ourselves and others. Amen.*

Suggested for Step 6

---

# NOVEMBER 20

*"The Lord also will be a refuge for the oppressed,*
*a refuge in times of trouble."*
Psalm 9:9

Psalm 9:9 contains a precious promise, and we need to trust it. At times, all of us need courage to face a new day. Some days are easier than others, but we need to stay close to our Lord so that we don't lose sight of the fact that he is in charge. He is a refuge to all who seek him. Nothing can overcome us as long as we stay close to him.

We have good reasons to feel powerless. We worry about our jobs, children, spouses, bills, health, even worry itself. Some times our best plans cave in like houses built on shifting sand. Then we begin to doubt God.

We need to hold onto the assurance that Jesus is with us. Then it will be easier to face the things we worry about. We worry because we lose sight of him, and crises cloud our vision. But if we commit ourselves to trust him and are willing to do our part to work through our circumstances, we will find that overcoming stresses will become easier.

PRAYER:

*Lord, help us to trust you. Help us to put you first in our lives so that we can rest in your care. Thank you for being our refuge in troubled times. Keep us close to you. Help us to be willing to share your love and the assurance of your presence with others. Amen.*

Suggested for Step 1

# NOVEMBER 21

*"Every one of us shall give account of himself to God."*
Romans 14:12

We need to remember Romans 14:12 not only while we are taking a personal inventory of our lives, but also when we confess our sins to Christ. Are we ready to admit the "exact nature of our sins," or will we smooth the rough edges a bit and make excuses? Will we cover up our destructive character traits or expose them? Only when we become honest with our Lord will we receive healing and his peace. Only then can we expect the possibility of wholeness in body, mind and spirit.

This is a good day to admit our wrongs and begin to change them. This is the time to say, "Okay," to the Holy Spirit and accept his comfort and assurance.

There is no use trying to hide from God because there's nowhere to hide. He knows everything. Confessing our sins, giving a true account of ourselves, is for our benefit, to enable us to experience his cleansing and peace. This is the only way to experience his forgiveness and healing transformation.

P R A Y E R:

*Loving Lord, thank you for listening to our confessions, for forgiving us and assuring us that they're off the record (cf. Jeremiah 31:34). Help us to be honest with you, contrite and ready to be healed. Fill us with your Spirit and remind us that you will be with us through the process of change. Amen.*

Suggested for Steps 5 and 10

# NOVEMBER 22

*"This is the day which the Lord has made;
let us rejoice and be glad in it."*
Psalm 118:24

Sunday, for some people, is the one day of the week that belongs to the Lord. That day they worship God and practice their spirituality. They read the Bible and pray more on that day than they do Monday through Saturday. But, every day of the week should be the Lord's day. Every day should be one of worship and praise. We can worship God in many ways and places and times besides in church on Sunday.

Every day is a brand new day; there has never been a rerun, even though we might be tempted to think so at times. Today is what we have *now*. We need not use it up by fretting about the past or worrying about the future. We live *today*! We live one day at a time.

We can make a new beginning today. We can make the change that we've needed for so long. Now, *today*, we can begin to make our dreams turn into realities. Today is the day to learn new things, to expand our minds and creativity beyond the stagnant status quo. Today we can make new friends, revitalize old friendships and forgive the hurts we've carried for so long. Today is our God-given day.

PRAYER:

*Divine Liberator, help us to appreciate today and utilize it to the fullest. Let us be creative in what we do. Let us use this day as if it were the last day we had to live. Help us to let go of the past and not worry about the future. Let us live fully today.* Thank you for today. Amen.

Suggested for Step 4

---

# NOVEMBER 23

*"Some people like to make cutting remarks,
but the words of the wise soothe and heal."*
Proverbs 12:18, *The Living Bible*

Unfortunately, when someone hurts us, we react with unkind words. We want to hurt back, and our words are our weapons. They often create wounds that take a long time to heal. Proverbs 12:18 reminds us that our words are sharp . . . they're cutting. Physical wounds heal quickly, but verbal abuse has long-lasting, damaging effects.

Children who are abused by their parents, teachers or other caregivers rarely develop healthy self-images. They accept the labels given them. Adults abuse one another, too; they say hurtful things that cannot be erased or taken back, and the damage may be irreparable.

Christ showed us how to respond to people who accuse, demean or insult. Some times he answered by his silence. Silence is a powerful motivator; in the wrong hands, it becomes a weapon of punishment. Often Christ responded with a word fitly spoken, but always with love. He did not use words to hurt or get even with people. We can learn from his example if we are willing to move beyond our hurt and anger. But first we need to let go of these negative feelings, and this will happen only when we are ready to forgive.

PRAYER:

*Gentle Savior, help us to remember your example when dealing with difficult people. Keep us from responding with cutting words. Give us patience with others. Help us to understand that they are hurting, that they're broken just as we are at times. Otherwise they would not be striking out at us. Amen.*

Suggested for Steps 8 and 9

# NOVEMBER 24

*"Every one helps his neighbor and says to his brother,*
*'Take courage.'"*
Isaiah 41:6

How do we respond to the challenge to help and encourage? Do we help our neighbors, our brothers and sisters, in difficult times? Do we make the effort to encourage them? Or do we briefly remark, "If you need anything, let me know." Some times we need to offer specifics like child care, lawn mowing, financial help or being available to talk with them.

Who are our neighbors? Who are our brothers and sisters? Are they the folks who live on our block, or are the boundaries of our neighborhood worldwide? We need to have a committed Christian concern for all of humankind. We must not limit our love and support to those who live next door or those we deeply care about.

We need to ask ourselves if we are doing everything we can to help people. We need to vote on important issues that affect people's lives. We need to think about who we vote into public office and what their goals and values are for humankind. We need to remember people of other countries in intercessory prayer. We need to teach our children to love and tolerate people regardless of race, color, creed and national origin.

PRAYER:

*Loving Father, teach us to love people as you love us and to be willing to minister to them as you minister. Help us to show our love for you by loving and helping others. Thank you for teaching us how to love courageously. Amen.*

Suggested for Step 12

---

# NOVEMBER 25

*"For me to live is Christ, and to die is gain."*
Philippians 1:21

I didn't understand Philippians 1:21 until I learned its historical context. The Apostle Paul wrote the scripture while in prison, when he did not know if he would be released or sentenced to death. He considered the two possibilities. On the one hand, if he lived, he would go on preaching the gospel of Jesus Christ. That would make him very happy. On the other hand, if he died, he would go to be with his Lord eternally. That would make him happy, too. Paul's faith was so firm that he was willing to accept either outcome with pride and dignity.

I'm not sure that many of us would have that strong a faith under such similar circumstances. Paul was not filled with despair; he had too much confidence in his Lord to doubt him. His faith is our example. We can attain the same kind of faith in our Lord when we are willing to seek his help.

We need to practice the Lord's presence as Paul did. When we are afraid, our Lord will calm us. When we doubt, we need only acknowledge our doubts and he will strengthen our faith. As we pray, can relax, knowing he will answer in ways best for us. Whatever our prison may be, we are assured that he is always with us.

PRAYER:

*Precious Lord, thank you for seeing us through fearful times. Thank you for your steadfast love that gives us the courage we need. Give us the kind of faith that Paul had so that we, too, will triumph over our circumstances. Help us not to fear death, but to say with Paul, "For me to live is Christ, and to die is gain." Amen.*

Suggested for Steps 1 and 10

---

# NOVEMBER 26

*"No man when he has lighted a candle puts it in a secret place,*
*neither under a bushel, but on a candlestick,*
*that they which enter in may see the light."*
Luke 11:33

Jesus used simple, understandable stories to teach spiritual truths. He did not use big words or technical terms. He did not speak so that only those with the best education could understand him. He spoke a universal language, one of love, compassion, commitment and involvement. The illustration of the candle is simple. What good would it do to light a candle and put it under a bushel basket? It would not light our way, nor would it help anyone else see any better in the dark.

Yet, many of us hide our light. We do not share our gifts. Not only do we fail to share our joy, but we fail to share our pain; so we fail to learn from others, and they fail to learn from us. How can we show Christ's love if we are unwilling to risk sharing ourselves in a very personal way? We need to talk about our strengths and our weaknesses. We need to express our joy and our sorrow. We need to laugh and cry with others. We need to believe that doing so is not only all right, but human.

PRAYER:

*Lord and Giver of light, help us to share our light with others so that they can learn to know you better. Help us to risk vulnerability and invite others to do the same. Thank you for opportunities to let our light shine so that others see your love. Amen.*

Suggested for Step 12

# THANKSGIVING DAY

*"Enter his gates with thanksgiving, and his courts with praise!
Give thanks to him, bless his name! For the Lord is good;
his steadfast love endures forever, and his faithfulness to all generations."*
Psalm 100:4,5

Today is the day we set apart for the purpose of giving thanks. We want to have, and should have, a spirit of thanksgiving every single day of the year, but this national holiday is for special thanksgiving to the God who has given us liberty to worship him freely and openly. He is the God who has stood by us. We have so many things to thank him for that they are beyond number.

Today we thank the Lord for all that is good in life. As we start this new day, we will begin to recount all of our reasons to be thankful. We are thankful for life, for our degree of health. We thank God for his guidance. We thank him for his love that surrounds us and warms our hearts.

Today we will give of ourselves and think positively. We will see truth and try to understand ourselves and others. We will work at being a blessing to others. We will risk trusting others and being trustworthy in return.

P R A Y E R :

*We give thanks to you, Lord, for your love is everlasting. We will look for you in others instead of seeing only their faults. Every person is your creation and therefore a person to love. Help us to see the good and the uniqueness of every individual, for in that specialness we see your signature.*

*Be with all who seek you and help them to find many reasons to rejoice. Let your presence be felt in such a way that they cannot deny it. Amen.*

Suggested for Step 12

---

# NOVEMBER 27

*"Faith is the assurance of things hoped for,
the conviction of things not seen."*
Hebrews 11:1

We want to see visible proofs of Christ's love for us. We want to see his nail-scarred hands. We demand answers to our prayers: positive, visible signs that he really hears and answers us. We doubt the veracity of his word. If we truly believed his word, we would not doubt. We cry, "Lord, I believe. Help my unbelief!" (Mark 9:24).

We need to develop faith that believes without demanding physical proofs, faith that is strong enough to conquer fear, faith that is worthy of the love and confidence Christ has shown us. We may wonder if it will ever be possible to have the kind of faith that honors God; but in order to attain that kind of faith, we have to study God's word. We need to pray, to wait upon the Lord for his direction and encouragement. The Scriptures relate many of the miracles that Christ performed. We need to take them at face value and believe in his ability to heal us. We need to stay close to him so that we will know his will for us. As we work on Step 7, we need to journal about our faith.

PRAYER:

*We want to be open to your leading, Lord. Fill us with determination to pursue faith in such a way that we won't be able to doubt. Bless others who struggle with doubt. Strengthen their faith so they can completely trust you and your promises. Amen.*

Suggested for Step 7

# NOVEMBER 28

*"Thou wilt show me the path of life:*
*in thy presence is fullness of joy;*
*at thy right hand there are pleasures for evermore."*
Psalm 16:11

If God is our Friend, let us be his close friends. We need to spend time with him every day. We need to talk with him, to listen, to worship, to seek his counsel, to ask for his help, to intercede on behalf of others, to thank him, to praise him, to learn more about him and about ourselves. Are we his close friends? Do we seek his direction first, or do we try to solve problems our own way first? We can talk to him about our jobs, our children, our marriages, our failures and our successes. He is the one Friend who fully understands and will stand by us, no matter how messed up our lives may be. We must willingly seek him.

Psalm 16:11 reminds us that we can have fullness of joy in God's presence. True and lasting joy comes from within. We can find it within ourselves. We do not have to be dependent upon other people to give us joy. Joy is a spiritual gift, a free gift from God because he loves us so. Joy adds to our positive experience of life. With God's help, we can feel it inwardly and exemplify it outwardly.

Our joy does not depend upon things or upon circumstances. Material possessions can give temporary joy, but lasting joy comes only from loving ourselves, God and others. This joy comes from serving him and others in a spirit of Christian love. We experience ever greater joy as we express our friendship with God in our thoughts, words and actions. As we inventory our lives, let's journal about whether or not we seek God's guidance every day and whether or not we experience the joy he gives so willingly.

PRAYER:

*Loving God, you show us the path of life and walk with us. You want us to know the richness of the joy we will find in close friendship with You. Help us to be willing to accept your friendship and the joy that comes with it, then enable us to share our joy with others. Amen.*

Suggested for Step 10

# NOVEMBER 29

*"God created man in his own image."*
Genesis 1:27

My mother was telling me about her childhood one day. She was born the ninth of ten children. Her mother died when she was only two. Her own father decided that she was of no use to him on the farm and left her at a Catholic orphanage. A married sister, 18 years older, took her from the orphanage to raise her with her two children. But her husband considered Mom a burden and let her know that. Their son was jealous of any attention Mom received from her older sister and often abused her.

When she was ten years old, Mom's stepmother considered her old enough to work as a servant, so she took her home. But she treated Mom far worse than a servant. She fed her own children and deprived Mother of proper nourishment. Some times she pushed Mother down the cellar stairs and beat her. Mom became weak physically, and she was emotionally scarred for life. Her health was so poor that she had to drop out of school when she was in the third grade.

All her young life, Mom was told that she was good-for-nothing. Five of her siblings died within two weeks during a diptheria epidemic, and she was too young to sort through what was happening and somehow come to terms with it. So, she developed a poor self-image and never really got over it.

PRAYER:

*Loving God, many people have grown up with the message stamped on their minds and spirits that they are worthless. Heal their brokenness and let them know they are worthwhile because you created them in your image. Help us to realize how important it is for us to treat one another responsibly. Teach us to be kind and nurturing and to see the strengths in others, not just their weaknesses. Help us to love ourselves and others as you love us. Amen.*

Suggested for Step 4

# NOVEMBER 30

*"Man looks on the outward appearance,*
*but the Lord looks on the heart."*
I Samuel 16:7

We constantly judge people by their outward appearance, rarely by the hidden qualities that are so important to God. How well dressed are they? Do they choose name-brand products? What kind of car do they drive? How large and expensive is their home? How much money do they make? What position do they hold? Are they socially involved with wealthy, well-known people? So on . . . and on . . . and on.

Appearances say little about the real person inside. God loves us whether we are rich or poor, famous or unknown, attractive or unattractive. The Lord looks upon our hearts. He does not care about worldly successes; he considers our spiritual successes.

We ought to try to see people as God sees them. What do their words and actions tell us of their relationship to the Lord? Do they love other people? Do they share God's love? Then we need to ask ourselves if our priorities are straight. What do we call success? Do our values reflect God's, or are ours more materialistic? If material possessions are more important that our relationships with God and others, our priorities are wrong.

PRAYER:

*Lord, help us to see that our hearts must be filled with your love, and when they are, that will be our claim to success! Help us to refrain from looking on the exterior, and enable us to see the inner beauty and strengths of people, not their weaknesses. Teach us to find good in others and to share your love with them. Amen.*

Suggested for Step 12

---

# DECEMBER 1

*"We are the children of God:*
*and if children, then heirs; heirs of God, and joint-heirs with Christ;*
*if so be that we suffer with him, that we may be also glorified together."*
Romans 8:16,17

Christmas is December, and December is Christmas. Christmas is *the* day for all of God's children. It is the day that marks the fulfillment of God's promise that his Son would be born of a human mother and become the Brother of us all. As his brothers and sisters, we are children of God and we inherit the possibility of salvation along with Christ. Therefore, we are not only promised eternal life, but also the possibility of healing through the transforming power of Christ . . . if we follow his will for our lives.

This makes us all significant and special. It doesn't matter how many gifts we received or how many people we had around us at Christmas. What does matter is that God has given himself to us, and if we work the 12 Steps, which contain the basic concepts of the Christian faith, we will find a personal, saving and healing relationship with the Christ who came to us at Christmas. Then we will feel constrained to share the joy of that experience with others.

Sharing what Christ has done and is doing for us is what Christmas and the twelfth step are all about. Unless we are willing to do this, we will miss true joy! Joy comes from *sharing* the overflow of God's grace that comes from a new sense of spirituality that resulted from the Christmas event.

Christmas is an expression of God's joy. *Sharing* Christ's message of love and forgiveness is *our joy*.

P R A Y E R:

*May our hearts overflow with the joy of Christmas and knowing more fully the love and forgiveness of Christ. Help us to know that true joy is bringing the atmosphere of heaven to earth. This, truly, is the Christmas event, and this is a new sense of spirituality. Help us, Lord, to be open to the Christ event in our lives this December. Amen.*

Suggested for Step 12                                    Vernon J. Bittner

---

# DECEMBER 2

*"They shall not sorrow any more at all."*
Jeremiah 31:12

God, speaking through his Old Testament prophet Jeremiah, promises a day in the future when sorrow and suffering will be over. Jeremiah 31:12 does not mean that we needn't expect to suffer now. As long as we live, we will be affected by losses of one kind or another; but the determining factors in the intensity of our suffering will be *how we react to losses* and *how close we are to our Lord*. If we develop a close friendship with him, he will enable us to overcome sorrow.

Let's look at our sorrow. Are we suffering because of the circumstances of our lives, because of the way we deal with them, or a combination of the two? My grief has been most profound when I've lost sight of my Lord, whether because tears dimmed my spiritual eyes or because I deliberately blocked him out of my life. Without him, my soul experienced a massive hemorrhage. But when I allowed him to come near, the pain lessened and I felt his comfort. My heart stopped aching and I began to hope in my Redeemer.

PRAYER:

*Lord, you have promised that in your 'presence is the fullness of joy"*
*(Psalm 16:11). We know this is true, even in our deepest sorrow. Help us to*
*turn to you when we grieve. Help us to seek comfort from Christian friends,*
*too. Enable us to use our experience of suffering to help others who suffer.*
*Amen.*

Suggested for Step 1

# DECEMBER 3

*"As he thinketh in his heart, so is he."*
Proverbs 23:7

Billions of dollars are spent every year
to help people who consider themselves worthless, unloved and somehow inferior to others. Some are in prisons, some in mental hospitals.
Some are in counseling programs. Many are trying to understand why
they have poor self-worth. Others either don't realize how distraught
they are, or they don't care, and continue to live destructive life styles.

Proverbs 23:7 reminds us how important our self-image is. What we
think about ourselves often determines what we think about others.
Often people with extremely poor self-images angrily refuse to trust anyone. They may even set themselves up to fail in relationships to prove
that they are unlovable and others are untrustworthy.

I've seen the truth in Proverbs 23:7, both from personal experience
and from observation of my family and friends. There have been many attempts at suicide, some successful. Several who tried to commit suicide
are or have been in prisons or mental hospitals. Several are addicted to alcohol and other drugs. They all have one thing in common: they believe
themselves unloved, unacceptable and of very little worth. They want to
kill what they hate most, themselves and their perceived failures. Some
just want to be relieved of the pain of living. But death by suicide is the
cheap solution to a problem. The death itself is not as tragic as the fact
that the person never really lived.

PRAYER:

*Loving God, we need to learn to love ourselves, to believe in our hearts*
*that we are lovable. Help us to give up any negative self-images we have held,*
*then to love ourselves as you love us. Help those whose lives as so filled with*
*pain that they've lost the will to live. Touch them with your healing. Amen.*

Suggested for Steps 4 and 6

# DECEMBER 4

*"Though he fall, he shall not be utterly cast down;
for the Lord upholds him with his hand."*
Psalm 37:24

At times we may feel that we have fallen from grace, that we have wandered so far from God that we will never again hear his voice of welcome. Some times the pit seems so deep and so black that we cannot find our way out. Then we hear his promise that even though we fall, we "shall not be utterly cast down; for the Lord upholds [us] with his hand." There is no pit so deep that Christ cannot reach down and lift us up to safe ground.

When we feel cast down, we need to remember that God's love makes all things possible and all things new. No situation is too difficult for the Lord to help us through. He can change the most difficult trial into a blessing. We need only claim the promise of Psalm 37:24 and seek him in humility and trust. Today let's take time to journal about the areas in our lives that need attention. We will better understand them if we put our thoughts down on paper.

PRAYER:

*Thank you, Protector, for your constant vigilance. Thank you for shepherding us, for lifting us from the murky waters of despair. You are truly kind and loving. Help us to become aware a little sooner that we need to stay close to you and trust you. Let us be willing to get rid of our curiosity that gets us to wander off on our own. Help others who stray and fall. Comfort them. Amen.*

Suggested for Steps 3 and 5

# DECEMBER 5

*"Look not every man on his own things,
but every man also on the things of others."*
Philippians 2:4

This verse calls us to do the work of Step 12, to "share the message of [God's] love and forgiveness with others and to practice these principles for spiritual living in all our affairs."

We underestimate what we can do for others. We have such poor self-images that we minimize our abilities and potential. As a result, we not only fail to recognize the gifts we already have, but we don't develop them. We need to see ourselves as we really are and to appreciate our God-given gifts. All that God expects is that we risk using our gifts to minister in his name. One gift may be to be a good listener. Perhaps we are called to share God's love by writing inspirational poetry. Possibly we are called to share through public speaking. I believe that God has called us all to share with someone who we are and where we've come from, because he has created us for relationships. Telling others our spiritual journeys is one of the most effective ways of working the twelfth step.

Your excuse for not trying may be "I can't do that. I'm too shy." Well, everyone has to start somewhere. An author has to risk writing his first book. A speaker has to give his first speech. A wounded healer (such as you and I) has to share his journey for the first time. It's difficult but not impossible. There is a difference between the attitude "I can't" and "I won't." Christ can help us to do almost anything if we are willing.

PRAYER:

*Loving Lord, help us to be willing to share with others and not just be wrapped up in ourselves. For those of us who lack confidence, this is difficult. Give us courage to risk sharing what you've done for us and help us to remember that we'll survive the process because you're with us.*

Suggested for Step 12

---

# DECEMBER 6

*"The Spirit also helps our infirmities:*
*for we know not what we should pray for as we ought:*
*but the Spirit itself makes intercession for us*
*with groanings which cannot be uttered."*

Romans 8:26

Paul wrote these words to the Christians in Rome. They wanted to learn how to pray effectively and yet realized that they needed the mind of God in order to accomplish his will through prayer. In the midst of persecution under the Empire, they must have been relieved to learn that the Holy Spirit intereceded for them according to the knowledge and will of the Father.

Christians now, as then, are challenged to a strong prayer life. When we think of prayer, many questions come to mind, questions to which no easy answers can be given. Do we maintain a regular prayer life? Do we believe in the power of prayer? What is the meaning and purpose of prayer for us personally? Do we expect anything to happen when we pray? Can we or will we accept God's answers to our prayers?

I remember when my only brother was emotionally ill. He attempted suicide on more than one occasion, and every time I was there to rescue him. I hurt for him because he was so filled with despair. Finally I started to pray for him in a different way. Instead of asking God to save his life, I prayed, "Please, Lord, give my brother peace even if that means through his death."

Not long afterward, he successfully ended his life. I felt devastated, even betrayed by God. Then I prayed, all too late, "Lord, I didn't mean it. Don't let him be dead." At the time, I didn't realize that God would not answer my prayers on behalf of my brother by triggering his death. My brother chose to end his life, and he didn't include God's will in his plan. Now I know that grief can cause us to feel guilty about some things over which we have no control.

PRAYER:

*Heavenly Father, teach us to pray confidently, knowing that you have our best interests in mind. Thank you for the privilege of approaching your throne in prayer. We know that we are not worthy on our own, but because you have chosen us to be your children. Your love makes us valuable. Help us to remember the needs of others when we pray, but enable us to refrain from taking responsibility for their actions. Amen.*

Suggested for Step 11

---

# DECEMBER 7

*"O taste and see that the Lord is good: blessed is the man that trusts in him."*

Psalm 34:8

Unless we trust Christ, turning our lives over to him will be difficult. Trust does not come easily for most of us. Those who do trust easily probably learned to trust as children. The important people they loved were there to love them in return. When they needed those people, they responded. Fortunately for them, their expectations were fulfilled. However, even the most ideal of homes is imperfect, so trust is a difficult word to put into action.

People from dysfunctional homes, where meaningful relationships did not exist, are deprived of needed love and acceptance. They hope, are disappointed and gradually decide that no one can be trusted. They may conclude that they are unworthy of anyone's love and respect.

We transfer our distrust of people to God. Why should he love us when others don't? Why should we trust him when we can't trust anyone else? Everyone has to answer those questions himself. If we have difficulty with trust, we could journal about the issue. Once we discover why it is hard to trust, we'll be in a better position to overcome the tendency to distrust others.

PRAYER:

*Kindly, gentle Lord, we struggle to trust, but we remember the times when we have been disappointed. Help us to believe that we can trust you because you will not let us down. Give us courage to open ourselves up to you and to others. Help us to know that you are with us as we make ourselves vulnerable to others. Thank you for being with us even when we don't sense your presence. Amen.*

Suggested for Step 3

# DECEMBER 8

*"The Lord gives wisdom:*
*out of his mouth come knowledge and understanding."*
Proverbs 2:6

To become "entirely ready" as suggested in Step 6, we need to seek wisdom from our Lord and from others whom we trust and respect. God will give us direction, inspiration and motivation, and we can trust him to want what is best for us. Some people are afraid to ask him for wisdom because they fear what he might expect of them in return. Still others confuse his will with their own and go ahead and do their own thing out of selfish desires.

If our Lord gives us wisdom, we can be sure that it will do us good, not harm. He is all-knowing and loving; he knows our needs before we ask, and he wants the abundant life for us. He will, however, allow us to make our own choices and go our own way even though that may be harmful to us. He will not cross the picket line of our free will.

P R A Y E R:

*Lord, help us to seek your wisdom and then be willing to yield to your will. You desire our healing. You desire our wholeness, and too often we stand in the way. Let us cooperate in the healing process and allow you to direct our lives as you see best. Help us to be available to others in their need as well. Amen.*

Suggested for Step 6

# DECEMBER 9

*"I am the Lord, I change not. . . .*
*Return unto me and I will return unto you, says the Lord of hosts."*
Malachi 3:6,7

When I was in training to become a chemical dependency counselor, I was surprised to see how many people had gotten off course and thought they had wandered too far from God to return. Some were alcoholics. Some were people who battered their spouses and children. Others had various problems requiring treatment. All were people who, in their pain, had turned away from God. In their self-imposed exile, they considered him a stranger.

When their lives became unmanageable from addictions and other destructive behavior, they weighed the positives and negatives of their lives and concluded that God could never forgive them. They couldn't forgive themselves, either. And as long as **they** alienated themselves from him, their recovery was improbable.

Fortunately for us, we know that God is ready to welcome us home to him the second we call to him, no matter how many times we drift into error. We need to return to him and accept his grace and forgiveness. All we have to do is tell him our pain and admit the sorrow that our alienation has caused us. Then we need to accept his forgiveness, forgive ourselves and do our best from that point on.

P R A Y E R:

*Heavenly Father, thank you for inviting us back into the fold regardless of how far or how often we wander from you. You promise to forgive us. Help us to forgive ourselves and trust you again. Amen.*

Suggested for Steps 1, 2 and 3

---

# DECEMBER 10

*"All men seek for thee."*
Mark 1:37

Jesus attracted people . . . people with different motives. Some sought him for good reasons, others for evil reasons. He was interested in every human being. He was willing to associate with sinners. He was not too wise to converse with those considered ignorant. He was not too involved in the pursuit of his own goals to take time for people who needed him. Although he was superior in every way to those around him, his humility touched them profoundly. He was as one of them as he ministered to their needs. He believed there was beauty and worth and truth in every one, and he saw their potential for good.

We should emulate Christ's ministry to the best of our ability. He loved the proud Pharisees (the teachers of the law), the wealthy scribes who were political friends of the Romans, the despised tax collectors, the poor fishermen and other people of the land, even the mixed-religion-and-race Samaritans. He ministered to the self-righteous and to the adulterous woman. Every one he met received the Lord's earnest consideration.

Are we willing to minister to all kinds of people, or are we too judgmental? We need to ask ourselves if we see beauty, good and trust in others like Jesus did. As we think about people whose behavior we don't like, do we see the potential for good that our Lord sees? Is a critical spirit one of our character defects that prevents us from having a healthier spiritual life style? Let's journal about our ministry to others.

P R A Y E R:

*Draw us nearer to you, O Father, and closer to your Son. We seek your guidance. Help us to work at becoming more like Christ every day, witnessing and ministering as he did on earth. Teach us to love people, all types of people, and to look for the good in them. Amen.*

Suggested for Steps 6 and 12

# DECEMBER 11

*"You have put gladness in my heart."*
Psalm 4:7

God has given all of us reasons to have gladness in our hearts. Whether we actually feel gladness or not will depend on our attitude as well as our relationship to our Lord. If we are close friends of his, we will be glad sooner or later, for his Spirit will fill us with joy. If we converse with him often, both speaking and listening, we will be open to his joy.

When we struggle with loss, we can still be aware, to whatever degree, of reasons for joy. But in order to experience the deep, satisfying joy of God in our hearts, we must know him as our Lord and Savior. We must do more than recognize our reasons to be joyful and thankful; we need to thank God for his gifts. We need to tell others of the magnificence of his love so they, too, will desire his presence in their lives.

P R A Y E R:

*Giver of all good gifts, thank you for the joy in our hearts. Help us to be more committed to finding strength in our lives than focusing on our weaknesses. Help us to be available to others who need to experience the joy of your love. Amen.*

Suggested for Step 11

# DECEMBER 12

*"When they saw him, they worshiped him, but some doubted."*
Matthew 28:17

Some times we doubt the Lord, his presence with us, his power, his wisdom, his love, his forgiveness. But we have no reason to doubt because experience has proved him true. When we earnestly seek him, we will find him very near.

It is when we're buried in pain that we forget to seek him. We may be angry and too rebellious to seek him because we've convinced ourselves that he could have prevented the pain if he'd wanted to, but he didn't want to. Often when we need him the most, we are too angry to reach out to him. When we lose faith in him, we're too confused and stubborn to confess our waywardness and ask him to forgive us. Then we do not get the help we need. We must be willing to turn back to him in love and repentance. He will welcome us back because he loves us.

P R A Y E R:

*Forgive us, Lord, for doubting you. Help us to know that when we pray, you will answer our prayers in some way, even though your answers may not be the ones we hope for. Fill us with the joy of expectancy that will keep our faith active. When we pray for healing and expect it, we can trust you to heal us.*

*We pray for others who struggle to believe but allow their humanness to get in the way. Help them to let go and let you lead. Teach them that faith endures even when reason and common sense say it should not, and then hope endures because faith believes. Bless others to be a blessing through their commitment to love even as you have loved us. Amen.*

Suggested for Steps 5 and 11

# DECEMBER 13

*"You will be hated by all for my name's sake.*
*But not a hair on your head will perish.*
*By your endurance you will gain your lives."*
Luke 21:27,28

The fact that we're followers of Jesus Christ may give us some automatic enemies, people who hate us because they hate him. We cannot expect to be immune from suffering; after all, our Lord himself suffered. What he says in Luke 21:27,28 is that if we stand firm, he will stand firm with us. He will see us through any situation if we trust him. And if we falter, he will help us.

Physical suffering, natural disasters and mistreatment by others are all possible sources of suffering; and if they touch our lives, we wonder if God still cares about us. If we ask ourselves the question, "Why me?" we might as well reply, "Why *not* me?" We may need to ask ourselves how committed we are to our Lord. We may well have to suffer for his sake and to love those who are unkind to us. Christ asks us to look beyond our hurt and desire the best for those who hurt us. He even asks us to pray for them. Perhaps this is something about which we should spend time journaling.

Finally, Jesus tells us that we need to *endure* the hatred of others in order to find wholeness and healing. Not one of us can save himself, of course; our Lord saves us. But, we can work on our spiritual growth. This is our part of our covenant with Christ; as he stands by us, so we are to stand by him. The Apostle Paul clarified this truth to the Christians at Philippi, about ten miles from the Aegean Sea along the Egnatian Way: "As you have always obeyed, . . . work out your own salvation with fear and trembling. *For it is God which worketh in you both to will and to do of his good pleasure*" (Philippians 2:12,13). The spiritual muscle to stand by our Lord is often developed through the discipline of pain.

PRAYER:
*When we are hated, O Father, help us to refrain from hating. When we are hurt, help us not to hurt back. When we are misunderstood, help us to understand. Help us to love those who hate us. We know that when we give all of our hurts and ourselves to you, you will enable us to work out our salvation, healing and spiritual growth. Amen.*
Suggested for Steps 8 and 9

# DECEMBER 14

*"A bruised reed shall he not break."*
Isaiah 42:3

I've often doubted the promise of Isaiah 42:3! When I felt overwhelmed by illness, the loss of my career and marriage, the death of my loved ones by suicide, I was quite sure that God broke bruised reeds. Yet as I look back, I see that God was there to help me through the trials, one at a time.

Part of the difficulty in coping was my tendency to hang onto my hurts and grief; I stockpiled them as trials came along. Gradually I learned the importance of resolving pain quickly. Pain and loss were not only excess baggage, but they drained me of the vital energy and faith to tackle each new day.

God was with me, and he gave me the strength I needed to endure. As long as I didn't feel sorry for myself and I dealt with only the immediate trial, I was fine. I had to comprehend my own powerlessness and turn the circumstance and myself over to God. I had to change my attitude of independence and allow other people to help and comfort me. I had to live one day at a time.

PRAYER:
*Lord, many times we feel that we are bruised reeds and wonder if you even care. Help us to trust you and to remember the promise of Isaiah 42:3. Help us to let go of past hurts and losses so that with your help, though bruised, we will not be broken. We can live in the health and wholeness of your love. Amen.*
Suggested for Steps 1 and 10

# DECEMBER 15

*"You are a chosen generation, a royal priesthood,*
*a holy nation, a peculiar people; that you should show forth the praises*
*of him who has called you out of darkness into his marvelous light."*
I Peter 2:9

The Apostle Peter, inspired to write by the Holy Spirit, was not making this promise only to the Jews. This promise includes the entire body of Christ, the priesthood of believers and we among them. God has chosen us to be his people, and that is a very special position to be in. We are to proclaim his glory, majesty and power to the entire world. He has called us out of the "darkness into his marvelous light." We are no longer slaves to the darkness; our ransom was paid, and the slave collars, if any exist, should be taken off.

Jesus Christ, our Brother, has given us many gifts. What shall we, his family, give him in return? The instructions in I Peter 2:9 are clear: we are to honor and glorify him . . . alone, with the family of God and to those who remain outside in the dark. We are to love him and ourselves and others. We are to forgive as we are forgiven. We are to *exercise* faith, and our good works will prove our faith. We are to intercede in prayer for others.

We are to be merciful as our Lord is merciful. The Apostle James warns us that "he shall have judgment without mercy, that hath showed no mercy" (James 2:13). That should make us think twice. As we work on the 12th step, we need to think about our Christian witness. How can we better demonstrate Christ's love? Let's pray and meditate on this important aspect of our lives.

P R A Y E R:

*O God, our help in ages past, our hope for years to come, help us to proclaim you to the world in positive, loving ways. Help us to be patient with those who are unsure of their faith and allow them the time they need to learn to know and love you. Help us to be merciful and forgiving. Amen.*

Suggested for Step 12

# DECEMBER 16

*"Whither shall I go from thy Spirit?*
*or whither shall I flee from thy presence?"*
Psalm 139:7

We cannot hide from God. He is everywhere, around and within us. Even when we cannot feel him or see him working, he is always with us. When we are being unlovable, we hope he's not watching, though we know better. If we continue to pretend, the Holy Spirit will soon remind us that we aren't being loving. If we become seriously depressed and believe that God has forsaken us, he's still there. As soon as we call him, he will answer.

He is with us in our joy. He laughs with us. He surrounds us with the beauties of nature and the warmth of loving people. He loves us. When we see a rainbow, we can remember his covenant with us. He wants the very best for us.

P R A Y E R:

*Thank you, Father, that we can never wander where you cannot find us. You are with us no matter where we go. You hear before we call. You comfort and strengthen us for each new day. And each new day is filled with the mystery of your love, so rich and boundless that we will explore it from now throughout eternity. Thank you for adopting us into your family. Amen.*

Suggested for Step 2

---

# DECEMBER 17

*"You have been a shelter for me
and a strong tower against the enemy."*
Psalm 61:3

Our Lord is our shelter, our strong tower. When we are frayed and battle-weary, we can retreat to him. When we are afraid, he will soothe and comfort us. His grace is abundant. His healing power penetrates our apprehensions. He calms our spirits and assures us that all will be well. We can gladly sing this chorus:

*"How marvelous! How wonderful!
And my song shall ever be;
How marvelous! How wonderful!
Is my Savior's love for me!"*

We can receive a great deal of consolation from the hymns of Christians who have tried and found that the Lord is true. He is all that the Scriptures tell us. Often when I need solace, I turn to my hymn book and read page after page of testimony to his love and grace.

P R A Y E R:

*Lord, some times we wonder how you can possibly love us, but you do and we know it. We thank you that you are willing to be our refuge and strength! Bless all who feel overcome by storms and enemy fire. Call the retreat to you and administer healing to the wounded. Amen.*

Suggested for Step 1

---

# DECEMBER 18

*"Glory to God in the highest
and on earth, peace, good will toward men."*
Luke 2:14

Bible scholars have discovered that a better translation of the Apostle Luke's words is this: "Glory to God in the highest and on earth peace to *men of good will.*" This makes more sense to me. Peace can only come to people of good will. Peace can only come to us if we love God and others as ourselves. We need to be more concerned about the happiness and security of our fellow human beings than we are about wealth, power and reputation.

Nations struggle to gain overlordship, to achieve superiority. Wars start and wars come to a bloody, bitter end. Weapons become more efficient and more deadly, and more people die. No one seems to learn from war.

Individuals strangle "the competition" on their way up the ladder of success, rationalizing that the final goal is worth the price. We are people with warring hearts and wounded spirits. We need to change ourselves before we can achieve peace on a larger scale. How much do we want the peace of God that passes all understanding?

PRAYER:

*Lord of peace, we pray that you will put good will into our spirits so that we will strive for peace. Help us to remove the the high walls and barbed-wire obstacles to peace, the hate, the prejudice, the greed and the selfishness. Help us to join hands with others to proclaim your message of "peace to men of good will." Amen.*

Suggested for Step 12

---

# DECEMBER 19

*"Though I bestow all my goods to feed the poor,
and though I give up my body to be burned, and have not love,
it profiteth me nothing."*
I Corinthians 13:3

Paul reminds us of what love is *not*. Many people believe that if they give enough money to the church and other charities, if they hold a church office, attend church and pray regularly, they are wonderful Christians. Paul tells us in I Corinthians 13:3 that the Lord wants much more—and better—of us than that. To serve God effectively, we must possess certain qualities of the heart, not just the wallet or the hands. To be a "doer" is sometimes an avoidance of deep commitment to our Lord and others.

When we read the 13th chapter of I Corinthians, we learn that God has given us great and beautiful gifts, but they are only as good as our willingness to use them to his glory. We need to value these gifts, share them and thank God for them. They were not given to us for our own glorification, but to enable us to become productive disciples of our Lord . . . to love God, ourselves and others. Discovering our giftedness takes time and effort. Journaling can help in the process of stretching our awareness of who we are and what makes us unique in God's eyes.

PRAYER:

*Gracious Father, grant that the gifts we have may be shared in such a way that others can see your reflection in us. Help us to develop our gifts and grant us grace to give you the glory. Help us to practice the greatest gift, <u>love</u>, so that we would not only discover our gifts, but the gifts of others. Amen.*

Suggested for Step 4

# DECEMBER 20

*"Hear now this, O foolish people, and without understanding; which have eyes, and see not; which have ears, and hear not."*
Jeremiah 5:21

As we near the end of this year, we need to think about whether or not we have ears but do not hear. We need to think about *how* we listen, *what* we listen to and *who* we listen to. Jeremiah 5:21 tells us that we need to develop two of our senses: our sight and our hearing. We need to be willing to discipline ourselves to listen to God in order to know his will for our lives.

We need to stop listening to the negative tapes of our past that tell us we're not worthwhile. We need to stop allowing people to abuse us by not treating us with love and respect. We need to separate from those who use us to their own ends.

We need to listen to what God has to say about us. We are his beloved children! We are worthwhile because he says we are. We are loved by him, and we are lovable. He has a plan for our lives if we will cooperate with him. He offers us healing and wholeness. He offers us comfort, strength and the assurance of his presence. We need to hear all of the wonderful things he offers because he loves us. We need to make a commitment to listen more carefully each day.

The more we develop the sense of hearing, the better we will be able to see God's manifold blessings in our lives and in those around us. We will see the reflection of our Lord's love in the loving, his humility in the humble, his mercy in the merciful, his purity in the pure, his peace in the peacemakers. When we have begun to exercise our spiritual ears and eyes, we will have just begun the abundant life our Lord intends for us.

PRAYER:

*Help us, O Father, to walk in the way of wisdom. Teach us to look and to listen. Help us to let go of the voices of the past that prevent our healing. Help us to give the tattered photo albums of our bad experiences to you and let you bury them in the depths of the deepest sea. Help all those who hear and see destructively, never finding serenity because they don't look and listen for you. Heal them. Amen.*

Suggested for Steps 3 and 11

260

# DECEMBER 21

*"If you leave God's paths and go astray,*
*you will hear a voice behind you say,*
*'No, this is the way; walk here.'"*
Isaiah 30:21, *The Living Bible*

God is here. If we listen closely, we can hear him speak to us. He will direct, encourage and comfort us. If we need the reminder, he will tell us we are missing the mark, that we had better check our compass because we're off the course of his will. He may let us feel guilty about areas of our lives that need changing and gently turn us to the Savior to confess our wrongs, receive his forgiveness and continue on in a more loving attitude.

We must listen to him and be open to his leading. We must let him help us correct our wayward ways. He is our loving Shepherd, and he wants the very best for us. We need to believe that and honor his transcendence in our daily lives.

P R A Y E R:

*Precious Shepherd, thank you for overseeing our lives and for correcting our course. Thank you for saying, "No, this is the way; walk here." For your protection, for your helpful and loving care, we praise and thank you. Help others to trust your superior sense of direction and turn the control of their lives over to you. Amen.*

Suggested for Steps 7 and 10

# DECEMBER 22

*"A man's gift makes room for him,*
*and brings him before great men."*
Proverbs 18:16

When doing a fourth-step inventory, let's look at our gifts. They change with time, and our abilities vary as our ages, health and circumstances of life change. If we've developed only one or two gifts, what will we do if the time comes when they're no longer needed or we can no longer use them? We need to explore new ways of sharing our giftedness.

Kinds of gifts depend on conditions. Our adult children may not need us in the way they did before. We may not be as active in the school or community as we used to be. We may have accomplished the goals we set some time ago. Yet God can still use us. Our gifts are still needed. Instead of feeling sorry for ourselves, let's find new ways to serve him. Let's ask God for the gifts that we need to accomplish today's activities and goals. When we develop new gifts to share with others, we will enjoy the blessing of being a blessing to others.

PRAYER:
*Almighty Father, thank you for our gifts. Tell us how to put them to the best use. Give us courage to explore and find new gifts. Help us to risk sharing them with others. Teach us your way, O God, and gently, firmly encourage us to follow it. Amen.*
Suggested for Step 4

# DECEMBER 23

*"He that loveth his life shall lose it,*
*he that hateth his life in this world shall keep it unto eternal life."*
John 12:25

When I think of letting go, I am reminded of Judson Van de Venter's famous old hymn, "I Surrender All":

*"All to Jesus I surrender,*
*All to him I freely give;*
*I will ever love and trust him,*
*In his presence daily live.*

*"All to Jesus I surrender,*
*Humbly at his feet I bow;*
*Worldly pleasures all forsaken,*
*Take me, Jesus, take me now."*

Step 3 is about this kind of complete surrender. We need to make the "decision to turn our wills and our lives over to the care of Christ as we understand him—hoping to understand him more fully." We must learn to love and trust him. We must be willing to practice living in his presence. We must be humble when we approach him and admit that we cannot manage our lives on our own. We may need to give up some worldly pleasures to follow him. We will certainly have to be willing to change destructive character traits with his help.

We need to decide whether or not we are really willing to "let go and let God." Are we willing to have Christ transform our lives? Are we willing to allow him to help us change what needs to be changed? Change is difficult. Even our friends and relatives may question change. The question is, have we hurt long enough? Will we allow him to heal us? Let's journal about this decision and why it might be hard to make.
PRAYER:
*Loving Lord, thank you for your willingness to be available to us when we call. Help us to be willing to give up the destructive aspects of our lives and accept your healing. Give us courage to say, "I surrender all." Amen.*
Suggested for Step 3

# CHRISTMAS EVE

*"Behold, a virgin shall be with child,*
*and shall bring forth a son,*
*and they shall call his name Immanuel,*
*which being interpreted is, God with us."*
Matthew 1:23

More love is expressed on this holy day than at any other time of the year. Church bells ring, and Christians around the globe praise God together. Friends and relatives gather for fellowship, and tonight or tomorrow, they will exchange gifts to express their love and respect. God's Spirit of love is in the air and in our hearts.

Christmas is a time of family tradition. Our family had a tradition of setting up the manger scene on Christmas Eve and then reading the Christmas story together. My children are carrying on the same tradition with their children.

When they were very young, my children thought that a merry Santa Claus would slide down the chimney with presents, but I felt it was important for them to know the true meaning of Christmas as soon as they could understand. Christmas is Christ. The tinsel, the mistletoe and holly, the red, white and pink poinsettias, the pine garlands and the grand old Christmas tree, the brightly wrapped and beribboned presents . . . can tempt us to forget the Giver and the Gift that made the angels sing in the shepherds' field outside Bethlehem.

We need to remember that not everyone will have a happy Christmas. Some do not have enough food, let alone presents. Not everyone knows about the incarnation of our Lord and how important he is to them for eternity. We need to pray for others who have less than we, and we need to share our Christ-child with them.

PRAYER:

*Gracious God, thank you for the gift of your Son, Jesus Christ. Help us to appreciate all that we have and be willing to share with others. Bless those who are suffering this Christmas and let them feel your love. Amen.*

Suggested for Steps 10, 11 and 12

# CHRISTMAS DAY

*"Unto you is born this day in the city of David a Savior,*
*which is Christ the Lord."*
Luke 2:11

Merry *Christmas!* This is the day we celebrate the birth of Christ . . . a day of joy, of peace, of love, of hope, of sharing the good news, of prayer, of thanksgiving for the gift of God's Son. Wherever and however you are today, dear friend, you are blessed because of the birth of Christ. You may be grieving over the loss of someone important. You may feel helpless and afraid. You may be lonely. You may be suffering physically, emotionally or spiritually.

Take courage! On the night that Jesus was born, shepherds were watching their flocks in a nearby field. The Scriptures tell us, "Lo, the angel of the Lord came upon them, and the glory of the Lord shone around about them. . . . And the angel said unto them, 'Fear not: for, behold, I bring you good tidings of great joy, which shall be to *all people*'" (Luke 2:10). Good news for *all* people. That includes you! Celebrate Jesus' birth; *he* is the one who can turn your sorrow into joy. If you are happy this Christmas, share your happiness with someone. If your are sad or sorrowing this Christmas, reach out and let others share their joy with you. That's what Christmas is all about: giving and receiving. We can share because God shared his best Gift with us. We can love because he first loved us.

P R A Y E R:

*Heavenly Father, we receive the Christ-child into our hearts this Christmas Day in a spirit of joy and thanksgiving. Help us to share the joy of his birth with everyone around us. We pray, especially, for those who do not feel the joy of Christmas and for those who do not yet know Christ. Help us to share his love effectively. Amen.*

Suggested for Step 12

---

# DECEMBER 26

*"Come unto me, all ye that labor and are heavy laden,
and I will give you rest."*
Matthew 11:28

Usually the day after Christmas is a day of rest. The excitement and preparations for Christmas are over and we wind down to a normal routine. The scramble for presents, decorating the house, social outings, cooking holiday foods and entertaining are done, at least until New Year's Day. We can rest with a feeling of satisfaction and hopefully experience the warm glow of love within the family that Christmas often deepens.

Unfortunately for many people, this "day after" can initiate a post-Christmas depression, especially for those who didn't feel the joy of Christmas. Some become suicidal. Thinking of this now is discouraging, but it is a reality that must be addressed if we honestly care about others.

If you still sense the joy of Christmas, share your joy with someone who needs you. Be a friend to someone who really needs a friend. Share your experiencing of letting go of things you have been powerless to change. Share your experience of resting in the Lord and receiving his comfort. You can help someone. Don't turn away! Love isn't love until you give it away.

PRAYER:

*Loving Father, thank you for the joy of Christmas. Help us to retain that joy throughout the year. Help us to go to you for rest when we need it. We pray for those who find the weeks after Christmas very difficult. Heal them so they can experience the joy of Christmas and the love of Christ once again. Amen.*

Suggested for Steps 3 and 12

# DECEMBER 27

*"Though we have never yet seen God,*
*when we love each other God lives in us*
*and his love within us grows even stronger."*
I John 4:12, *The Living Bible*

If you were unable to speak or write, how would you communicate your Christian values? Could people tell just by being with you that you were a Christian? Could they tell simply by knowing you as a person that you were a child of God? Would your love and belief in Christ be visible in your treatment of others? Would the promise that you have as his child radiate so others could see?

We demonstrate God's love by the way we love ourselves and others. People should not have to guess whether or not we are Christians. If we live for him as well as share his name, they will know that we have a close friendship with him.

We need to grow stronger in his love. If we love him and others, he will fill us to the brim with the Spirit of love. Our Lord instructs us, "Love one another even as I have loved you."

PRAYER:

*Creator, Lord, we know that even though we cannot see you with our bodily sense of sight, we can see you with our spiritual sight. You are reflected in all that is beautiful and right. Thank you for your presence within us. Thank you that we grow more and more in the likeness of your Son as we allow you to manage our lives. Thank you for your love that surrounds and strengthens us. Help others to learn to love and trust you. Amen.*

Suggested for Step 12

# DECEMBER 28

*"That we henceforth be no more children, tossed to and fro,*
*and carried about with every wind of doctrine, by the sleight of men,*
*and cunning craftiness, whereby they lie in wait to deceive."*
Ephesians 4:14

There are times when we feel like we are tossed to and fro. We feel powerless and don't know where to turn. Our faith may falter when we need it most. God may seem so far away that we wonder if he is even there.

Lake Erie, shallowest of the five Great Lakes in the northern United States, is also the most treacherous. A shallow lake is much more fierce in a storm because it doesn't have stabilizing depth. The waves whip into a fury.

Many of us are like Lake Erie, shallow and easily disturbed by every wind of trouble, by every problem, every burden. Only when we learn to trust Jesus Christ will we develop stability and inner peace, the security we need to endure. We can gain from the times of powerlessness if we are willing to turn to our source of strength. Once we give him our burdens, we will cease to toss to and fro.

P R A Y E R:

*Heavenly Father, give us the faith to trust you for all things. Deepen our convictions so that we will trust you to still the waves of doubt and fear. Help us to quiet ourselves so that we can hear you whisper, "Peace, be still." Help us to grow so that every day we will lessen the shallowness of our souls. Thank you for your abiding peace and comfort. Amen.*

Suggested for Step 1

---

# DECEMBER 29

*"As unknown, and yet well known;*
*as dying, and, behold, we live;*
*as chastened, and not killed."*
II Corinthians 6:9

Some of us see only the suffering in our lives. We are so busy counting our losses that we don't look at our gains. We spend so much time in self-pity that we don't have time to work on healing. We need to see the hope in II Corinthians 6:9, yet this hope is only possible when we surrender our wills and lives to Christ. We need to be willing to give up the pain and be open to seeing the gain.

> *"Measure your life by loss and not by gain,*
> *Not by the wine drunk, but by the wine poured forth;*
> *For love's strength stands in love's sacrifice,*
> *And he who suffers most has the most to give."*
> —Source unknown

The only way we can have more to give as a result of suffering is when we are willing to be used by our Lord in the way he sees best. We need to trust him to lead us through the suffering to a greater glory.

Significantly, the time we need to trust the most is when we feel the least trusting. When our lives are the most broken, we may feel that our faith is lacking. We need to turn to our Lord to heal our brokenness. We need to work harder on our faith because our strength is reduced by fatigue. Maybe this means that we need to seek out our Christian friends because it will be with them that we most fully experience the comfort and support we need.

PRAYER:

> *Lord, thank you for the hope in II Corinthians 6:9. At the most difficult times of our lives, you give us hope. Help us to remember that although we may be cast down, we are not destroyed. You are always with us to give us confidence. Thank you for your presence and strength that continually enable us to become more victorious in you. Amen.*

Suggested for Steps 1 and 3

---

# DECEMBER 30

*"Therefore be ye also ready;*
*for in such as hour as ye think not shall the Son of man come."*
Matthew 24:44

The year has ended, and some of us did not take life very seriously this year. Now as we prepare for the new year, we think of the things we haven't done and the things we would like to do. We assume we will still be around (that is, alive) in the new year. If our lives have been destructive to ourselves or others, it's okay because we believe we have time to set things right *tomorrow.*

But, life may have a surprise for us. Every day we step into the unknown, believing we'll always have another day to do things differently. We believe we have lots of time to make peace with God, either before we die or before Christ returns. People die suddenly every day, and though we may be shaken, we didn't die and don't believe we will. We're going to be around for a long time yet.

Of course, we don't want to spend our lives being gloomy and always expecting the worst from life. Life can be difficult enough without making it harder by catering to feelings of apprehension, imagining all of the evil and painful things that might or could happen. We need to believe in life, to believe that the unexpected is not always bad. We need to make sure that we work on changing the areas of our lives that need changing. Let's stop procrastinating. As we work on the tenth step and take a daily inventory, let's journal and ask ourselves if we would feel good about our lives if we knew they'd end today. What would you do differently?

PRAYER:

> *Grant us, O God, to meet this new day with cheerful hope. Remove gloomy fears and renew a simple, childlike faith within us. Help us to be willing to change the areas of our lives that need changing. Amen.*

Suggested for Step 10

# NEW YEAR'S EVE

*"Take therefore no thought of tomorrow;*
*for the morrow shall take thought for the things of itself.*
*Sufficient unto the day is the evil thereof."*
Matthew 6:34

Today is the last day of the year. People are busy thinking up resolutions for the coming year. They plan to accomplish all the things they didn't get around to this year.

As we review this past year, are we carrying any unfinished business over into the new year? Do we have an unresolved grief that is still pulling us down and keeping us from living the abundant life in Christ? Is there anyone we have failed to forgive because of hurt or false pride? We cannot afford to drag these negative emotions and behaviors into the new year with us. There will be enough new challenges to face squarely. We need the energy to live one day at a time.

We need to remember the importance of living one day at a time with God's help. We can't change yesterday, and we don't have control over tomorrow. We must release the hurts of yesterday and banish the grievances of the past. We must allow our spirits to be joyful and full of hope. Today is a new day! Before us is a new year! We are free to start fresh, new lives, to live in harmony with God, ourselves and others. We bless this day and will be a blessing this day.

PRAYER:

*Loving Father, we come to the end of this year, cognizant of our failures and disappointments. Some of us come tired and in need of renewal. Some of us come refreshed and ready for the new year. Help us to see that every day is a fresh beginning for us. Grant us courage to face the future with confidence and help us to let go of the past. Amen.*

Suggested for Step 10

Spiritual growth is the desire of many people. The *Twelve Steps for Christian Living* as outlined in the book and study guide *You Can Help With Your Healing* provide the planned format and climate for spiritual growth in the context of a small group.

The book *Breaking Free* and the accompanying study guide were especially designed and written as a 12-step guide for spiritual and emotional intimacy for individuals and couples. This can be used in a small-group setting or by couples or individuals.

If you are interested in more information about either of these books and study guides or a *starter packet* for beginning these groups, write to or phone:

INSTITUTE FOR CHRISTIAN LIVING
P.O. Box 22408
Minneapolis, MN 55422
(612) 593-1791